▪ RELOCATING

D070052Z

DATE DUE

7/17/97	

ARCTIC VISIONS

Gail Osherenko and Oran Young
GENERAL EDITORS

The Arctic has long appeared to outsiders as a vast, forbidding wasteland or, alternatively, as a storehouse of riches ready for the taking by those able to conquer the harsh physical environment. More recently, a competing vision paints the Arctic as the last pristine wilderness on earth, a place to be preserved for future generations.

Arctic Visions confronts these conflicting and simplistic portraits, conceived in ignorance of the complexities of the circumpolar world and without appreciation of the viewpoints of those indigenous to the region. Drawing upon an international community of writers who are sensitive to the human dimensions, Arctic Visions will explore political, strategic, economic, environmental, and cultural issues.

The Arctic has always been a place of human and natural drama, an arena for imperial ambitions, economic exploitation, ecological disasters, and personal glory. As the region gains importance in international affairs, this series will help a growing audience of readers to develop new and more informed visions of the Arctic.

Arctic Politics: Conflict and Cooperation in the Circumpolar North, Oran Young, 1992

Arctic Wars, Animal Rights, Endangered Peoples, Finn Lynge, 1992

Arctic Adaptations: Native Whalers and Reindeer Herders of Northern Eurasia, Igor Krupnik, 1993

Relocating Eden: The Image and Politics of Inuit Exile in the Canadian Arctic, Alan Rudolph Marcus, 1995

RELOCATING
· EDEN ·

The Image and Politics of Inuit
Exile in the Canadian Arctic

ALAN RUDOLPH MARCUS

· DARTMOUTH COLLEGE ·

Published by University Press of New England
Hanover and London

Dartmouth College
Published by University Press of New England, Hanover, NH 03755
© 1995 by the Trustees of Dartmouth College
All rights reserved
Printed in the United States of America   5   4   3   2   1
CIP data appear at the end of the book

• CONTENTS •

PART 2: SOUTH OF EDEN
RELOCATION OF THE INUKJUAMIUT

PART 3: THE FLIGHT FROM EDEN
RELOCATION OF THE AHIARMIUT

PART 4: REASSESSMENT

· ILLUSTRATIONS ·

Maps

Tables

Figures

· ACKNOWLEDGMENTS ·

A great many people have been especially helpful to me during my research. I am indebted to the staff of the Scott Polar Research Institute where this research was undertaken (Marcus, 1993), my supervisor Piers Vitebsky, my graduate tutor Andrew Holmes at Clare College, and Oran Young at Dartmouth College. I would like to thank the many people I interviewed for this study (given in appendix D), including the Inuit living in the Canadian Arctic communities of Arviat, Grise Fiord, Inukjuak, and Resolute Bay, without whose cooperation this work would not have been possible.

The archivists at the National Archives of Canada, the Department of Indian Affairs and Northern Development, the Hudson's Bay Company Archives, and the Prince of Wales Northern Heritage Center were of substantial assistance, particularly when faced with my large photocopying requests. The Inuit organizations, Inuit Tapirisat of Canada, Makivik Corporation, and Avataq Cultural Institute were always helpful, as were the staff of the Polar Continental Shelf Project and the Royal Commission on Aboriginal Peoples. A research grant from the National Science Foundation (DPP-9113103), together with travel grants from the American Friends of Cambridge, the Sir Bartle Frere's Memorial Fund, the Brian Roberts Fund, Clare College, the Frederic William Maitland Memorial Fund, and the Smuts Memorial Fund, made it possible for me to conduct extensive archival research and fieldwork in Canada. The people who generously allowed me to copy their photographs, which are reproduced in this book, are Bob Pilot (figs. 4.1, 4.3, 8.3), Jaybeddie Amagoalik (figs. 3.5, 4.2), Reuben Ploughman (fig. 3.3), and Geert van den Steenhoven (figs. 5.1, 5.2, 5.3, 5.4, 5.5, 6.1). Permission to reproduce other photographs and illustrations has kindly been given by Avataq Cultural Institute (figs. 3.2, 3.6), *The Globe and Mail* (fig. 2.5), *The Beaver* (fig. 1.3), and the National Archives of Canada (figs. 1.2, 1.4, 2.1, 3.1, 3.4, 3.7, 8.1). Among those individuals who patiently interpreted for me in the communities were Elizabeth Allakariallak, Larry Audlaluk,

Anne Gardener, Gailey and Siasi Iqaluk, Martha Irkok, Lena Napayok, and Moses Nowkawalk.

I am also grateful to Mark Achbar, Evano Aggark, John Amagoalik, Terence Armstrong, Susan Baer, Carol Baker, Gillian Beer, Ellen Bielawski, Barbara Bodenhorn, Noel Broadbent, Patrick Burden, Brian Chambers, John Crump, Jens Dahl, Richard Diubaldo, Andrea Doucet, Brian Finch, Martha Flaherty, Ross Gibson, Shelagh Grant, Barrie Gunn, Jack Hicks, Lise Lyck, Ken MacRury, Nicki Maynard, Sheila Meldrum, William Mills, Ian Moir, Anne Morton, Anna Ohaituk, Markoosie Patsauq, Bob and Lois Pilot, Reuben and Lily Ploughman, Yvonne Privett, Doreen Reidel, Derek Roche, Graham and Diana Rowley, Sam Silverstone, Ben Sivertz, Richard Valpy, Paul Watson, Doug Whyte, Kari and Peter Williams, Bob Williamson, and Renee Wissink.

I would like to thank those folk who kindly read drafts of the book and gave their comments, including Michael Bravo, Peter Clancy, Yvon Csonka, William Dunlap, Stuart Mackinnon, Mark Nuttall, Geert van den Steenhoven, Maria Tippett, and Ian Whitaker, and my editors at University Press of New England, together with series editors Oran Young and Gail Osherenko, have provided helpful comments and encouragement and shown great patience awaiting the manuscript. I am most grateful to my copy editor, Jane McGraw, and to Rosemary Graham and Martin Whittles, who offered their invaluable editorial and proofreading skills. My family have provided the guiding support throughout this endeavor. My father and mother, Rudolph and Laura Marcus, and my wife Barbara have helped immeasurably. I would especially like to thank my brother Ken Marcus, who was together with me at Clare College, for his incisive criticisms and helpful contributions during this work.

Cambridge   A.R.M.
December 1994

· ABBREVIATIONS ·

ACND   Advisory Committee on Northern Development
DIAND   Department of Indian Affairs and Northern Development
DNANR   Department of Northern Affairs and National Resources
DOT   Department of Transport
DRD   Department of Resources and Development
HBC   Hudson's Bay Company
NSO   Northern Service Officer
NWT   Northwest Territories
OIC   Officer in Charge
RCAF   Royal Canadian Air Force
RCAP   Royal Commission on Aboriginal Peoples
RCMP   Royal Canadian Mounted Police
USAF   United States Air Force

Officer ranks within the RCMP:

Cst.   Constable
S/Cst.   Special Constable
Cpl.   Corporal
Sgt.   Sergeant
Insp.   Inspector
Supt.   Superintendent

· TERMINOLOGY ·

The Canadian federal department that has had responsibility for the administration of the Canadian North has evolved through various restructuring efforts and name changes over the years. From 1873 to 1935 it was the Department of the Interior, then the Department of Mines and Resources, and in 1950 became the Department of Resources and Development, only to be renamed in 1953 the Department of Northern Affairs and National Resources. That name remained until the latest change, in 1966, to the present Department of Indian Affairs and Northern Development. To avoid confusion, unless one of the above departments is referred to by name I will simply call it "the Department." The Hudson's Bay Company will be referred to as "the HBC" or "the Company," the Royal Canadian Mounted Police will be referred to as "the RCMP" or "the Force," and the Anglican and Catholic missions will at times be referred to collectively as "the Churches."

The word "Eskimo" is not an indigenous term; its origin is controversial and more recently the term has been interpreted as having pejorative connotations (Damas, 1984: 5–7; Woodbury, 1984). The aboriginal people who have been popularly known to the outside world as Eskimos call themselves "Inuit," which means "people." "Inuk" means one person. (Those Inuit who live in the western Arctic and the Mackenzie Delta region call themselves "Inuvialuit.") White people are called *Qallunaat* in "Inuktitut," the Inuit language. Until the 1970s, officials used the word Eskimo, which I will use in direct quotations or in that context; otherwise I will use the term Inuit. Several terms in common usage are employed here: the High Arctic Islands include those islands north of Lancaster Sound that in 1954 were given the name the Queen Elizabeth Islands. The community of Port Harrison in northern Quebec was known by the Inuit as Inukjuak, which is the name of the town today. Both names are used in this study, depending on the context.

A distinct Inuit social group is known as a "band" and used to be comprised of a number of "camps" containing extended family units. The identity and geographical location of an Inuit band is described by the suffix -*miut*, meaning "people of." The Inuit living in the area of Port Harrison are the "Inukjuamiut" (people of Inukjuak). The other band of Inuit I will be discussing is a group of Caribou Inuit known as the "Ahiar-miut" ("people dwelling inland"), who live in the Keewatin District. The transliteration of Inuktitut into Roman orthography is complicated by the number of Inuit dialects, thus the spelling of people's names and of words can differ greatly. For example, the name Ahiarmiut has over time been spelled several ways, including Ihalmiut (Mowat, 1952) and Ahear-miut (Rudnicki and Stevenson, 1958). Except for those words used in direct quotations, I will adopt the spellings the Inuit use themselves and the dialect appropriate to the geographical context. The translations have principally been provided by John MacDonald with assistance from Leah Otak and Louis Tapardjuk of the Science Institute of the Northwest Territories Igloolik Research Center, Professor Louis-Jacques Dorais of Laval University, and Larry Audlaluk of Grise Fiord.

· RELOCATING EDEN ·

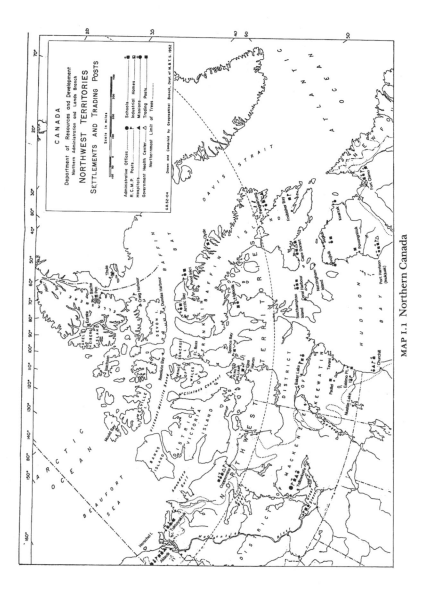

MAP I.1 Northern Canada

· INTRODUCTION ·

This book presents a cultural history of a series of dramatic events that took place in the Arctic in the 1950s, during which the Canadian government relocated groups of Inuit (then known to outsiders as Eskimos) northward to unoccupied lands. Examining the circumstances surrounding these acts and seeing how they correspond to the government's overall strategy for northern expansion opens up a number of areas for inquiry. The motivations, responsibility, and justification for the moves are of primary interest, as is the need to identify how media representations of aboriginal people are shaped and manipulated by officials, novelists, and filmmakers. Another theme I wish to explore is the way Inuit and Whites conceive 'a sense of place' and attach meaning to Arctic environments. Perceptions of nomadism and homeland are germane to this discussion.

An underlying question in this unfolding narrative relates to how history is represented. A particular challenge in historiography arises when faced with two distinct cultural interpretations—one based on an oral tradition and the other on written accounts. When considering historical events from cross-cultural perspectives involving southern texts and northern contexts, they can reveal profoundly different viewpoints which appear shrouded in myth. For instance, did officials and Inuit view the relocation projects as migrations, or as deportations? Were they conceived of as imaginative utopian experiments to re-create an Edenic way of life in the High Arctic, or were they intended as punitive acts of translocation?

I have entitled this book *Relocating Eden*; for the purposes of this study, the metaphors of Eden and utopia are effectively interchangeable. Eden is traditionally viewed in biblical terms as an original, ideal state granted by God or nature, whereas utopia is an ideal of the future that one must strive for through social reform. Analytically, the concepts of Eden and utopia are quite distinct, but the relocation planners coupled the two: for them, the utopia of the future consisted in restoring the Eden of the past.

On 25 August 1953, thirty-four Inuit men, women, and children were placed on board a barge and taken to the government eastern Arctic patrol ship CGS *C.D. Howe*, which lay anchored off the coast of Hudson Bay. They were members of the Inukjuamiut Inuit who had been living near the Port Harrison settlement on the Ungava Peninsula in northern Quebec (see maps 1.1 and 3.1). The families were selected by officials to participate in what the government described as a voluntary migration experiment. The project involved transporting the group twenty-two hundred kilometers to the High Arctic Islands, where Canada's two northernmost colonies were to be established for them on Ellesmere and Cornwallis Islands. This relocation was envisaged as the prototype for an ambitious initiative to resettle Inuit throughout the unoccupied regions of the High Arctic.

Why were these pioneer migrants, or "chosen people," encouraged to find a new homeland in this Arctic Eden? Why was the government intrigued by the idea of repopulating the far North and shifting Inuit from one part of the Arctic to another? Although Canada is one of the largest countries in the world, most of its populace live within a hundred-mile-wide strip along the southern border with the United States. The Northwest Territories and the Yukon comprise over one-third of Canada's territory, yet this region has an extremely low population density. Before 1950 the government exercised a laissez-faire policy of minimal intervention in the North. The Canadian government offices that had principal administrative responsibility for the North were the Department of Resources and Development (hereafter referred to as "the Department") and the Royal Canadian Mounted Police (RCMP). At this time, the majority of Canadian Inuit were living in camps on the land and were depending on its natural resources for much of their diet. The small settlements and frontier outposts dotted about the North (see maps I.1 and 1.1) usually consisted of a few buildings, occupied by a trader, perhaps a missionary, and a Royal Canadian Mounted policeman. There were few schools or nursing stations in the Arctic in the early 1950s and no government administrators. The settlements were supplied once a year by ship, at which time the Inuit would be given brief medical examinations by the ship's doctor. In contrast, the post-1959 period was characterized by a process of accelerated acculturation and centralization, during which all of Canada's Inuit were resettled by the government into purposely built northern towns.

In the 1950s, the government searched for policy paradigms and technological solutions for developing Canada's northern frontier. One senior official spoke metaphorically of viewing the Arctic as a laboratory wherein one might conduct experiments with the nine thousand Canadian Inuit in order to improve their standard of living (Phillips, 1955: 106). The project to repopulate the Queen Elizabeth Islands in the High Arctic, which the Inuit had abandoned several hundred years ago during the Little Ice Age, was one such bold social experiment. Some reformers saw the project as a means of creating a refuge for the Inuit, away from the corrupting influences of Western civilization. The relocation would provide them with a fresh start, it was argued, so that an ideal Inuit community in the far North might flourish under benevolent and firm police supervision. Although some officials may have viewed the Arctic as a field laboratory, and other Whites perceived the Arctic environment as a generic, snow-bound space, the Inuit had a decidedly different view of place. Ideas of wilderness, frontier versus homeland, and the associative value of place will be explored later in this text. The literature on the role of place and landscape is extensive, and several works are especially applicable, such as *The Power of Place* by Agnew and Duncan (1989), *Ulysses' Sail* by Helms (1988), and Jackson's (1989) *Maps of Meaning*. My discussion of place embraces a binary examination of geographical and anthropological aspects. In this regard, two important works on Inuit perceptions of landscape and other cultural factors are Brody's *The Living Arctic* (1987), and *Arctic Homeland* by Nuttall (1992).

The representation of the Inuit and the influence of stereotypes and myths are fundamental to identifying the links between imagery, popular thinking, and government policy. Ironically, the Inukjuamiut selected for the 1953 relocation had been projected on cinema screens throughout the world as symbols of the happy, smiling Eskimos, the "noble savages" in the classic film *Nanook of the North* made by Robert Flaherty in 1922. At that time, the government had limited contact with the Inuit. Thirty years later, though, momentous changes were taking place in the Canadian North, both in terms of the accelerated militarization of the Arctic by American and Canadian forces as a result of the Cold War and in the increase in government intervention. The government's Inuit relocation program during the 1950s coincided with the introduction of the welfare state to the North and was influenced by three primary factors: a desire to reform the Inuit, humanitarian interests, and geopolitical considerations.

The Whites' concern about the erosion of native self-reliance was linked with a conservative appraisal of their ability to sustain themselves on the available natural resources. In short, the government feared that the welfare state might make the Inuit more dependent on Whites rather than on what the land and its resources might continue to provide. Welfare benefits, in turn, would alter the economic relationship between the state and the Inuit. In the 1950s, geopolitical issues involving sovereignty were highlighted by the presence of large numbers of American military personnel in the Canadian Arctic and by the fact that the Inuit were virtually the only Canadian citizens living in one-third of Canada's territory. The government therefore placed increasing importance on the status of Inuit living standards and on their occupation of the land.

In this study, the intricacies of a larger issue are also explored: the attempt by seemingly benevolent and paternalistic external agencies to reform the native for his "own good" and to clothe their actions in moralistic rhetoric. Officials perceived that a kind of primitive Arctic Eden was in danger of being destroyed. Having bitten the apple offered to them in the form of relief (public welfare) and other state benefit payments, the residents of this Arctic Eden appeared to be abandoning their traditional ways and "loitering" around the small northern settlements. Officials referred to certain areas of the North as being "overpopulated" and suggested that, by physically removing Inuit from the settlements and returning them to their natural environment, they might be restored to their traditional and seemingly idyllic way of life. Studies such as Piven and Cloward's (1972) classic text, *Regulating the Poor*, on the functions of public welfare are relevant to this issue, in addition to literature on the connection between welfare and punitive strategies such as *Punishment and Welfare* by Garland (1985), H. Johnston's (1972) *British Emigration Policy 1815–1830, "Shovelling out Paupers,"* and *The Reform of Prisoners 1830–1900* by Forsythe (1987).

A contention I make in this book, namely, that Inuit relocation experiments were wedded to a reformist ideology, has been presented in the context of other relocations, notably in Constantine's (1991) revealing study of "Empire Migration and Social Reform, 1880–1950." When discussing the rehabilitation component of the relocation projects, several works have been particularly useful, including *The Decline of the Rehabilitative Ideal* by Allen (1981), *A Just Measure of Pain* by Ignatieff (1978), and Foucault's (1977) *Discipline and Punish*.

A second case study presented in this book focuses on another band of Inuit known as the Ahiarmiut, who lived near Ennadai Lake in the Keewatin District of the Northwest Territories (see map I.1). The Ahiarmiut were the subject of perhaps the most famous book written about the Inuit, Farley Mowat's *People of the Deer*, published in 1952. The entire band of Ahiarmiut was relocated four times by government officials during 1951–58. The multilayered analogies between the relocations favor a comparative study. The relocation of the Inukjuamiut in 1953–55 and the Ahiarmiut in 1957 (see appendices A and B) were the foremost examples of a government policy designed to move Inuit into unoccupied wilderness sites in order to isolate them and minimize external contact. Six months after the Ahiarmiut were relocated "voluntarily" in 1957, seven had died. Their deaths and those of other Inuit in the Keewatin District in the winter of 1957–58 signaled an end to this form of experimentation. The government reversed its Inuit resettlement policy and embarked on a plan of assimilation through centralization by encouraging all Inuit to move from small camps into larger settlements during the late 1950s and 1960s (Diubaldo, 1985: 9; Mackinnon, 1989: 165).

The government's motives for the relocations and the social implications of the experiments have since become the subject of much controversy and political debate in Canada. A series of public inquiries, investigations, and reports was conducted by the Parliamentary Standing Committee on Aboriginal Affairs in 1990 and by the Canadian Human Rights Commission in 1991. In April 1993, forty years after the High Arctic relocation experiment was initiated, Canada's first Royal Commission on Aboriginal Peoples conducted public hearings in Ottawa on the government-sponsored resettlement project. For five days during the April hearings, twenty-five Inuit from the Arctic communities of Resolute Bay, Grise Fiord, and Inukjuak presented their testimonies about the relocation. Across Canada, viewers watched the live, televised broadcasts of the proceedings and witnessed emotional scenes as Inuit elders recounted their disturbing memories.

The Royal Commission was appointed in 1990 with the responsibility of investigating a wide range of political, economic, and cultural issues of significance to native peoples. The inquiry into the 1953 relocation experiment, which has included oral testimonies and revisionist studies, has challenged official accounts (a detailed commentary on the documents has been written by Grant [1993]). Central to the commission's investigation was the need to interpret the radically contrasting perceptions of the relocation experiment. The Inuit spoke of the hardships of resettlement and of their inability to leave the High Arctic colonies and return home to Port Harrison. The Department claimed that these stories were exaggerated and that there was little evidence of hardship. Independent studies and reports have suggested that the relocation was implemented as an experiment in social reform and for sovereignty purposes (Grant, 1991; Marcus, 1992; Soberman, 1991), whereas the Department and its former officials claimed that the operation was motivated solely by humanitarian concerns (Canada, 1955a; Canada, 1993b: 134–36). Roger Tassé, a former deputy minister of justice, and Mary Simon, past president of the Inuit Circumpolar Conference, were asked by the commission to conduct a preliminary review of the case. Tassé and Simon (1993) reported that there were serious discrepancies in the findings about the relocation, and that Inuit viewpoints had "not been addressed in an entirely fair and just manner by the government."

In June 1993 the Royal Commission conducted further hearings in which former civil servants, government investigators, academic researchers (including the author; see appendix C), and others presented their views on the relocation. The occasion served as a precedent, in that for the first time, former senior government officials were invited to account for their actions before a Royal Commission that included a majority of commissioners of aboriginal descent. The officials who testified included Gordon Robertson, former deputy minister of the Department of Northern Affairs and National Resources (DNANR), commissioner of the Northwest Territories, and clerk of the Privy Council (Canada's most senior civil servant); Ben Sivertz, former chief of the Arctic Division, director of the Lands and Administration Branch of the DNANR and commissioner of the Northwest Territories; and Graham Rowley, secretary of the Advisory Committee on Northern Development.

The commissioners included co-chairman René Dussault, justice of the Quebec Court of Appeal; co-chairman George Erasmus, former grand chief of the Assembly of First Nations; Bertha Wilson, retired justice of the Supreme Court of Canada; Paul Chartrand, professor, Department of Native Studies, University of Manitoba; Viola Robinson, former president of the Native Council of Canada; and Mary Sillett, former president of the Inuit Women's Association of Canada. At times, the hearings became confrontational when the commissioners closely questioned officials about actions they took pertaining to the relocation. Gordon Robertson criticized the commission's investigation, stating that it was "a travesty of justice" for the officials responsible for the relocation to be "held up to ridicule" today for actions they had taken forty years ago (Canada, 1993b: 137). His comment raises an interesting point: who amongst the politicians, civil servants, officials, novelists, and the public should take responsibility for the relocations and their repercussions? Can one make such value judgments in retrospect, employing perhaps a different ethical protocol than that practiced in the 1950s? In the course of this study, I intend to address the issue of responsibility, examining the question of who knew what and when they knew it.

When first researching the history of Inuit migrations and relocations, I found some excellent studies on traditional patterns of migration (Graburn, 1969; Freeman and others, 1976; S. Rowley, 1985b); other studies largely examined the post-1960 period, during which resettlement was used to promote centralization and wage employment for the Canadian Inuit (D. Stevenson, 1968; Williamson, 1974; Williamson and Foster,

1974). With a few notable exceptions (Jenness, 1964; Ben-Dor, 1966; Freeman, 1969, 1971, 1984), however, few texts concentrated on the relocation experiments of the 1950s themselves. These studies were either based primarily on anthropological (Freeman, 1969) or on archival research (Jenness, 1964; Diubaldo, 1985), but they did not synthesize the two. Since the completion of the present study, two excellent complementary texts have appeared (Royal Commission on Aboriginal Peoples, 1994; Tester and Kulchyski, 1994).

Because a number of the participants in the relocation projects are still alive and a great wealth of government records has become newly available, I felt there would be advantages to taking a twofold approach, combining fieldwork and archival research. The data I have collected are of four kinds: published material, unpublished documentation from archival and private sources, systematic interviews, and participant observations. I conducted fieldwork in four Inuit communities—Arviat, Grise Fiord, Inukjuak, and Resolute Bay—to interview the relocation survivors, their offspring, and other members of the hamlets (see appendix D). In southern Canada, I interviewed former and current civil servants involved in northern administration, Royal Canadian Mounted policemen, missionaries, and traders who were connected with the relocations or the Inuit groups involved (see appendix D). This story has a large and diverse cast of characters, and for a number of them I have provided biographical sketches (see appendix E). Many of the documents cited in this study are government memoranda and reports that, at the time they were written, were intended for private, internal review only. They often provide, therefore, candid observations and insights about the events that took place. During the course of earlier research (Marcus, 1990), I uncovered a number of key documents in the National Archives of Canada in Ottawa on the relocation to Resolute Bay and Grise Fiord (Bolger, 1960a; Fraser, 1960b; Hinds, 1953b; J. C. Jackson, 1956; Jenkin, 1960; Larsen, 1954b; Macdonell, 1964; Sivertz, 1956a; A. Stevenson, 1951b). In addition, I discovered important material within the Alex Stevenson Collection in the Prince of Wales Northern Heritage Center in Yellowknife (Marcus, 1992), which is also used in this study.

This book is divided into four sections. In part 1 (chapters 1 and 2), causal factors behind the government's Inuit relocation policies are explored. In chapter 1, I describe the symbolic representation of the Inuit hunters in Canadian and American films and literature, together with the manner in which those perceptions might have influenced and reflected government attitudes and policies towards the Inuit. In particular, a connection is identified between the government's articulations about an "Eskimo problem" in 1952 and its subsequent attempts to find remedial solutions, of which the relocation experiments formed a prominent part. Chapter 2 examines the reasons for the government's decision to target for relocation the Inukjuamiut living in the area of Port Harrison in Arctic Quebec. The linkage is then explored between a social-reformist policy, in which relocation was a means of shifting "surplus" Inuit populations to unoccupied areas of the High Arctic, and the government's geopolitical initiatives to colonize those areas to demonstrate Canadian sovereignty.

Part 2 (chapters 3 and 4) describes the first case study, which involves the relocation by boat in 1953–55 of Inuit from Port Harrison to the distant locations of Resolute Bay and Grise Fiord in the High Arctic. Although the relocations were inspired by initiatives within the government to implement a reformative ideology suffused with metaphors from the Garden of Eden, these experiments were viewed at the time by some officials and by the Inuit as being only partly beneficial. The language the government used to describe the relocation projects and the keywords it employed, including "voluntary migration," "rehabilitation," and "experiment," are an essential element in the reconstruction of events.

In part 3 (chapters 5, 6, and 7), the second case study is considered, involving the relocation of the Ahiarmiut in 1950 to Nueltin Lake and in 1957 to Henik Lake. Chapter 5 examines the Ahiarmiut's encounters with officials, which ultimately led to their relocation away from their homeland at Ennadai Lake. The operation ended in tragedy, with the seven deaths mentioned earlier and with the incarceration of several more Inuit. Chapter 6 searches for the factors behind the Ahiarmiut deaths in the investigative reports and reviews transcripts of the criminal trial of Kikkik that followed. The manner in which the Department controlled the discourse of the relocation and its role in shaping public perceptions of the Inuit deaths are analyzed in chapter 7.

Part 4 (chapter 8) assesses the aftermath of the relocations and their implications for the Inuit and for the government's northern policies. Despite the largely altruistic and idealistic motives that may have been part of the government-sponsored relocations, the native persons interviewed for this study have presented dystopian perspectives of the events. These views challenge the assumption that the relocation projects were executed with "informed consent." At the end of this section, I draw together the metaphors discussed in earlier chapters regarding Eden, utopia, and migration, and their relationship to a sense of place, to suggest how they can be used to interpret the relocation experiences.

· PART 1 ·

PROBLEMS AND SOLUTIONS

1

IMAGES OF THE INUIT

Film Imagery of the Happy-Go-Lucky Eskimo

The film *Nanook of the North* is arguably the most popular and enduring cinematic representation of the Inuit (see fig. 1.1). By coincidence, the Inuit featured in the film were from the same group of Inukjuamiut living on the east coast of Hudson Bay who were relocated thirty years later to the High Arctic. The film was made by Robert Flaherty, an American mining engineer and explorer turned filmmaker. When the film was first distributed in 1922, it was premiered in London, Moscow, and New York, where it was paired with Harold Lloyd's box-office success, *Grandma's Boy*. The film presented audiences across the world with a vivid image of Inuit life in the Canadian Arctic.

Such was the public's fascination with the "happy Eskimos" that ice creams were soon being sold as "Nanuks" in Germany, "Esquimaux" in France, and "Eskimo Pies" in Britain and America. When the hunter who played the role of Nanook died of starvation two years after the film was made, his death was mourned as far away as China (Brody, 1987: 21). For the audiences, Flaherty's native film stars reinforced the image of "noble savage" Eskimo hunters. In Western popular culture, *Nanook of the North* remains today the quintessential iconographic representation of Inuit life.

One of the reasons for the film's success was its personification of the Eskimo. Flaherty structured his film by focusing on a single family. The hunter Nanook, his wife Nyla, and their children and dogs became the family through whom Flaherty intended to dramatize aspects of Inuit life. There were few people in the audiences who watched *Nanook of the North* who had ever come into contact with the Inuit; yet, perhaps

FIGURE 1.1 Nanook (Alakariallak) from the film *Nanook of the North,* 1922.
Credit: Robert Flaherty

because of a desire to view hunting societies and the Inuit, in particular,
as an original, primitive version of our own society, the film portrayed
a family with whom audiences could readily identify (Fienup-Riordan,
1990: xix; Toren, 1991: 277). Nanook and his family were shown per-
forming everyday activities—building a house, sleeping, playing games,
traveling, obtaining food. How they went about these activities, and the
setting in which they took place, provided the exotic elements of the
story. The immediacy of the scenes was heightened by the strong characterization of Nanook. The viewer was captivated by Nanook's comedic

mannerisms and the resourceful techniques he employed to accomplish his daily tasks.

As anthropologist Margaret Mead has recalled, the film was initially viewed as an ethnographic account of Inuit life (Rombout and others, 1979: 71; see also Asch, 1992: 197). Although some theorists might have been contented with the broad cinematic view that "the space of film is the space of reality" (Heath, 1981: 25), other critics were dissatisfied that the film was not accurate in various details (Calder-Marshall, 1963). For example, in the film Nanook wears polar bear pants, which were not worn by northern Quebec Inuit but by those living in northern Greenland. Ironically, the one scenario Flaherty tried and failed to film was a polar bear hunt (R. Flaherty, 1924). Flaherty's film employed a certain amount of artifice to achieve its representation of Inuit life. Nanook's name was not really Nanook, which was a screen name (a transliteration of *nanuq*, meaning "polar bear" in Inuktitut); in fact Nanook was played by an Inuk called Alakariallak. Nanook's family was also fictitious; they were simply members of the Inukjuamiut whom Flaherty had selected on an individual basis. The role of Nanook's wife, Nyla, was played by Maggie Nujarluktuk, who was actually Alakariallak's daughter-in-law.

Irrespective of some critics' disenchantment with the quality of the film's realism, the belief "that film can be an unmediated record of the real world is based on the idea that cameras, not people, take pictures" (Ruby, 1982: 125). Though others have referred to Flaherty as "the father of the documentary," it had not been his intention to document a scientific set of images. He was more interested in creating a dramatic representation that reflected the essence of traditional Inuit life. He remarked: "I am not going to make films about what the white man has made of primitive peoples; . . . what I want to show is the former majesty and character of these people, while it is still possible—before the white man has destroyed not only their character, but the people as well" (cited in Barnouw, 1974). By naturalizing the Inuit, Flaherty portrayed them as paragons of simplicity and virtue (Fienup-Riordan, 1990: xvi).

The external perception of "Eskimo" identity was thus transformed from that of a strange and little-known people who lived at the top of the world to that of human beings who pursued activities like everyone else, albeit in a more "primitive" and exotic way. *Nanook*'s power as a symbol was significant because its uninformed audiences assumed that the film was providing them with a panoptic view of Eskimo culture; however, as Ann Fienup-Riordan (1990) explains in her perceptive study *Eskimo Essays*, Nanook's iconographic image obscured the reality and diversity of North American Inuit, the majority of whom did not live in igloos. Although the face of Nanook became known and was marketed around the world, the Inukjuamiut continued their lives in much the same way as before Flaherty's visit, with little or no knowledge of their widespread fame.

Thirty years after the making of the film, the Inukjuamiut and other Inuit living in northern Quebec were no longer considered by officials as "happy-go-lucky Eskimos" but rather as an economically depressed people living in an "overpopulated area" (Eskimo Affairs, 1952b). It was the transformation of the Eskimo from the noble savage of the 1920s presented in *Nanook of the North* to the welfare-dependent "white man's burden" of the 1950s that altered the government's essential relationship with the Inuit. By replacing its former policy of minimal social intervention with one of financial provision, Ottawa was no longer responsible *to* the Inuit; rather, it became responsible *for* them. To claim state aid was to relinquish one's private freedom, allowing the state to exert control over those who came to depend on its resources for their survival (Piven and Cloward, 1972: 22; Garland, 1985: 48). Within the context of "welfare colonialism," the government now had a prerogative to organize resettlement projects to ameliorate the standard of living of the Inuit and reduce state dependency (Paine, 1977).

Nanook Reborn as Joseph Idlout

In 1952, the documentary film *Land of the Long Day*, directed by Doug Wilkinson and financed by the Canadian Film Board, was shown in cinemas in Canada and the United States. It could almost be a more realistic color version of *Nanook of the North*. Indeed, it was Wilkinson's intention to appropriate the Nanook model for his film and to adopt Flaherty's dramatic device of focusing on a single Inuit hunter and his family (Wilkinson, personal communication). He recruited a highly skilled hunter, Joseph Idlout, for the starring role. The film was set in the High Arctic at Idlout's camp, one hundred kilometers from the settlement of Pond Inlet on North Baffin Island. Idlout's realistic persona, as presented in the film, aptly suited the mythical Nanook mold. Like Nanook, Idlout is depicted as a resourceful, industrious, and highly successful hunter, with a gentle disposition and a good sense of humor. True to the Nanook stereotype, Idlout and his extended family are presented in the film as "happy, smiling Eskimos," but with a difference. Through his use of narration, Wilkinson's characterization of Idlout is intended to symbolize the acculturated, modern Inuk.

Like Flaherty, Wilkinson concentrated on scenes of Inuit life, without showing interactions with Whites. Unlike Flaherty, who feared for the victimization of the Inuit by Western imperialism, Wilkinson wanted to present an integrated cultural figure. In his depiction of an ideal Inuit hunter, he made a point of showing material items the Inuit had long adopted from Western culture, including firearms, metal animal traps, and telescopes. Whereas Flaherty's Nanook was largely frozen in an atemporal, "traditional" state, Idlout had mastered the use of Western tools and incorporated them into his own culture. The only Western article in *Nanook of the North* was a gramophone, which Nanook treated as a great novelty. This encounter with modern technology was a joyous one, suggesting that Western civilization had yet to have any detrimental impact on Inuit society. For Idlout, there were no such novelties. Wilkinson's lens conveyed the impression that Idlout had already established a happy and fruitful association with Western culture. The message in *Land of the Long Day* appeared to be that the cultural encounter that had taken place during the thirty years between Wilkinson's film and *Nanook of the North* had left Inuit society resilient and unscathed.

Both Nanook and Idlout were transposed into iconographic symbols by Western society. The likeness of Nanook appeared on ice-cream wrappers, and Idlout was featured on the back of the Canadian two-dollar bill. Despite the differences in acculturation, they also shared an identity "off camera": they were "real people," *Inummariit*, who lived close to the land and typified traditional Inuit culture (Brody, 1975). Flaherty's and Wilkinson's efforts to capture the spirit of the *Inummariit* by living with the people, studying their culture, and selecting Inuit actors contrasted with many later cinematic attempts to portray "traditional" Inuit life. In one such film, *Savage Innocents*, made in 1960, actor Anthony Quinn played the leading role of "Inuk," while the other Inuit roles were performed by Japanese actors. In comparison with these contrived images, the Nanook and Idlout representations were fated to be extended, for, as I will explain in chapter 3, Nanook's kinsmen and Joseph Idlout himself were selected to join a government relocation scheme to the High Arctic.

Stark Images of Another North

In the early 1950s, the authors Farley Mowat and Richard Harrington unveiled images of Inuit deprivation and starvation that stood in sharp contrast to the popular image of happy Eskimos presented in *Nanook of the North* and *Land of the Long Day*. Mowat's work in particular was to have a profound impact on public perceptions of the Inuit and on the government's Inuit administration policies (Burch, 1986: 130).

Farley Mowat was born in Belleville, Ontario, in 1921, served as a brigade intelligence officer with the Canadian Forces in Europe during World War II, and left the army with the rank of captain. He was funded by the Arctic Institute of North America to undertake a biological survey in the Canadian Arctic in the summer of 1947. The following year, he was employed by the Canadian Wildlife Service to conduct wolf surveys in the same region of the Keewatin District. Mowat established his camp near Ennadai Lake (see map 5.1), where he came into contact with Inuit who were members of the small band of Ahiarmiut. Having decided to write about his experiences with them, and drawing on the work of Tyrrell (1897), Birket-Smith (1929a), Rasmussen (1930), and Downes (1943), Mowat published his first book, *People of the Deer*, in early 1952. The book was highly controversial, sold extremely well in North America, and quickly became an international best seller.

People of the Deer received a large number of enthusiastic reviews from critics, especially in the United States and England. "It is 'inspired' writing in the best sense and gives us a respect for human life that we are in the danger of losing," exclaimed the *San Francisco Chronicle* (Voiles, 1952: 21). "Here is a really great book," reported *Saturday Review* (Sanderson, 1952: 17). British readers were informed by the *Times Literary Supplement* (1952: 599) that "this is the most powerful book to come out of the Arctic for some years"; and the *Library Journal* recommended the book, stating that it was worth reading "for its high literary quality alone" (Henderson, 1952: 359). "A new classic," wrote the reviewer for the London *Sunday Times*: "Mr. Mowat writes of the vanishing Ihalmiut [Ahiarmiut] with passionate sympathy and indignation" (Mortimer, 1952).

In terms of the story it told, Mowat's *People of the Deer* was a tragedy. It thus contrasted dramatically with Flaherty's *Nanook of the North*, which had elements of a slapstick comedy (such as the now-classic scene depicting Nanook in a tug-of-war with a seal). In his book, Mowat dramatized his experiences while living with the Ahiarmiut and described their recent history and decimation by starvation. The author blamed the group's demise on neglect by the authorities. Whereas Wilkinson's *Land of the Long Day* offered an optimistic appraisal of Inuit acculturation, Mowat's book, published in the same year, presented a darker side of the cultural convergence of Inuit and White societies. The story concerns a single band of Inuit, but Mowat presented the Ahiarmiut in a more contemporary mode as emblematic of the difficulties affecting Inuit across Canada at the time.

People of the Deer criticized the tripartite control of the North exercised by the Hudson's Bay Company (HBC), the Royal Canadian Mounted Police (RCMP), and the Catholic and Anglican Churches. It condemned the government for not taking a more active role in the North and focused public attention on the "plight of the Eskimo." As a result, the Canadian government came under sustained attack for wanton neglect of its northern citizens. The prime minister received hundreds of letters from people around the world who became concerned about the Canadian Inuit after reading Mowat's book. This letter was representative of many:

I simply want you to know that I care about those people who live in the North and that I am sure I represent many, many more who do care too. Since governments act when weight of public opinion requires it, please place me on the side that says act. . . . May I hope that apathy and immovable mass can be moved by government action. (Howell, 1952)

The Department responded to Mowat's polemical narrative by attacking the factuality of the book and the credibility of the author. When the book was serialized by *The Atlantic Monthly* and published in a condensed form in *Reader's Digest*, the Department's Deputy Minister Hugh Young (1953a) informed the editors that the book was factually incorrect and that its "sweeping charge is simply untrue." Young insisted that Mowat had only brief contact with the Inuit, was not an expert on Inuit culture, and that contrary to Mowat's descriptions the Caribou Inuit were probably as well off as most other Inuit. Several Canadian journals published reviews critical of *People of the Deer* by officials who had worked in the North: the *Canadian Geographical Journal's* reviewer described it as "a dangerous book . . . because it is likely to have a wide distribution." Because it attacked the activities of the Company and other agencies working in the North, the reviewer warned that it was a prejudiced book and one likely to do more harm than good (Leechman, 1952).

The strongest attack on *People of the Deer* came from a Department official, Dr. A. E. Porsild, chief botanist for the National Museum of Canada. The National Museum was under the Department of Resources and Development, and Porsild conferred with his colleagues in the Department during 1952–53 about steps they should take to denounce the book and its author. Porsild saw the book as a seditious text and wrote letters to the editors of popular magazines stating that the thirty-one-year-old Mowat was "unscrupulous, . . . posing as an authority on Eskimo and arctic problems." Furthermore, Porsild postulated that "there never was such a tribe" and that Mowat had created the Ahiarmiut "solely as a vehicle for his attack on Government administration and on the 'wicked' traders" (Porsild, 1952a). Porsild might have based his assumption on the fact that the Fifth Thule Expedition of 1921–24, in their classic study of the Caribou Inuit (Birket-Smith, 1929a), did not come across the Ahiarmiut (nor did they journey to Ennadai Lake). Research, however, has confirmed that the Ahiarmiut were a distinct band living in the general area of Ennadai Lake from the midnineteenth century, and that they had contact with traders (and occasionally with the police and explorers) from that time until 1949 (Csonka, 1991).

Porsild's notorious attack on *People of the Deer* culminated in a review article he wrote for the Hudson's Bay Company's journal *The Beaver* in June 1952. As a scientist, Porsild was disturbed by what he perceived as various factual mistakes. His didactic approach was to state that Mowat did not spend as much time in the Arctic as he said he did, and that he had overestimated the decline in the Caribou Inuit population. Porsild (1952b) suggested that Mowat be given the Inuk nickname *Sagdlutorssuaq*—"Great Teller of Tall Tales." Mowat prepared a lengthy rebuttal that addressed each of Porsild's charges, but *The Beaver* apparently declined to print it (Mowat, personal communication).

Richard Harrington's book, *The Face of the Arctic*, was published in the same year as *People of the Deer*. Harrington was a well-known photographer who had traveled across the North and wrote a number of articles for *The Beaver* and other Canadian periodicals. He based his book *The Face of the Arctic* on five journeys he had made through the Arctic in the 1940s and '50s. The book was intended to give a realistic, overall perspective of life in northern Canada. The text comprised accounts of Harrington's adventures and contact with native peoples and was accompanied by striking photographs. Although words can *describe*, the camera has the power to *authenticate* (Beloff, 1985: 16). In the book's third chapter, "Portrait of Famine: Padlei, 1950," Harrington presented stark images of starving Caribou Inuit and their dogs in the region of Padlei in the Keewatin District. The portraits of Inuit taken in "starvation camps" showed a people living in desperate circumstances. In one photograph of an Inuk "near death," Harrington provided the ironic caption, "Note Government identification tag," which was hanging around the starving woman's neck (see fig. 1.2). The author's message was clear, implying that the government had tagged the Inuit but not looked after them.

Harrington's book, which was published a few months after Mowat's, was perhaps more informed because the author had years of experience in the North. It was well received, but the reviews it received were more sedate than Mowat's. Trevor Lloyd (1952: 7) reviewed *Face of the Arctic* for the *New York Times*, noting: "The book is attractively written and beautifully illustrated." The reviewer for the *New York Herald Tribune* similarly stated: "Here is a well-written book by a sensitive and sensible observer who is a magnificent photographer and who describes and interprets in a relaxed and thoroughly likeable, satisfactory fashion" (Stefansson, 1952:

FIGURE 1.2 Inuit woman at "starvation camp" near Padlei, featured in *The Face of the Arctic* by Richard Harrington, 1952. Credit: National Archives of Canada

1). The reviews were commendatory, but the book did not elicit the same passionate storm of controversy generated by *People of the Deer*. Nevertheless, the two books by Harrington and Mowat were complementary. Harrington provided the photographic evidence of Caribou Inuit starvation, and Mowat, whose *People of the Deer* included no photographs in the first edition, created a dramatic portrait of Caribou Inuit life, noting the steep decline in their numbers due to famine. Whereas Harrington's book presented images of starvation principally as a reality of Inuit life, Mowat used similar imagery as an indictment of the government's Inuit administration policy, or lack thereof.

The fact that both books were printed by American publishers meant that the Canadian government faced the humiliation of receiving a considerable amount of correspondence from the American public and negative publicity in articles published in American newspapers and periodicals. Issues Mowat raised in *People of the Deer* were subsequently debated in the House of Commons. Mr. R. Knight, MP for Saskatoon, told the House: "This book by Farley Mowat caused a great deal of controversy, and it is really a terrible—and I am using a mild word—indictment of the authorities who are at present responsible for Eskimo affairs" (Canada, 1953d: 773). Two years after the book made its debut, it was still the subject of a House of Commons debate between the minister of Northern Affairs and National Resources, Jean Lesage, and MPs. *People of the Deer* was "a book which I think should deeply touch our consciences," said one opposition MP (Canada, 1954c: 1243). In keeping with the Department's attempts to discredit the book and its author, Lesage countered by repeating that the story was an invention of Mowat's imagination. He suggested that the thing to do "would be to take that book from the factual shelves and put it on the fictional shelves of the library because it is based on false and partial information" (ibid.: 1244).

In the late 1950s, Mowat admitted that his book's dramatic treatment did not adhere entirely to the facts. "I became so angry about the awful conditions under which they [the Caribou Inuit] were forced to exist as a result of neglect by their fellow-Canadians," he recalled, "that I wasn't too careful about documenting my findings. Because I was vulnerable on certain points, a concerted effort was made to discredit the whole story" (*Toronto Telegram*, 1959). As might be expected, the imbroglio between the government and Mowat only increased the public's interest in the matter.

Henry Larsen's Views on Inuit Welfare

"The average Canadian citizen has no conception of how the once healthful and resourceful Eskimo has been exploited to such a degree that he now lives a life comparable to that of a dog," observed Henry Larsen (1952c), a senior official in the RCMP.

Two months before Mowat's stark depiction of Inuit life became public, Insp. Larsen had recorded his critical views on conditions of Inuit life in the North in reports to his superior, the commander of the RCMP, Commissioner L. H. Nicholson. Larsen described, for example, what he had found when inspecting Inuit camps in the eastern Arctic:

The Eskimos generally have drifted into a state of lack of initiative and confusion. Conditions generally are appalling. Never has there existed so much destitution, filth and squalor as exists today, and in the opinion of some people the conditions under which some natives live is a disgrace to Canada, surpassing the worst evils of slum areas in cities. Bad sanitary and economic conditions are gradually undermining the health of these people and if not checked will ultimately result in their extermination. (Larsen, 1951)

Larsen's comments were purely for internal consideration, and the contents of this memo to Commissioner Nicholson were not made public. Larsen later recorded that he was determined to do what he could to bring out the facts about Inuit conditions (Larsen, n.d.: 994). He was acutely aware that there was a difference between the Canadian public's popular conceptions of the Inuit and the reality of life in the North. Larsen informed Nicholson: "The sordid conditions existing amongst Eskimos are not known to the general public 'outside,' whose knowledge of the Eskimos generally is that gleaned from glowing accounts which appear in the press occasionally and from romantic photographs in the magazines" (Larsen, 1951). Larsen's comment was made only a few months before the publication of *People of the Deer*. His observation reinforces the impression that public perceptions of Inuit life were still conditioned by stereotyped, happy-go-lucky images like that of the idealized Nanook, hence the great impact of Mowat's book, which aimed forcefully to debunk those views.

Commanding the RCMP's "G" Division, Insp. Henry Larsen supervised its forty-one detachments in the Northwest Territories, the Yukon, and northern Quebec. These detachments were responsible for the maintenance of law and order in the regions, for the symbolic display of Canadian sovereignty, and for Inuit welfare. The government recognized that the "enforcement of law and order and the laws of the Northwest Territories were considered to be a minor part of the R.C.M. Police duties in the Arctic," because "Eskimos as a race are law-abiding and there is little crime" (Eskimo Affairs, 1952b: 2).

Inuit welfare therefore became one of their primary concerns, especially when family allowance payments of six to eight dollars per month per child began being disbursed to the Inuit around 1945–48 (other Canadian children had been receiving these benefits since the 1944 Family Allowances Act). The Inuit called family allowances *kakkalaanituq*, "something for babies." This sudden infusion of money into the Inuit economy represented a major source of income for the Inuit. In 1945 the Old Age Pensions Act was passed, which provided the Inuit with an additional form of income. The RCMP were given the responsibility of supervising not only the distribution of family allowances but also other transfer payments, including old-age benefits and pensions for the blind, and of approving government relief (public welfare). Previously, relief had been allotted on an ad hoc basis at the behest of the local HBC store managers dotted about the Arctic. Replacing the former laissez-faire attitudes, the new relief policies were designed to centralize, rationalize, and professionalize the provision of state benefits to the Inuit (Garland, 1985: 50).

The RCMP also served as representatives in the Arctic for other government departments, including National Health and Welfare, Citizenship and Immigration, National Revenue, and the Post Office, on whose behalf they issued game and hunting licenses and fur-export permits, and acted as postmasters and medics. The Department was almost wholly reliant on the RCMP for implementing its Inuit administration policies. Larsen, who served as head of "G" Division during 1949–61, was therefore in a highly responsible and influential position. He was also an unconventional policeman with what were somewhat radical ideas for the time, and he became an advocate for improving the standard of living of the Inuit.

Henry Asbjorn Larsen was born in Norway in 1899. He went to sea at the age of fifteen, eventually became a Canadian citizen, and in 1928 he joined the RCMP and was assigned as a first mate to their new Arctic patrol vessel *St. Roch*. As the only member of the Force with previous Arctic sailing experience, Larsen was soon promoted to skipper and, after five years, was given command of the ship. When the *St. Roch* overwintered in the Arctic, Larsen made long patrols by dog sled to visit Inuit camps and settlements. Bassett (1980: 30) has written that the Inuit gave Larsen (fig. 1.3) the nickname *Hanorie Umiarjuaq* ("Henry with the big ship"). In the eastern Arctic, the Inuit called him by the nickname *Pallursialuk*, which means "the big one with the eyes slanted downwards" (MacDonald, personal communication). He became a popular figure, known throughout the North, and was described as having a charismatic personality. A crew member recalled Larsen's effect on people:

The skipper was well known, well liked, but above all well respected both by Inuit and Whites. Of course he had his share of curious customs. One of them was to stand on deck during a violent gale and sing hymns at the top of his voice. Now sailors are a superstitious lot and this hymn singing didn't go down well. But it was a sight to see his short, stocky figure standing there as though he was daring the Arctic to do its worst. (Bassett, 1980: 27)

From 1928 to 1948, Larsen patrolled the Arctic in the *St. Roch* and made several historic voyages. In 1940–42, Larsen and his eight-man crew became the first Canadians to complete a voyage through the Northwest Passage, a journey that took twenty-eight months. In 1944, Larsen again took the *St. Roch* through the Passage, westward through

FIGURE 1.3 Insp. Henry Larsen and Inuit women featured on the cover of *The Beaver*, September 1952. Credit: The Beaver/Canada's National History Society

a more northerly, uncharted route, after which he entered the history books as the first man to sail the Northwest Passage in both directions. He became a national hero, and he and his crew were awarded the Polar Medal by King George VI.

After twenty-one years serving the Force as master of the *St. Roch*, Larsen was promoted to inspector and moved to Ottawa in 1949, where he was given command of "G" Division. He became particularly concerned about the worsening social and economic conditions of the Inuit after the war. As a principal official responsible for their welfare, he adopted a forthright manner in pursuing policies designed to enhance their well-being. Larsen's memos to the commissioner are illustrative of his disputatious approach. Since they were written by a person outside the Department who had more knowledge of Inuit life and northern conditions than did most other senior officials in Ottawa, these documents provide a valuable alternative perspective of conditions in the North.

In Larsen's report to Commissioner Nicholson following his 1951 inspection patrol of the eastern Arctic, he defined the components of the "Eskimo problem" as he perceived them and produced a strong indictment of the government's Inuit administration policies. He candidly drew attention to the contrast between his perspective on the state of northern affairs and the Department's position. Larsen (1951) noted that his comments in the report were made from a purely humanitarian point of view; they were his own personal observations and a summary of information he had received during the past summer from reliable, confidential sources. He then proceeded to focus sharp criticism on the status quo, stating that the government had been lax in protecting the Inuit economy.

Like Farley Mowat, Larsen was unequivocal about whom he blamed for the decline of the Inuit—almost everyone with a white skin: "The Eskimos have been exploited over the years by the traders, missionaries, and other white persons living in the North." With the sharp decline in the price of white fox fur and the coincidental introduction of social-benefit payments, Larsen highlighted what he saw as the key socioeconomic dilemma: the Inuit were becoming dependent on family allowances and relief and on the goods they obtained for the furs they trapped rather than being dependent mostly on game they hunted.

One of the Department's senior officials, James Cantley, was asked to comment on Larsen's report. Cantley (1951) found a similarity in this report to others he had received from "well-meaning people" who looked at Inuit problems from a purely "humanitarian point of view." Cantley thought Larsen's comment that conditions in the North were appalling was an exaggeration. The Department's response was defensive, and Larsen recorded that he and his men in the field were beginning to be a bit disheartened by continually sending in reports without getting results. "All we could do was to report," said Larsen, "not to rectify or make policies for improvements which had been badly needed for years" (Larsen, n.d.: 996). Not confident that the Department would change its policy of minimal intervention and place greater emphasis on Inuit welfare, Larsen recommended that a Royal Commission be created to investigate the government's treatment of the Inuit. He wrote:

I have heard people say that the administration responsible for Eskimos failed in its handling of Eskimo affairs and that present conditions call for the appointment of a commission to fully investigate all matters pertaining to Eskimos. I, myself, am of the opinion that an independent Government commission should be appointed for that purpose, to travel into the country and visit the camps at different times of the year, summer and winter and see at first hand how the Eskimos exist. (Larsen, 1951)

The government was not interested in an outside investigation into its northern administration policies, however, and Cantley thought the suggestion of a Royal Commission did not seem very practicable. He replied that it would take too many years to obtain information about local conditions and it would be too costly an exercise. Besides, he concluded, the causes of the "Eskimo problem" were quite well realized by most people who have had any extensive experience in the Arctic (Cantley, 1951). Forty years after Larsen's original suggestion, a Royal Commission on Aboriginal Peoples was finally appointed to address problems of the North. At the time, however, Cantley did find merit in Larsen's proposal that a meeting be organized by the deputy minister of resources and development as soon as possible to bring together agencies working in the North to discuss the "Eskimo problem." Six months later, the first "Conference on Eskimo Affairs" was held.

Publicly Identifying the "Eskimo Problem"

Their voices became silent as white men told them what to do, what to trap, what to wear, how to think and how to die. The Eskimos were no longer the proud Inuit who had mastered the toughest climate on earth; they became just "the Eskimo Problem." (Phillips 1959b: 20)

When *People of the Deer* was published, the Department was caught unawares by the international reaction. By informing the Canadian public about "the plight of the Eskimo," Mowat's book served as a catalyst, making it a political necessity for the Department to be seen as taking steps to address the problems of Canadian Inuit who were confronting starvation, epidemics, and poverty (Zaslow, 1988: 272). The North was assuming a higher profile in the national consciousness, and there was increasing interest in the circumstances of its aboriginal inhabitants. As Larsen's reports indicate, there was also growing realization within the RCMP and the Department that something should be done to improve social and economic conditions in the North.

Public response to Mowat's book and increasing pressure within the government for changes in northern social policy had the combined effect of prompting the Department to take up Larsen's idea to organize a Conference on Eskimo Affairs, to be held on 19–20 May 1952. The

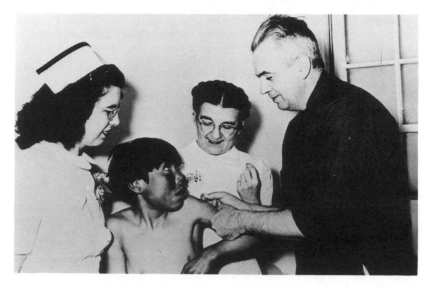

FIGURE 1.4 Inuit boy receiving inoculation from medical staff at Port Harrison, 1947.
Credit: Richard Harrington/National Archives of Canada, PA-129925

meeting was opened by the minister of the Department of Resources and
Development (the Department), and chaired by Major-General Hugh
Young, who held the joint position of commissioner of the Northwest
Territories and deputy minister of the Department. Fifty-eight officials
from eight government departments and agencies, including the RCMP,
the Anglican and Catholic Churches, the HBC, and representatives from
the U.S. embassy, attended the conference. By organizing this high-
profile conference, the Department was hoping to demonstrate publicly
its ability to deal effectively with the deteriorating situation.

One purpose of the conference was to encourage greater dialogue
between the different agencies working in the North and to discuss possible solutions to what was labeled the "Eskimo problem." The very act
of naming and classifying social problems often gives people the impression that the state understands what is wrong and can control the situation through its apparatus (Clark and Dear, 1984: 98). When establishing a "problem–solution" frame of reference, perhaps we should ask to
what extent social "problems" can in principle be solved or whether the
responses simply lead to new situations that will in turn become problems (Vitebsky, 1986: 11).

At the conference, the "Eskimo problem" was defined as having three
components: an unstable economy, poor health, and a growing dependence on government benefits. Health was of particular concern, for the

Canadian Inuit had an extremely high infant mortality rate of 200 per 1,000 births and reportedly the highest incidence of pulmonary tuberculosis in the world (Mackinnon, 1989: 163). Since the late 1940s, the Department of National Health and Welfare had been running an extensive program of x-raying and immunizing the Inuit (see fig. 1.4), removing many of them to southern hospitals for treatment of tuberculosis (by 1956 almost 20 percent of the Canadian Inuit population were in southern hospitals) (Diubaldo, 1985: 104–5). The act of holding the conference was, in fact, an admission for the first time that there was "a problem" and that it would take the talents of a number of agencies to come up with solutions and then to coordinate their activities in the North.

In the early 1950s, the Department was handicapped by its limited northern presence. The headquarters staff was in Ottawa, and, other than a few welfare teachers in Arctic settlements, it had no field staff north of the tree line (Clancy, 1987a: 192). It was therefore imperative that the Department seek the cooperation of the RCMP, who had a growing number of Arctic field staff, and the Department of National Health and Welfare, the Department of Transport, and nongovernmental agencies in pursuing its initiatives.

As a result of the conference, the Eskimo Affairs Committee was formed to act as a consultative body to the Department. It consisted of senior officials from the organizations most active in the North. The committee met twice yearly to discuss northern policy, although no Inuit were even invited to address the committee until 1959. Within the framework of welfare colonialism, this practice encouraged a "silencing of the cultural other" (Toren, 1991: 277) and reflected the nature of discourse between the Whites and the Inuit throughout the development of the Department's relocation policies in the 1950s.

The Fur Trade and Inuit Dependency

Of principal concern at the 1952 conference was the instability of the price of white fox fur. The sale of white fox fur had been the keystone of Inuit economic well-being. The Inuit trapped the white fox (*tirigan-niaq*) and sold the fur to the traders. In fact, the entire Inuit economy in the eastern Arctic was largely based on this one commodity, which was a speciality item used mainly in European and South American markets for trimming on coats and accessories such as ladies' stoles rather than for the mainstream garment trade (Cantley, 1950b). The drastic decline in white fox fur prices, from $35 a pelt in 1945 to a temporary low of $3.50 in 1950, was accompanied by a postwar inflationary increase in the prices of store goods in the North (Wright, 1953). In fact, the price of "essential goods" being traded at northern posts effectively doubled in the three-year period between 1946 and 1949 (Clancy, 1991: 201). These two factors had a disastrous effect on the Inuit economy. The Whites had created a commercial fur market on which the Inuit were now dependent, diverting their attention from subsistence activities and thereby creating a form of internal colonialism (Dryzek and Young, 1985: 126). This model of colonialism can occur when an affluent industrial society possessing an uncontrollable need for raw materials comes into contact with small communities located in a sparsely populated region rich in natural resources (ibid.: 136).

The wide fluctuations in the price of white fox fur reflected the character of the international fur market, which itself was strongly dependent on economic conditions and fashion trends. The total market value of white fox trapped in the Canadian Arctic varied from a high of $3,015,350 in 1923 to a low of just $167,040 in 1950 (Canada, 1951a). The income Inuit received from their fur trapping was tied not only to the fashion market but also to the cyclical fluctuations in the white fox population. The white fox had a four-year cycle during which highs and lows could vary greatly, with the peak occurring in the third year. These factors placed many Inuit in a peculiar dependency relationship with the Company and other traders (Brody, 1975: 22). No cash changed hands; until the late 1950s and early 1960s, the Inuit in the eastern Arctic were bound by a system of credits that were established at their nearest trading store or with the RCMP. The Inuit depended on the trader for advances to purchase supplies and store items. A "grubstake" or debt (*akinitsaq*, "something to be paid") would be advanced to good trappers against the fur catch they were expected to harvest. Unless there was more than one trading store in the settlement, the Inuk and his family would be completely beholden to the trader and dependent upon his goodwill.

Although officials considered the decline in Inuit spending power largely as an "Eskimo problem," Mowat and Larsen (1952c) believed that the Inuit were vulnerable in settlements to "the endless exploitation of Traders and Missionaries." Larsen held the traders responsible for turning the Inuit from hunters of meat into trappers of fur-bearing animals (see Brody, 1975: 21). He argued that the Inuit were tied to a fur economy on which it was impossible for them to exist given the small returns they obtained for their furs combined with the comparatively small individual catches of fur (Larsen, 1951). Larsen (1952c) was also alarmed that former HBC traders now employed in the administration appeared to have taken over the reins of the Department. He was alluding to the fact that James Cantley, a former Company trader, had recently been put in charge of the Department's Arctic Services Section.

The Company and the Department labeled an Inuk an "inefficient trapper" or "indigent" if he did not trap ten foxes a year, or an average of fifty foxes over a five-year period. Even though he might be a good hunter and provider of food for his family, for lack of fox furs he could be denied credit and supplies by the traders in times of deprivation. "Inefficient trappers" were eligible for government relief when the local Company manager or RCMP constable deemed it to be appropriate. This system was a way of regulating the poor, whereby relief was granted on condition that the individual behaved in a certain way and worked as required (Piven and Cloward, 1972: 22). If an "efficient trapper" was in need of relief because it was a poor fox year, he was considered to be the responsibility of the HBC, who might give him Company relief. The Company's debt policies were applied according to the trader's evaluation of the character of a trapper and his ability to catch fox, supplemented by considerations of his distance from the post, family size, and amount of time spent on the land (Clancy, 1991). Relief carried an "efficient trapper" during the lean years, and in the good years it allowed him to devote less time to hunting out of necessity and more time to his trap lines.

One solution to the "Eskimo problem" discussed at the 1952 conference was for the government to stabilize the price the Inuit received for white fox fur. There was a precedent for using price supports, as in the agricultural stabilization programs that were increasingly common in Canada by the late 1940s (ibid.: 205). The Department decided, however, not to commit itself to direct government support by setting a guaranteed price. Insp. Larsen informed the commissioner that there was only one way to check the continuation of these bad conditions— by establishing a Crown Company to conduct all trading with the Inuit and to replace all other traders (Larsen, 1951). For Larsen and many other Canadian officials, the Danish administration of Greenland was the model to follow.

Greenland presented the paradigm of a people "peacefully pursuing its primitive native ways" while being almost completely isolated from detrimental outside influences (Cantley, 1950b: 6). Trade with Greenlanders was controlled by a national Greenlandic trading company. The Greenland government's paternalistic colonial policy until 1950 was to regulate imports and exports so as to ensure that the Inuit would continue to have a subsistence lifestyle based as much as possible on the country's natural resources. The appeal of his fellow Scandinavians' policies in Greenland to Larsen was obvious. Rather than allowing the HBC to continue to control the Inuit economically, Larsen saw advantages in reforming the trader-Inuit relationship, envisaging a strong paternalistic role for his proposed Canadian Crown trading company. In an attempt to place social control before profit, Larsen (1951) proposed that a benevolent Crown trader could monitor and assist Inuit hunting and only sell those goods which would be beneficial to the Inuit way of life.

If the Department had accepted Larsen's suggestion for a Crown trading company, it would have meant breaking the monopoly of the Hudson's Bay Company and probably nationalizing its trading operations. That idea was obviously not popular with the HBC, which was one of Canada's most powerful private companies, nor with its former employees who were now working in the Department, such as Alex Stevenson and James Cantley. Cantley (1950b) had already investigated the feasibility of forming a Crown trading company in a detailed study commissioned by the Northwest Territories Council in 1949 and entitled "Survey of Economic Conditions among the Eskimos of the Canadian Arctic." As the consultant selected to undertake the survey, James Cantley had substantial northern experience. He was formerly an assistant fur trade commissioner for the Company, and in 1938 he had established a rival firm, the Baffin Trading Company, Ltd. Cantley tried to discourage the idea of stabilizing the price of fur, or of forming a Crown trading company, and informed the Northwest Territories Council that in his opinion a Crown company would not offer any advantage over the continuation of trade by private traders if the Department supervised their activities (Cantley, 1951; Jenness, 1964: 82).

Competition to Exert Social Control over the Inuit

The opposing points of view within the agencies responsible for northern administration in the early 1950s were typified by those expressed by James Cantley and Henry Larsen. Larsen advocated that the RCMP should take a more active role in developing and implementing Inuit administration policy. He believed that the RCMP could play a very important part in "rehabilitating the Eskimos," provided the proper policies were adopted (Larsen, 1952c). Larsen asked Commissioner Nicholson whether the Inuit were to be controlled more or less entirely by the traders or whether the RCMP could ensure that, with the government's help, the Inuit would be relocated to new communities.

Cantley argued for the opposite approach, believing that police control of Inuit relief should be curtailed:

When the responsibility for the issue of relief was taken from the traders and vested in the R.C.M. Police and later, when the administration of family and old age allowances was also added to the Police duties, two distinct sources of supply were opened to the Eskimos. Previously they had to look to the trader for everything they needed and as the average trader was not prone to giving much for nothing, they had to get out and earn their living either by hunting or trapping. Now they have found that if they cannot or will not stand on their own feet they can go to the Police and get at least sufficient relief or family allowances to keep them going without having to work for it or pay it back. The effect over the past few years has been to encourage the natives to look to the Police for free issues of necessities and to the trader for the non-essentials which furs and other produce will buy. From that it is only a step to complete dependence. (Cantley, 1950b: 46)

Cantley felt that the increased powers given to the RCMP for Inuit welfare upset the special relationship between the Company and the Department. The new arrangement, he said, had greatly reduced the interest many post managers had in Inuit affairs, without ensuring that family allowances were put to the best possible use. Cantley argued that the Department was "handicapped in using the Police," because they were not directly responsible to the Department but to Police headquarters, where there might not be understanding or agreement on the Department's policies (ibid.: 48). His solution was not to create a Department field staff but to form a closer alliance with the Company, building on the old working relationship between the two agencies. Cantley's proposal was controversial and appears to have been influenced by his background as a fur trader and former senior employee of the Company. His bid for control was blunt, stressing that a much more practical approach to Inuit problems could be made if the RCMP were relieved of all responsibility for the supervision of economic and welfare matters and if this responsibility was resumed entirely by the Department.

In practice, if the Department had adopted the policy revisions Cantley was proposing, it would have meant reverting to the former system whereby Company managers were essentially given field responsibility for Inuit welfare. The struggle between the Department and the RCMP for control of Inuit welfare was influential in the development of the government's Inuit relocation policies. Indeed, fundamental discrepancies between policy and implementation can be traced to the interdependent (and at times strained) relationship between the two agencies (as will be discussed in chapters 7 and 8). Cantley's proposals in 1951 to limit police control were never pursued because of two significant events that took place the following year: the publication of Mowat's *People of the Deer* and the resultant Conference on Eskimo Affairs, which demonstrated the Department's need to find new solutions to northern problems. It would have been politically untenable at that point for the Department to give government control of Inuit affairs back to the Company.

Because it needed to appear to be developing a progressive posture, the Department had little choice but to rely on the goodwill of the RCMP to implement its policies. Cantley's position as chief of Arctic services lasted only two years before he was effectively demoted during a structural reorganization of the Department. In late 1953, it was renamed the Department of Northern Affairs and National Resources, and Gordon Robertson was appointed deputy minister. The Department's new senior officers, Robertson, Ben Sivertz, and Bob Phillips, had all been transferred from the Department of External Affairs. Unlike Stevenson and Cantley who were fur traders turned government officials, the new triumvirate had no previous northern experience. Their expertise from External Affairs was more in the area of geopolitics and diplomacy—an indication of the redefined role the Department under its new name was expected to play in an increasingly politicized and militarized North (Paine, 1977: 13). The linkage between growing geopolitical concerns and the development of an Inuit relocation policy will be discussed in chapter 2.

Bringing Order to a "Disordered" People

Having identified the "Eskimo problem," officials sought to take remedial action. The Department viewed the North as being in a chaotic state and as a difficult region in which to exert effective social and economic control. Most Inuit spoke no English, and few officials spoke Inuktitut. It was difficult for the administrators to keep track of the people, because the Inuit were seminomadic and stayed at a variety of seasonal camps throughout the year, often returning to the settlement only for purposes of re-supply. To make matters worse, they had similar Christian names and no surnames (Whites did not usually call the Inuit by their Inuktitut names). Their economy was in crisis, they were highly susceptible to disease and starvation, and the police were constantly reporting that Inuit were beginning to "loiter" around settlements. Even though the Inuit numbered less than ten thousand, they were spread across a vast expanse of territory. The harsh weather conditions often complicated access to the region from the south and hindered the transportation of people and supplies.

In the interests of "good administration," officials adopted measures indicative of a Western taxonomic approach to transform Inuit society into a more manageable entity. The problem for the taxonomist is how to devise a simple classificatory system that others can easily adopt (Knight, 1981: 131); thus, at the time of the 1941 census, the Department assigned to all of the Canadian Inuit individual numbers, called "E-numbers," that referred to the "E"-district in the eastern Arctic where they were apparently living. In 1945, officials drew artificial boundaries on maps of the North, classifying the Inuit into twelve "Eskimo Registration Districts" (see map 1.1). They thus created a system that could be developed and controlled, laying the foundations for a new social order in the North. Officials acknowledged that the system would provide "useful information on movements of the population" (*The Arctic Circular*, 1953a). There were nine districts in the eastern Arctic, and three "W" districts in the western Arctic. A person with the number E9-162, for example, lived in the E9 Port Harrison district. These numbers were commonly referred to as "disc numbers," because each Inuk was given a disc to wear around his neck to facilitate his identification by officials (hence Harrington's picture in figure 1.2). The registration district and number were stamped on one side, and the reverse side featured a crown with the words "Eskimo Identification" printed above it and "Canada" below.

As a labeling process, assigning disc numbers was a form of cultural inscription that began when the Churches baptized Inuit with anglicized names, such as Mosesee, Jonasee, Philipusie, and Lukasee, and the traders called them "indigents" or "efficient trappers." Once given disc numbers, Canada's Inuit were viewed by officials in Ottawa less as an anonymous mass and more as an organized collection of identifiable individuals, although the Inuit were the only Canadian civilians required to wear identification discs. E-numbers were used for twenty years, until the late 1960s when the Department assigned surnames to the Inuit in an operation logically entitled "Project Surname."

After serving as officer in charge of the annual eastern Arctic patrol in 1955, Department official Bob Phillips reflected on the voyage in a report to his deputy minister, Gordon Robertson. It could be useful, commented Phillips (1955: 106), to "think of 9,000 Eskimos as a laboratory experiment and to give the imagination full rein on what might be done to improve the culture." After classifying the Inuit, the Department, in fact, did undertake numerous social experiments in its northern "field laboratory." New cottage industries were introduced to the North on a small, experimental scale. There were sheep-herding and horticultural experiments at Fort Chimo and eider duck farming in Cape Dorset. Yaks were imported in an experiment to see if the Inuit could be encouraged to abandon a hunting lifestyle for that of yak herdsmen. Boat-building projects were tried at Lake Harbour and Tuktoyaktuk, and a handicrafts program was begun at Port Harrison. All of these ventures were conducted on a trial basis in the attempt to diversify the Inuit economy so that it would become less dependent on the proceeds from white fox fur (Diubaldo, 1989: 178).

In assessing the economic opportunities and regional problems of

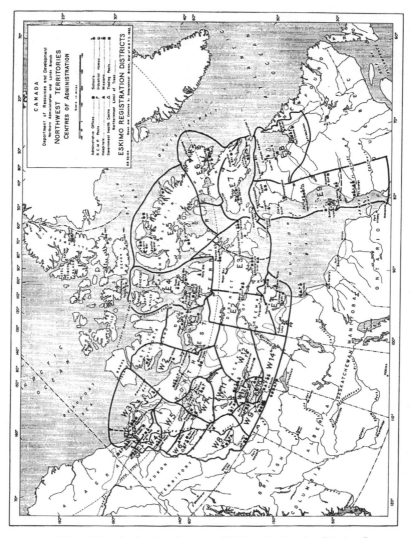

MAP 1.1 Map of Canada showing the twelve "Eskimo Registration Districts," 1953.

the North, the Department defined certain areas as being overpopulated and others as underpopulated. Because the Department was able to establish that relief costs were rising unevenly in different Eskimo registration districts, relocation could be proposed as a tool for population redistribution (Constantine, 1991: 62–64). Some Inuit were relocated to sites of employment: for example, from the "overpopulated" area of Fort Chimo to the army base at Churchill in 1953. Others were moved to unoccupied regions, as when Inuit from the "overpopulated" Port Harrison district were relocated to the High Arctic in 1953–55. Whether it was yak herding or resettlement, the Department's imaginative utopian schemes were constantly referred to as "experiments." Most of the attempts to introduce new industries to the North failed, with the dramatic exception of handicrafts (Zaslow, 1988: 275). Relocation experiments stood apart from the other forms of field laboratory work in that they involved the dislocation of a populace, causing complex social repercussions that I shall discuss in the following chapters.

2

THE PEOPLE OF THE CROWN

At the 1952 Conference on Eskimo Affairs, it was suggested that the Department develop an Inuit relocation policy: "Movements could be initiated from over-populated or depleted districts," the document concluded, "to areas not presently occupied or where the natural resources could support a greater number of people" (Eskimo Affairs, 1952b: 4). That year, Inuit from Arctic Quebec were selected for relocation to the High Arctic. This government experiment raises two main questions: Why were Inuit from Port Harrison in the southern Arctic selected for relocation to the High Arctic? and, How did the relocation fit into the government's overall Inuit administration and northern development policies? In this chapter, I will explore the political and social-reformist motivations behind the relocation experiments and examine how they were related to broader Inuit resettlement initiatives in the Canadian North.

Port Harrison and the Problems of Arctic Quebec

When Robert Flaherty first visited Port Harrison in the early 1900s, its only permanent structure was a Revillon Frères trading post, which had been established in 1909. In 1920–21, while Flaherty was living there and filming *Nanook of the North*, the Hudson's Bay Company also established a trading store at Port Harrison. Other agencies began to establish services, and a settlement gradually formed. An Anglican mission was built there in 1927, and in 1935 a radio transmitter, operated by the Department of Transport, was installed and an RCMP detachment established. A radiosonde station was opened in 1943, where Joseph Flaherty, the

Inuk son of filmmaker Robert Flaherty, was employed to carry out general maintenance. Port Harrison was the first Arctic settlement to have a federal nursing station, built in 1947. A welfare teacher was assigned to the settlement, and a federal day school was constructed in 1951. By the 1950s, most of the Inuit were still living in camps, and Joseph Flaherty's was one of the few Inuit families to live in a house in the settlement, provided for them by the radiosonde station.

The Inuit name for Port Harrison, Inukjuak, means "the giant person." The community is situated at the mouth of the Innuksuak River. Ruins of stone houses from the Dorset period (1000 B.C.–A.D. 1100) indicate that this area had been inhabited by Inuit for a considerable time. By the end of the nineteenth century, the Inuit living in the area, the Inukjuamiut, were probably trading with the HBC post at Great Whale River, three hundred kilometers to the south (E. A. Smith, 1991: 116). At the turn of the century, Anglican missionaries were visiting Inuit camps in the Port Harrison area and teaching the Inukjuamiut to read syllabic script, as the Rev. E. J. Peck, "the Apostle of the Eskimos," had done earlier at Great Whale. With the use of bibles and hymn books in Inuktitut, the Inuit of the eastern Arctic became literate in syllabics (ibid.: 117). The Inukjuamiut started using firearms between 1860 and 1910 (Willmott, 1961: 2). By the early 1950s, about four hundred Inuit lived in the vicinity of Port Harrison, in camps mostly along the coast within eighty kilometers of the settlement (see fig. 2.1). The only Inuit who actually lived in the settlement, which had a White population of about twenty to twenty-five people, were those who were employed by the various agencies in the community.

At the time of Robert Flaherty's death in 1951, the place where he had filmed scenes of "traditional" Inuit life thirty years before was considered by the Department as a problem area. Four events had occurred in 1951 that created this situation from the Department's point of view: the four-year fox population cycle was at its lowest point, so relatively few foxes were being caught; the fur market had crashed, and the prices the Inuit were able to obtain were low; government relief had been increased to offset the low earnings from fur; and family allowances had just been introduced and were seen as encouraging greater Inuit dependency on Whites. Furthermore, a number of Inuit camps were clustered around Port Harrison and Fort Chimo, the two largest White settlements in northern Quebec.

The Conference on Eskimo Affairs (1952b) identified northern Quebec as one of the "most densely populated" and poorest Inuit regions in Canada. According to Cantley's economic survey of 1950, based on population statistics for 1949, Arctic Quebec had the highest Inuit popu-

FIGURE 2.1 Inuit winter houses near Port Harrison, 1948. Credit: Richard
Harrington/National Archives of Canada, PA-146917

lation density in the 923,000-square-mile area of the Canadian Arctic
(see table 2.1; Cantley, 1950b: 16).

It was estimated that the Canadian Inuit population comprised about
2,154 families, with an average of 3.9 persons per family. On this basis,
the area per hunter would be roughly four times that shown in table 2.1.
Cantley pointed out that almost 30 percent of the Canadian Inuit population was concentrated in the region of "New Quebec" (northern or
Arctic Quebec), which comprised only about 15 percent of the total land
area and 17 percent of the total coastline available to the Inuit in the
Canadian Arctic. Cantley conceded, though, that it could be misleading to generalize and make judgments solely on the basis of population
distribution data. There were some large land areas, such as Ellesmere
Island, where Inuit could not make a living at all, and other areas of
quite limited size, such as the Mackenzie Delta, where relatively large
populations could secure a livelihood. The population capacity of a particular area could only be assessed by taking into account all aspects of
the region (Cantley, 1950b: 17). It would appear that Cantley included
the Inuit population of Labrador in his "New Quebec" total, which
would account for the discrepancy between his summations and those

TABLE 2.1: Estimated Canadian Inuit
population distribution in 1949

Regions	Population	Land area (mi^2) per capita
Eastern Arctic		
New Quebec	2,465	57
Keewatin	1,525	138
Baffin Island	2,405	95
Western Arctic		
Cambridge Bay	433	199
Coppermine	602	241
Aklavik	1,007	111

Source: Cantley, 1950b.

TABLE 2.2: Government census
of Inuit population in 1951
(areas refer to the registration districts shown on map 1.1)

Northwest Territories	
Eskimo Point (E1)	446
Baker Lake (E2)	413
Chesterfield (E3)	427
Southampton Island (E3)	220
Spence Bay (E4)	462
Pond Inlet (E5)	908
Pangnirtung (E6)	591
Lake Harbour (E7)	716
Frobisher Bay (E7)	298
Fort Chimo (E8)	31
Port Harrison (E9)	330
Other Areas (Craig Harbour)	16
Total — Eastern Arctic	4,858
Cambridge Bay (W1)	295
Coppermine (W2)	624
Aklavik (W3)	1,080
Total — Western Arctic	1,999
Quebec	
Fort Chimo (E8)	627
Port Harrison and Moose Factory (E9)	1,162
Total — Quebec	1,789
Labrador	847
Total Canadian Inuit population	9,493

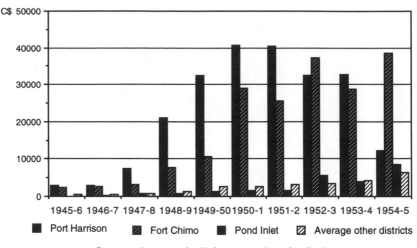

FIGURE 2.2 Comparative annual relief payments issued to Inuit, 1945–55.
Source: Canada, 1956a.

given in the official 1951 census (which distinguished between Labrador and Quebec populations). According to the 1951 census figures (see
table 2.2), northern Quebec had a population of only 1,789 Inuit, or 18
percent of the total Canadian Inuit population of 9,493 (*The Arctic Circular,* 1953b: 42). If one includes the 361 Inuit listed as living on the
offshore islands adjacent to northern Quebec (but administered within
the Northwest Territories), the figure rises only to 23 percent—still substantially below Cantley's estimated 30 percent.

An examination of the records of government relief issued to Inuit
yields striking comparative data. During the ten-year period from 1945
to 1955, northern Quebec received $484,000 in relief payments out of
a total of $830,000 the government paid to the Inuit, including those
on Baffin Island, the west side of Hudson Bay, the western Arctic, and
the Mackenzie Delta region (Canada, 1956a). The Inuit in Quebec, who
made up 29 percent of the total Inuit population, were therefore receiving 59 percent of all federal government relief being expended on
the Inuit. For eight of those ten years, Port Harrison received by far the
highest level of relief of all Inuit districts, only to be surpassed by Fort
Chimo in northern Quebec in 1952–53 and 1954–55, as indicated in
figure 2.2. In 1950–51, Port Harrison received $40,603 in relief, sixteen
times as much as the $2,554 paid on average to the other Inuit districts.
In 1951–52, Port Harrison relief payments were $40,337, whereas other
districts averaged $3,081.

The per capita relief levels for the twelve Inuit registration districts

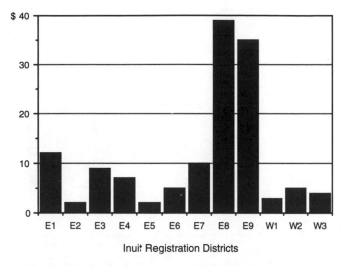

FIGURE 2.3 Comparative levels of government relief the Inuit received per capita in the twelve Inuit registration districts for the year 1951. *Sources: The Arctic Circular,* 1953b; Canada, 1956a.

(consisting of nine eastern Arctic districts, E1–E9, and three western Arctic districts, W1–W3, shown on map 1.1) for the census year 1951 reveal the comparative magnitude of government relief payments, shown in figure 2.3. Northern Quebec was divided into two registration districts, E9 Port Harrison and E8 Fort Chimo. In the E8 Fort Chimo district, 658 Inuit received a total of $25,465 in relief in 1951, or $39 per capita. The E9 Port Harrison district had an Inuit population of 1,492 in 1951 and received a total of $52,258, or $35 per capita. This district, which included the Moose Factory sub-district, comprised Port Harrison and eight other settlements on the east coast of Hudson Bay (see map 1.1). The E9 and E8 districts compared unfavorably with other Inuit regions, including the E5 Pond Inlet district that received $2 per capita and the E6 Pangnirtung district that received $5 per capita. Dismay about the escalating relief benefits paid to the E8 and E9 districts was summed up in a single note from the director of the Lands and Development Branch to the acting deputy minister of the Department: "We are distributing altogether too much relief in these northern Quebec areas" (R. A. Gibson, 1950).

According to a 1952 government financial report, the Inuit registration district with the highest level of family allowances in Canada was the E9 Port Harrison district, which up to that time had received $161,773 in benefits, followed by the E5 Pond Inlet district, NWT, which had re-

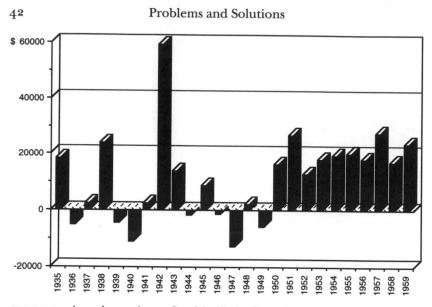

FIGURE 2.4 Annual operating profits of the Hudson's Bay Company Port Harrison post, 1935–59. *Source:* HBC, 1935–59.

ceived a total of $122,303, and the E8 Fort Chimo district, which had received $111,334 (Crozier, 1952). Moreover, in a study of Port Harrison's average Inuit family income for 1951, 61.8 percent was shown to derive from social benefits (31.2 percent from family allowances and 30.6 percent from government relief), whereas only 12.7 percent came from the proceeds of fur trapping. In the postwar market economy, it was no longer feasible for the Inuit to subsist solely by living off the land, but in the early 1950s the Department felt it was costing too much to provide for the welfare needs of Inuit in districts such as Port Harrison. There was thus an economic motive for finding a solution to this inverse relationship—fur prices having sharply decreased and the provision of social benefits having greatly increased. It comes as little suprise that the E9, E5, and E8 districts, which had received the highest levels of social benefits, were targeted for relocation experiments in 1953.

In fact, this assessment of benefits received was not an accurate economic picture. When officials drafted their charts and graphs to assess Inuit earnings, they were only including cash income. This paradigm of dependency, which formed the backbone of the "Eskimo problem" argument, failed to take into account the monetary equivalent for the local food sources that sustained the Inuit on a high protein meat diet, the dwellings they constructed, and the skin clothing they made for themselves. These factors would have provided the Department with a more balanced picture of the subsistence economy of the time, showing a lesser degree of dependency even when relief levels were at their highest.

The Port Harrison district, with the high profile its record level of benefits had attracted, was thus in an exposed sociopolitical position and fertile ground for potential "rehabilitation" experiments. The records of the Hudson's Bay Company provide other details. Of the twelve to fifteen Company posts in the eastern Arctic, Port Harrison was almost consistently one of the three most profitable posts. A review of the post's annual accounts between 1935 and 1959 (shown in fig. 2.4) demonstrates that until 1950 profits fluctuated a great deal. As in the case of other posts, the fluctuation essentially mirrored the four-year fox cycle: the harvest of furs was highest in the third year. At Port Harrison, the Company was also in competition with the Revillon Frères post until 1936 (when it bought it out) and with a Baffin Trading Company post during 1939–49. When, in 1950, the Company became the sole trader and provider of goods to the settlement, profits increased and remained strong thereafter.

"White Man's Handouts" and the Reform Movement

Canada's economic boom and international focus on the Arctic regions prompted Prime Minister Louis St. Laurent's decision to revise the government's Inuit administration policies. In a major speech delivered in the House of Commons in December 1953, the prime minister conceded that in the past the government had administered the North "in an almost continuing state of absence of mind" (Canada, 1953c: 696). Public concern about Canada's neglect of its northern citizens led to fundamental policy changes. The early 1950s thus brought new initiatives to improve what was perceived as the low Inuit standard of living (Rea, 1968: 298–99).

Thirty years after Flaherty's classic film *Nanook of the North* was made, depicting the happy and proud Inuk hunter and his family, administrators in Ottawa were faced with what they perceived as the moral degradation of the Inuit. If poverty was a disease, then the cure—relief payments—was equally undesirable. Officials struggled with a fundamental moral dilemma. Figures such as Nanook and Idlout crystallized the White perception of the Eskimo as the ultimate, self-reliant individualist (Fienup-Riordan, 1990: xv). Relief, it was argued, was destroying the moral character and independence of the Inuit (Eskimo Affairs, 1952b). The Whites found this development particularly disconcerting, because their image of the Inuit was an idealized image of themselves. The self-

sufficient Eskimo contributed to the frontiersman myth, which served as
a role model for North Americans, a model that contrasted with the re-
gressive image of soft, European city-dwellers (Cross and others, 1970).
Dependency on relief was anathema to the Canadian self-image. Cantley (1950b: 45–46) had already forewarned against adopting generous
social welfare measures:

> While it is important that the native should be protected as far as possible against
> privation and exploitation, it is more important that this protection should not
> be carried to a point where they will lose all initiative and become completely
> dependent. Yet this is the trend under our present administrative policy. The
> actual needs—as opposed to the desires—of the average Eskimo are small; gen-
> erally, as long as he can obtain a minimum of food, clothing and shelter without
> exertion on his part he will be satisfied. It is therefore very easy for him to adapt
> himself to a relief economy and to beg rather than work for a bare subsistence.
> Unless this trait of the Eskimo character is fully understood by all concerned,
> grave mistakes can easily be made.

The government was not alone in criticizing the modern changes to
the Inuit way of life. Indications of a growing class of Inuit dependents
soon raised a disapproving public response (Piven and Cloward, 1972:
149). Reporting on the outcome of the Conference on Eskimo Affairs,
the *Toronto Globe and Mail* on 22 May 1952 stated: "Knowing that there is
always government aid to fall back on, the Eskimo in some parts of the
north has lost a certain amount of his interest in hunting and fishing for
a living" (Bain, 1952). An article in the *Wall Street Journal* in December
1952, based on these reports and others, attacked Canada's Inuit administration policy (McKenna, 1952): "The debut of the welfare state in the
Arctic," it contended, "meant they [the Inuit] didn't have to hunt seals
or catch fish anymore."

The Union Oil Company of California used the *Wall Street Journal*
article as the basis for a full-page advertisement in the 16 February 1953
issue of *Newsweek* magazine. Featuring a stereotypical, joyful Eskimo, it
stated that the Eskimos' new life under the welfare state was "soft and
easy" because they had complete security. As a result, they had "lost all
vigor and *ambition*" (italics theirs). Euro-Americans often viewed the Inuk
as a more primitive version of themselves, both noble and base, and some
of them saw any loss of self-reliance as an indication of what the welfare
state might do to the rest of society (Clancy, 1987a: 194; Fienup-Riordan,
1990: xv). This controversy surrounded the postwar introduction of the
welfare state in North America, as it did in Western Europe. In the caption to a cartoon of an Eskimo smoking, the advertisement moralized:
"Enslavement by *security* isn't something that happens only to Eskimos.
In fact, millions of people all over the world see nothing wrong with a

welfare society" (Union Oil, 1953). This contention was an old argument repackaged—that paupers could earn greater self-respect by providing for themselves than by relying on the state (H. Johnston, 1972: 12). The language used in the *Wall Street Journal* article and the Union Oil advertisement summed up the views expressed by officials at the 1952 conference. It was the message the conference delivered, rather than the event itself, that made an impact on the public (Edelman, 1977: 142). This kind of adverse publicity did little to enhance the public's perception of the government's methods of handling Inuit welfare.

Executive Officer Bob Phillips (1955: 109) explained the Department's dilemma about the rise of the welfare state and the dependency on relief as an incentive for expanding its Inuit resettlement initiatives:

In the south a family of three children may receive about $200 a year in family allowances depending upon their ages. This is less than eight per cent of the average family income and it can be no more than a supplement to the bread-winner's earning power. In the Arctic the same family finds that the same allowance money is not eight per cent but perhaps forty or even eighty per cent of the cash income for the year. Hence these goods, which in the Eskimo land are becoming increasingly not luxuries but necessities, the Eskimo gets not by earned income but by what is psychologically a form of relief. It is little wonder then that even Family Allowances can be a dangerous form of paternalism in the Arctic.

The present stage of paternalism is the greatest danger to the Eskimo future. The longer they depend upon Government payments for a disquieting proportion of their daily bread the more difficult it will be in future to establish them in a life where ninety per cent of their income must be earned. Those who have had some acquaintance with both Indians and Eskimos sometimes make the contrast between the irresponsible Indians who are waiting always for handouts and the noble independence of the Eskimos. My fear is that we are encouraging the same state of irresponsibility among the Eskimos as is found in the Indians. It is not too late to arrest the trend but it is possible to do so only by drastic measures including wide resettlement.

The author's usage of "bread" as a biblical metaphor for income and the stereotypical Nanook image of "noble independence" underscored the prevailing point of view amongst officials that relief and family allowances were collectively seen as "white man's handouts." Because the Inuit were legally entitled to government benefits, it is not clear how Phillips hoped to reduce state paternalism. Defining relations between the center and the peripheral sectors of society was a major dilemma of "welfare colonialism" (Paine, 1977: 3). Phillips's comparisons of Indians and Eskimos typified the connection between the "Indian problem" and the "Eskimo problem" in the 1950s. At the same time, government officials in the United States were discussing their "Indian problem" and the "Negro problem." The "Indian problem" was seen to be poverty, state dependency, alcoholism, lack of economic opportunities, and segregation. The Indians, and increasingly the Inuit, were perceived by the Whites to have strayed from a state of innocence to a state of cultural decay and ecological imbalance with nature. An example was the view of many Whites that the decline in the caribou population, or "caribou crisis," of the 1950s was in large part due to over-hunting by Indians and Inuit (Clancy, 1987b), whereas cyclical fluctuations in caribou population levels could have been a more important factor.

The popular perceptions of the Indian and the Eskimo were quite different. The Indian as typified cinematically in cowboy westerns was seen as cunning and warlike, in contrast to the smiling Nanook Eskimo (Brody, 1987: 19). Although Phillips and other officials saw both the Indians and the Eskimos as "irresponsible," they hoped that the likeable Eskimo was still redeemable. As a possible solution to Inuit dependency on "white man's handouts," Phillips raised the issue of resettlement. The theory was that if aboriginal people were resettled to urban areas, they might obtain wage employment. Conversely, if they were resettled further out on the land, away from the "bad influences" of settlement life, they might once more become self-sufficient. In both cases, resettlement was regarded as a social-reformist tool to induce self-reliance. The Department's quandary about whether to relocate the Inuit north or south during the 1950s will be discussed in chapter 8.

Inuit Settlement Patterns and the Argument for Rehabilitation

Although the Department was concerned about Inuit dependency on relief, as publicized by the 1952 conference, it was also disconcerted by the nontraditional Inuit dwellings being constructed around settlements. In his October 1951 report to RCMP Commissioner Nicholson, Insp. Larsen made it clear that he was particularly unhappy about the new, semipermanent Inuit dwellings, which he found to be made from discarded boards, odds and ends of burlap, canvas, and other waste material. The "accumulation of filth and dirt inside these habitations is indescribable," he stated (Larsen, 1951). In a popular magazine article, senior Department official Bob Phillips (1959b) called the Inuit "slum dwellers of the wide-open spaces." Featuring a picture of a small, makeshift, wooden dwelling, Phillips stated: "Except for those who have built shacks like this one from refuse, no Canadian Eskimo owns a home. Most are forced to live in the cold and damp of igloo and tent." Larsen (1951) claimed that poor clothing, poor dwellings, filth, and squalor had a detrimental effect on the health of the Inuit and, together with malnutrition, contributed to their high incidence of tuberculosis. These views of Whites reflect the cultural collision that resulted in disgust at the way Inuit "traditional" culture was being transformed by contact with Western influences. By permitting the Inuit to camp around the settlements rather than encouraging them to move continuously in search of game, officials, Larsen cautioned, were allowing the wrong form of northern development. His solution to this problem was a radical one: "Many of these habitations should be destroyed by burning and I would suggest that next year the Medical Health Officer on the Government Vessel, 'C.D. HOWE' should pay particular attention to sanitation matters at each settlement and give orders to rectify all unfavourable conditions" (Larsen, 1951: 2).

Larsen's hygienic ideals reflected the notion that cleanliness was an outward manifestation of inner order and that dirtiness was a sign of slothfulness (Ignatieff, 1978: 101). Cantley (1951) did not look favorably on Larsen's idea of burning native homes. He felt it would be impractical for medical officers to assume such a responsibility and noted that, before the police destroyed Inuit habitations, they should make provision for other forms of shelter. Although he thought Larsen's suggested course of action was too drastic, Cantley praised Larsen's comments about the unsatisfactory change in Inuit lifestyle: "No exception can be taken to Inspector Larsen's statement that the Eskimos are better off while living in small communities and moving from place to place hunting" (Cantley, 1951: 4).

As a result of this moral concern, the Department's officer in charge of the 1951 eastern Arctic patrol, Alex Stevenson, received orders that "consideration should be given to the feasibility of breaking up the present concentrations of population around the main centres" (Sinclair, 1951). Inspector Larsen was convinced that, by dispersing Inuit who lived around settlements and relocating them to sites rich in game, their standard of living would improve:

At the present time there are concentrations of Eskimos at certain places, which, if they could be broken up by providing the Eskimos with boats and other means of travel, would I feel result in a better standard of living for the Eskimos in so far that they would have a better chance of obtaining more meat and skin clothing and thereby living more their native way of life. (Larsen, 1951: 3)

Larsen took this approach one step further and advised Commissioner Nicholson in September 1952: "I also have in mind a plan to relieve the overpopulation of some areas." He suggested that they transfer, by Department of Transport vessel, to Craig Harbour, Cape Sabine, and Dundas Harbour "several needy families to these places where colonization by them appears to be suitable and feasible" (Larsen, 1952c).

Self-Reliance, Resources, and Relocation

Officials at the 1952 Conference on Eskimo Affairs agreed "that the immediate need was to assist the natives to continue to follow their traditional way of life as hunters" (Eskimo Affairs, 1952b: 4). They thus sought to keep the native "native," despite the growing intrusion of the postwar modern world into northern society (Diubaldo, 1989: 173). Relocation was seen as a way of returning the Inuit to a self-reliant state by removing them from areas considered to be overpopulated. To rehabilitate the Inuit selected for relocation, it was necessary to move them to sites thought to be rich in game. Officials emphasized the plan's advantages for better conservation and utilization of food resources. This point had been developed previously in Cantley's report in 1950:

Experience with the primitive races in both Canada and Greenland has shown that if the natives are to live off the resources of the country, they must be distributed in small communities over as wide an area as possible. There are few places where the resources are sufficient to support a large population for any length of time, but there are innumerable places where a few families can hunt and obtain a living indefinitely. They will have seasons of moderate abundance and extreme scarcity, just as their forefathers had, but overall they will obtain, not luxury, but at least a higher standard of living than could ever be provided for permanently in larger communities. (Cantley, 1950b: 28)

The "voluntary" relocation of Inuit to better hunting areas in the High Arctic was characteristic of resettlement activity organized by the Hudson's Bay Company in the '20s through the '50s. In 1925 the Company relocated a group of Inuit to Southampton Island from Chesterfield Inlet, Baffin, and Port Burwell. In 1934 a group of Inuit were relocated by the Company from Baffin to Devon Island at the suggestion of the Department of the Interior; and in 1936 the Company relocated Inuit from Devon to Arctic Bay on Baffin Island (Jenness, 1964: 59–64). An Inuit relocation to Somerset Island was organized by the Company in 1937 when it established a new post at Fort Ross (A. Stevenson, 1977), and in 1944 the Company considered a proposal to move the entire Inuit population off the Belcher Islands in southern Hudson Bay to Prince of Wales Island in the High Arctic (Cruickshank, 1944). In 1947 the Company relocated Inuit from Somerset Island to the Boothia Peninsula (Jenness, 1964: 61). Some of these moves were "successful" from official perspectives; others proved not to be viable economically. In a number of cases, the Inuit expressed a desire to return to their homeland. This clash of interests will be discussed further in chapter 4.

It was against this background of relocation activity that Alex Stevenson and Henry Larsen discussed the feasibility of relocating Inuit from

Baffin to Devon Island and to Ellesmere Island in 1950. Because a colonization experiment on Devon Island in 1934–36 had failed (Jenness,
1964), the Company and the Department had not undertaken to relocate Inuit to the north of Lancaster Sound. The RCMP had gained
some experience in resettling Inuit to the High Arctic when it moved
one or two families at a time, to be employed by detachments on Devon
and Ellesmere Islands, in the '20s through the '40s. The Department's
consultations with the RCMP in 1950 about a joint relocation project
in the eastern Arctic took place concurrently with the Department's discussions with the Company about an Inuit resettlement project in the
western Arctic. The Department and the Company held talks at a senior
level to discuss the feasibility of relocating Inuit to Banks Island and
establishing a trading post there to supply them. The Company was not
interested, but the Department was sufficiently keen to go ahead with
the plan that it funded the resettlement operation in 1951.

Northern Quebec became a target for relocation in the early 1950s
when the Company considered a project for moving Inuit from the south
coast of the Hudson Straits to Boothia Peninsula. Initially, the Department looked at the possibility of relocating Inuit from Quebec to Baffin
Island in 1952, but then organized relocations in 1953–55 from Quebec
to Ellesmere and Cornwallis Islands in the High Arctic. The project was
to be the first Inuit relocation wholly organized and implemented by the
Department together with the RCMP. The relocations that had taken
place during the '20s through the '50s had similarities in the way they
were conceived and executed. The Inuit also had common experiences
in how they responded to resettlement. I will discuss these moves when
considering the two principal case studies.

Geopolitical Perceptions of the Northern Frontier

The idea of moving Inuit to potentially better hunting areas to promote
self-reliance and that of moving people to lands that were unoccupied
were sometimes linked. Canada and other circumpolar countries, like
nation states elsewhere, have resorted to relocating people to a particular
region to demonstrate territorial sovereignty through "effective occupation." The relocation in 1953–55 to Resolute Bay and Grise Fiord could
be seen as this kind of resettlement, combining social reform with territorial occupation.

At the 1993 hearings of the Royal Commission on Aboriginal Peoples,
the government's motives for relocating Inukjuamiut in 1953–55 were
discussed at length (Canada, 1993a and 1993b). The debate centered on

FIGURE 2.5 "Using the Inuit as human flagpoles," cartoon by Anthony Jenkins, 4 December 1992.
Credit: Reprinted with permission from *The Globe and Mail*

whether the Department relocated Inuit to the High Arctic to establish effective occupation of unoccupied islands and demonstrate Canadian sovereignty. The newspaper cartoon in figure 2.5 reflects the Inuit claim that the main reason they were relocated was to establish colonies of Canadian citizens in the High Arctic. The issue is clearly controversial, and the government has never formally conceded that sovereignty was a reason for moving the Inuit.

Canada's claim to the northernmost Arctic Islands, known since 1954 as the Queen Elizabeth Islands, has been subject to a sensitivity towards foreign incursions. Until the late 1940s, the Queen Elizabeth Islands had been uninhabited for several hundred years. Britain transferred the Arctic Islands to Canada on 31 July 1880 by an Order-in-Council. In preparing for the transfer, an official stated that "the object in annexing these unexplored territories to Canada is, I apprehend, to prevent the United States from claiming them, and not from the likelihood of their proving of any value to Canada" (Great Britain, Colonial Office, 1879). Exercising sovereignty over polar territories can present certain unique difficulties (Greig, 1976: 173). From 1900 to the early 1930s, Canada was prepared to forestall rival claims to its northernmost Arctic Islands, not just from the United States in its exploration of the area but from

Norway and Denmark as well. During the 1920s, as in the more distant past, Inuit hunters from the Thule region on the northwest coast of Greenland hunted musk-oxen on Ellesmere Island. When the Canadian government informed Denmark that Greenlanders were not allowed to hunt on Ellesmere, the Danish government replied that in their opinion Ellesmere Island was *terra nullius*, an unoccupied "no man's land" (Morrison, 1986: 253).

Canada at once realized the need to assert its claims to the Arctic Islands and make a symbolic demonstration of Canadian sovereignty. In 1922 it therefore established RCMP detachments at Craig Harbour on Ellesmere Island and Pond Inlet on North Baffin Island (Morrison, 1985: 168). The government accepted that territorial sovereignty had to be more than a passive declaration based on right of discovery; there had to be evidence of administrative activity (Morrison, 1986: 254). J. B. Harkin of the Department of the Interior stated the case for linking RCMP and Inuit occupation of Ellesmere Island:

To securely establish Canada's title, occupation and administration are necessary. Therefore, next spring [1921?] an expedition should be sent north to locate two or three permanent police posts on Ellesmere land. This probably should be followed by the transfer of some Canadian Eskimos to the island. (Cited in McConnell, 1973: 469)

The government's plans during the '20s through the '50s was obviously to use the RCMP and the Inuit together to establish a physical presence in areas of the High Arctic where it was considered necessary to demonstrate effective occupation. Further RCMP detachments were established in the Arctic Islands at Pangnirtung on Baffin Island (1923), Dundas Harbour on Devon Island (1924), Bache Peninsula on Ellesmere Island (1926), and Lake Harbour on Baffin Island (1927). At Dundas Harbour, Craig Harbour, and Bache Peninsula, the only resident Canadian nationals were RCMP officers and their few Inuit employees who had been moved there from Greenland and Baffin Island to serve as guides and hunters for the policemen.

As a way of exercising sovereignty, the government in July 1926 passed P.C. 1146, a regulatory act designating the northern islands between meridians 60 and 141 a special Arctic Islands Preserve, which gave the RCMP a further legal instrument for discouraging Greenlandic hunters. In the previous year, an amendment to the Northwest Territories Act had been introduced to require scientists and explorers wishing to enter the Northwest Territories to obtain a license. The Hon. Charles Stewart, minister of the interior, noted in the House of Commons debate on the bill in June 1925 that "there is no intention to collect any taxes. . . . What we want to do is to assert our sovereignty. We want to make it clear that this is Canadian territory and that if foreigners want to go in there they must have permission in the form of a license" (Canada, 1925).

Mr. Stewart explained the reason for taking the action at this time: "Here we are getting after men like MacMillan and Doctor Amundsen, men who are going in presumably for exploration purposes, but possibly there may arise a question as to the sovereignty over some land they may discover in the northern portion of Canada, and we claim all that portion" (ibid.).

Other countries had shown an interest in the Canadian High Arctic Islands. American explorers had spent a period of extensive activity in the region, which began with De Haven's search for Franklin (1850–51) and the expeditions of Hayes (1860–61), Hall (1871–73), Greely (1881–84), Peary (1896–1902, 1905–06, 1908–09), Cook (1907–09), and Mac-Millan (1913–17, 1923–25). Norway's claim to the Sverdrup Islands in the northern archipelago was based on the explorations of Otto Sverdrup (1904), who declared that the lands he had discovered west of Ellesmere Island on his explorations of 1898–1902 had been claimed in the name of the Norwegian king. The dispute over the ownership of these islands was not settled until 1930, when the Norwegian government formally recognized Canada's title to these uninhabited islands. As compensation, the Canadian government paid Sverdrup $67,000 for his original maps, diaries, and documents of the expedition (Barr, 1984). While reaching this agreement with Canada, Norway was in the process of asserting its claims to eastern Greenland. On the grounds that Greenland came under Danish sovereignty, the Danish government in 1931 began legal proceedings against Norway before the Permanent Court of International Justice (Inch, 1962).

Given the reduced threat to Canada's sovereignty over the Arctic Islands north of Lancaster Sound and the difficulties in supplying the detachments during the country's economic depression, the RCMP posts at Dundas Harbour and Bache Peninsula were closed in 1933 (Craig Harbour was closed between 1927 and 1933). In this case, the government was admitting that, because of the peculiar geographic and climatic conditions of polar regions, the international legal requirement of effective occupation can be difficult to fulfill (Svarlien, 1960). In 1934 the Department of the Interior in collaboration with the Hudson's Bay Company initiated an experiment to people the Arctic Islands with Canadian Inuit (an idea put forward by Harkin around 1920 [McConnell, 1973: 469]). The 1953–55 Inuit relocation from Port Harrison to the High Arctic has certain significant similarities to the 1934 resettlement project undertaken jointly by the Hudson's Bay Company and the Department. In both cases, ten Inuit families were moved from what were described as "overpopulated" districts to unoccupied areas of the High Arctic. Inuit families from three Baffin Island settlements were recruited for the 1934 relocation to Devon Island. Alex Stevenson observed that when the Department of the Interior suggested that the HBC use the former RCMP buildings on Devon Island as a base for the 1934 relocation, it demonstrated "sovereign rights in the Arctic Archipelago by greater occupation than one or two RCMP detachments" (cited in Grant, 1993: 25). Although the government stated that the goal of both the 1934 and the 1953 projects was to assist the Inuit in finding better game, others have concluded that, as "colonization projects," the schemes had the objective of securing "effective occupation" and demonstrating sovereignty (Barr, 1977; Grant, 1991; Marcus, 1992).

The Department had stated publicly that the 1934 relocation was authorized "in the interest of good administration" (Canada, 1935–36). "Good administration" could be interpreted in various ways, but in this case a document dated 1935 in the government's files provides a more complete explanation:

In addition to the placing of the Eskimos in new regions where game is more abundant and work more regular, there is the angle of occupation of the country, now that aerial routes, mineral developments, and other reasons make possible the claims of other countries to part of Canada's Arctic, which now reaches to the North Pole. To forestall any such future claims, the Dominion is occupying the Arctic islands to within nearly 700 miles of the North Pole. (Cited in Jenness, 1964: 58)

Canada was not alone in using Inuit relocation as a means of establishing effective occupation of disputed territory (Marcus, 1994). In 1925 the Danish government relocated a group of eighty-five Inuit from the village of Angmagssalik in Greenland to establish the more northerly settlement of Scoresby Sund. The operation was conceived of when Norwegian activity along the east coast of Greenland was interpreted as compromising Danish sovereignty. By creating a permanent Inuit settlement at Scoresby Sund, "the whole of this huge district would automatically become a monopoly under Danish government administration" (Mikkelsen, 1927: 214; see also Mikkelsen, 1933 and 1951). The assertion of sovereign rights over Arctic territory has an interesting history on the island of Ostrov Vrangelya (Wrangel Island), which lies between the East Siberian Sea and the Chukchi Sea. The occupation of Ostrov Vrangelya was initiated by Vilhjalmur Stefansson and American entrepreneurs in 1923 when they brought twelve Alaskan Eskimos to the island (Barr, 1977). The Russian government responded by removing the foreigners in 1926 and establishing a permanent Eskimo settlement of sixty people, who were brought over from Chukotka. In 1981, since the native peoples were no longer required to be there for sovereignty reasons, they were all returned to the mainland (Tichotsky, personal communication). There have been a number of other examples of governments using the relocation of native peoples for geopolitical purposes. These three instances have been cited simply because they occurred in a circumpolar setting within thirty years of Canadian plans for relocating Inuit to the High Arctic in the 1950s. This form of relocation was not unique.

Re-establishing "Effective Occupation" of the High Arctic

Any threat to Canadian nationhood has usually come from the south (Slowe, 1990: 80). Relief from Canada's sovereignty worries about the Arctic Islands during the 1930s was dispelled by an uneasiness about American activities there in the 1940s. In 1946 Canadian officials were informed that the United States was preparing to construct several weather stations in the High Arctic Islands to collect climatic information as a defense measure and to guard against Soviet attack. Canada's Department of External Affairs managed to obtain a copy of a report prepared by a U.S. Air Coordinating Committee and was alarmed to learn of the report's recommendation that U.S. Army reconnaissance flights be conducted in the sector west of Greenland to "determine whether islands exist which might be claimed by the United States" with a view to establishing weather stations (Canada, 1977: 1546). Canadian External Affairs realized that, if the Americans established the weather stations without Canadian participation, "Canadian sovereignty might be diminished if not endangered" (ibid.: 1562). Canada was therefore able to persuade Washington to delay plans for the weather stations for one year, until 1947, after which Joint Arctic Weather Stations (JAWS) were established by the Americans, with Canadian participation, at Resolute Bay, Eureka Sound, Mould Bay, Isachsen, and Alert.

In the late 1940s and early 1950s, the Canadian government felt the need to adopt measures that once again would "show the flag" and demonstrate its effective occupation of the High Arctic Islands according to the requirements of international law. Whereas in the past Canada had been content with a modest symbolic display of sovereignty, effective occupation was now required to "consolidate sovereignty" (Morrison, 1986: 247). In the 1950s the government needed to contend not only with the Greenlanders, who were hunting on Canadian soil, but also with the Americans, who were increasing their defense-related activity in the area. The Permanent Court of International Justice, in its decision on the 1933 "Eastern Greenland Case," referred to effective occupation as a sufficient basis for a claim to sovereignty based upon continued display of authority (Inch, 1962: 35). Canada's claim to sovereignty over the northernmost Arctic Islands had been unchallenged since the 1920s; nevertheless, in the early 1950s there were fears that the failure to maintain effective occupation of these remote and unpopulated areas might call Canadian claims of sovereignty into question, especially if a country like the United States gradually increased its occupation of that territory. In his 1950 "Report on Canadian Sovereignty in the Arctic" for the government, Dean Vincent MacDonald advised that Canada's title to its Arctic territories be asserted and maintained "upon the ground of effective occupation alone as the chief and most satisfactory ground of reliance." Mr. Hamilton, a member of Parliament, was later to echo that view in the House of Commons: "This great northland of ours is not ours because it is colored red on a map. It will only be ours by effective occupation" (Canada, 1958g).

With the aim of renewing its demonstration of Canadian authority over the High Arctic Islands, the RCMP was instructed to re-establish a detachment at Craig Harbour (open 1923–27 and 1933–40). When the RCMP did re-open the operation in September 1951, Alex Stevenson represented the Department at the ceremony, which was attended by Insp. Larsen and filmed by a newsreel cameraman. Stevenson (1951b) immediately sent a wireless message to J. G. Wright at the Department in Ottawa: "The flag was raised today in fine, clear weather that marked the opening of the Craig Harbour detachment [which is] now the most northerly active detachment." Stevenson completed his message with "Sovereignty now is a cinch."

Some officials were concerned that the Inuit who were occupying Ellesmere were not Canadian but Greenlandic and that there was no way for the government to assert Canadian sovereignty over that region. In connection with re-establishing an RCMP detachment at Bache Peninsula (Alexandra Fiord) on Ellesmere Island, Larsen informed Commissioner Nicholson in 1952:

The advantages of placing our Detachment directly across from Greenland would be that we then would have full control and supervision of Greenland Eskimos and others travelling back and forth, and over hunting activities they may engage in. As you already know, we had a Detachment established at Bache Peninsula in 1926, primarily for the maintenance of sovereignty. (Larsen, 1952a)

Commissioner Nicholson responded to Larsen's request by sending a confidential memorandum to Major-General Young, the Department's deputy minister. Nicholson (1952) informed him that a new detachment at Alexandra Fiord could maintain some surveillance over that part of the Ellesmere coast visited most frequently by Greenland natives. Cantley (1952a: 8) concurred and then linked the proposed relocation project to Ellesmere, stating that "the occupation of the island by Canadian Eskimos" would discourage Greenlanders from crossing over and hunting in the region.

While the Canadian government discussed the establishment of detachments at Alexandra Fiord and Craig Harbour, the United States Air Force (USAF) was constructing a massive military installation and air base at Thule on the northeast coast of Greenland, across Smith Sound from Craig Harbour and Alexandra Fiord. The American military also proposed to establish an early warning radar station on Cobourg Island (Canadian territory), opposite Craig Harbour (Canada, 1990a: 1201). Minutes of a meeting of the Cabinet chaired by Prime Minister St. Laurent on 19 January 1953 and classified as "top secret" show that Lester Pearson, secretary of state for external affairs, raised questions about U.S. military activity in the Canadian Arctic (Canada, 1953a). He pointed out that transient U.S. officials both civil and military outnumbered Canadian transients in the Arctic archipelago during the summer months. Pearson stated that "everything pointed towards an increase in U.S. activity in the Arctic during coming years." Pearson was responding in part to a briefing that had been passed to the Privy Council Office citing various recent infringements of Canadian sovereignty by American forces operating in the Arctic (Canada, 1990a: 1194–96). The incidents included unauthorized use of the Alert air base on Ellesmere Island by the USAF in 1950–52, and a USAF attempt to prevent the Canadian government ship *C.D. Howe* from anchoring at Padloping Island (Canadian territory) in 1952. That same year, the USAF Thule air base on one occasion instructed a Royal Canadian Air Force (RCAF) Lancaster aircraft to cease aerial photography of Canadian territory along the coast of Baffin Island. The largest U.S. project being planned was the establishment of the Distant Early Warning (DEW) line, a chain of forty radar stations extending across the Arctic. The USAF was also studying the possibility of constructing air strips on both Ellesmere Island and Baffin Island for landing their heaviest freighter aircraft and jet fighters. Pearson's position was summarized thus:

If Canadian claims to territory in the Arctic rested on discovery and continuous occupation, Canadian claims to some relatively unexplored areas might be questioned in the future. He [Pearson] was concerned about the de facto exercise of U.S. sovereignty, examples of which were numerous during the last war in other parts of Canada, and it seemed clear that an increase in U.S. activity in the Arctic would present risks of misunderstandings, incidents and infringements on the exercise of Canadian sovereignty. (Canada, 1953a)

Pearson strongly urged the Cabinet to direct the Advisory Committee on Northern Development (ACND) to report on what means might be employed to preserve or develop the political, administrative, scientific, and defense interests of Canada in that area. The prime minister's reply was that "it was within the realm of the possible that in years to come U.S. developments might be just about the only form of human activity in the vast wastelands of the Canadian Arctic. This was the problem which had to be met" (ibid.). In December 1952, for example, a secret Privy Council Office document noted, with reference to the Joint Arctic Weather Stations: "We have maintained our tenuous position by providing half the staff, but in the entire Archipelago we have less than 50 men. . . . Any new U.S. activity is bound to change the delicate balance of manpower in the northern Arctic" (Canada, 1990a: 1197). Rowley (1953) at the ACND confirmed that the joint weather stations did not provide the form of sole occupation desirable for demonstrating Canadian sovereignty in the Arctic archipelago. The Privy Council Office advised that extreme care must be exercised to preserve Canadian sovereignty in remote areas where Canadians were outnumbered and outranked (Canada, 1990a: 1198). Furthermore, it stated:

It may well be in future that our claim to some relatively unexplored areas will be shaky indeed. I am not now worried by formal claims; . . . of much grater concern is the sort of *de facto* U.S. sovereignty which caused so much trouble in the last war and which might be exercised again. There have already been incidents which, if they had reached the public ear, might have embarrassed the government.

It was thus not only desirable but a sine qua non that the new police detachments being established in the High Arctic Islands in the early 1950s have a human population to administer, and it was essential that they be Canadian citizens. On 10 August 1953 at an interdepartmental meeting with the RCAF to discuss the relocation to Resolute Bay and Grise Fiord, Ben Sivertz of the Department pointed out that "the Canadian government is anxious to have Canadians occupying as much of the north as possible and it appeared that in many cases the Eskimo were the only people capable of doing this" (Canada, 1953b). The prime minister in the House of Commons on 8 December 1953 affirmed that "we must leave no doubt about our active occupation and exercise of our sovereignty in these northern lands right up to the pole" (Canada, 1953c). The point about human activity was essential, for while fully defining "effective occupation," Heydte (1935) had emphasized:

Effectiveness seems to be best illustrated by the actual display of sovereign rights, the maintenance of order, and protection. But as a matter of fact sovereign rights can be exercised only over human beings, in inhabited lands; a certain order can be maintained only amongst human beings, i.e., again in inhabited countries; and protection too can be granted only to human beings.

Establishing the new RCMP detachments with their Inuit components in the High Arctic was thus a sovereignty objective, as was the Cabinet decision in 1953 to approve the establishment of customs and immigration offices at twenty-two northern points, eight of which were in the High Arctic Islands. Prime Minister St. Laurent expressed his government's sovereignty concerns and the need for additional measures when speaking before the House in 1953: "There are quite a number of non-Canadians going into that territory. We felt that it was very important to have the situation such that whenever they went there they realized they were in Canadian territory and in territory that was administered by Canadian authorities" (Canada, 1953c).

The prime minister's speech mirrored the rhetoric of Mr. Stewart thirty years earlier when he introduced legislation in the Commons requiring explorers to obtain a license (Canada, 1925). Though neither the United States nor any other country after the 1930s showed an inclination actually to threaten Canadian sovereignty in the High Arctic, the government still, at times, *perceived* a potential threat. The perceived need to fortify Canada's effective occupation of the Arctic Islands was a response to the reality of geography and Cold War geopolitics. Canada's "own security is probably made more difficult to provide for," explained the prime minister, "by the fact that this northland of ours is between these two great world powers [the United States and the Soviet Union]" (Canada, 1953c). "Occupation" became a key word in public debates about the Arctic Islands. In May 1954, Jean Lesage, minister of northern affairs, reaffirmed in the House of Commons that "we should do everything to assert our sovereignty in those Arctic islands, of which Ellesmere is the most northern" (Canada, 1954d). A member of Parliament, Mr. Fraser (of Peterborough), inquired as to whether the RCMP post on Ellesmere Island was flying a Canadian flag. Lesage responded that there were two Canadian flags flying because there were two posts. He underscored the fact by making the point that "there is no question of our sovereignty, and there is no question of occupancy. We occupy that island."

If there was no question of sovereignty, as the government has persistently maintained, then why was the issue continually being addressed? In August 1956 in the House of Commons, the MP Mr. Harkness expressed the view that public sensitivity to the presence of American forces had "caused a considerable number of Canadians to think pretty seriously about what our situation is in the north, [and] the extent to which our control of that area still remains in our hands" (Canada, 1956b). Throughout the 1950s, the importance of maintaining the new Inuit colonies at Resolute Bay and Grise Fiord was associated with the Canadian government's heightened concern about occupation of the Queen Elizabeth Islands. In August 1958, the then minister of northern affairs, Alvin Hamilton, stated in the House of Commons that "you can hold a territory by right of discovery or by claiming it under some sector theory but where you have great powers holding different points of view the only way to hold that territory, with all its great potential wealth, is by effective occupation" (Canada, 1958h).

In November 1960, C. M. Bolger, the Department's administrator of the Arctic, completed a confidential report for his supervisor, Ben Sivertz, on the relocation to Resolute Bay and Grise Fiord. Bolger (1960b) explained that, although the Inuit at Grise Fiord had not had the opportunities for employment that those at Resolute Bay had, nevertheless "this community also serves a distinctly useful purpose in confirming, in a tangible manner, Canada's sovereignty over this vast region of the Arctic." Sivertz (1960b) described the report as "a very good review" of the situation.

Ultima Thule: Reoccupation of the High Arctic Islands

In a confidential memo dated May 1954 for the Advisory Committee on Northern Development (ACND), the Department's policy guidelines for the release of information on the North were outlined:

The first object of public information on the north is to emphasize that the northern regions are as much a part of Canada as any other area in the country. It is important that all Canadians should be aware of this fact in order that the measures to stimulate and encourage the development of our northern frontier will be supported and sustained. It is also important that the rest of the world should be aware that the Canadian Arctic is not an "Ultima Thule" but is being effectively occupied, administered and developed by the Canadian Government and people. (G. Rowley, 1954)

The document's use of the phrase *ultima Thule* refers to a "distant unknown region." In the 1950s, the government sought to ensure that all of its Arctic Islands, including those strategic areas that lacked a permanent population of Canadian nationals, be reoccupied if possible. The 1953 Resolute Bay and Grise Fiord colonization scheme was partly designed to use native peoples to demonstrate occupation of a territory (Diubaldo, 1989: 175). This process of resettlement in the 1950s was an integral part of the government's overall desire to "Canadianize" the North. "Canadianization" or "re-Canadianize" were nationalistic terms used by officials (Canada, 1990a: 1201) for a policy designed to secure and demonstrate effective occupation. In the mid-1950s, the Department took pride in the fact that the prime minister and members of the Cabinet had made many public statements on the growing importance of the North and on the growing attention to be focused on that area (G. Rowley, 1954). This development was being done because "it is the logical extension of the development of Canadian nationhood. . . . Canada is developing the north merely because it is Canada."

During Canadian efforts to repopulate its High Arctic Islands with Inuit in the early 1950s, government officials thought there should be no public statements suggesting that sovereignty was a reason for this activity. The demonstration of effective occupation of the Arctic Islands was a politically sensitive issue, and the ACND told the Department that:

No emphasis should be placed on Canadian claims in the north lest we seem to be on the defensive. Canada owns all the lands shown on official maps of Canada and we recognize no differences in degree of control between any of the northern islands and counties in a southern province. We do recognize, however, that the maintenance of sovereignty in any part of Canada requires continuous, effective administration which there now is and will continue to be. (ibid.)

The ACND's statement was indicative of the government's longstanding concern about how other countries might perceive Canadian sovereignty over the Arctic Islands. In May 1946, for example, the head of the External Affairs' legal division, E. R. Hopkins, advised the department's political division: "It is my view that we should not raise any question concerning our sovereignty in the Arctic. . . . It would not be wise to indicate that we entertain any doubts with regard to our sovereignty" (Canada, 1977: 1547). This testament to the nation's sensitivity about Arctic sovereignty placed particular emphasis on the number of symbolic measures necessary to "wave the flag."

Before World War II, RCMP detachments had been the primary means of displaying a largely symbolic Canadian presence in the Arctic archipelago. This was the purpose of the RCMP's floating detachment, the *St. Roch*, which went through the Northwest Passage under the command of Henry Larsen. As a cost-savings measure, when the war began the RCMP reduced the number of its Arctic posts from thirteen to seven. In the postwar period, the process of Arctic Canadianization took several forms: opening additional RCMP detachments (making a total of nineteen in 1950 and twenty-four in 1960), increasing the numbers of Canadian scientists, civilian, and military personnel in the North, and taking over supply roles from the United States for the High Arctic weather stations.

Peopling the North by assisting Inuit to settle on unoccupied Arctic Islands was a natural component of a northern Canadianization policy. Rather than explaining to the Inuit the nature of the policy, however, the government adopted the explanation that the move was being arranged to offer them better hunting opportunities. Either officials thought it was a useful inducement, feeling that the political motive was too secret or too difficult to explain, or they sincerely believed that the moves would satisfy both a group's need to obtain food and a country's need to secure its territory. Whatever the actual motives of the governments concerned, the appeal of better hunting was used by the Danes at Scoresby Sund, the Russians at Ostrov Vrangelya, and the Canadians at Devon Island, Resolute Bay, and Grise Fiord. It was also used in concurrent attempts in the early 1950s to attract Inuit to Banks and Herschel Islands.

The Eskimo Loan Fund and Resettlement Initiatives

In the early 1950s, the government explored various options for re-establishing permanent Inuit populations on the northern Arctic Islands. The first step towards colonization was to establish trading stores on the islands so that the Inuit would not have to return to the mainland to trade. Initially, Cantley sought the assistance of the Company in establishing new stores, for example on Banks Island in the western Arctic. During his struggle to wrest field control from the RCMP and give it back to the Company (see chapter 1), Cantley (1950b: 49) had tried to reassure the Northwest Territories Council that, if a suitable plan for direct cooperative action between the Company and one responsible Department were proposed, they would willingly cooperate. When Cantley approached the Company about establishing a store on Banks Island, however, they responded that it was an uneconomical proposal, and the Department therefore had to ask for police cooperation.

In 1953 the Department created an "Eskimo Loan Fund" with the Treasury Board so that returnable advances could be made to Inuit groups or individuals for purchasing necessary supplies and equipment (Eskimo Affairs, 1952b: 3). The Loan Fund was apparently set up to facilitate the Department's resettlement plans, although this purpose has not been suggested in the available literature. A memo of March 1953 outlined the five "assisted Eskimo projects" to be financed under the fund (Cunningham, 1953). All five were connected with resettlement.

The first three loans were for establishing government trading stores, to be operated by the RCMP, at the proposed Inuit colonies at Cape Herschel (Alexandra Fiord) and Craig Harbour on Ellesmere Island, and at Resolute Bay. The fourth loan was to equip Inuit for trapping and resettling on Banks Island, and the fifth loan was to purchase trade supplies for a new RCMP-operated government store on Herschel Island (see map 1.1).

In the case of Banks Island, the Department wanted to encourage Inuit trappers who had formerly lived on the island (and were known as Bankslanders) and were now living in the Mackenzie Delta to return permanently to Banks. In 1951–52, the Department experimented by making advances to fifteen families, many of whom had hunted on the island in previous years. They were equipped by the Department and realized a profit each year, thereby establishing a precedent that emphasized that the advances were "self-liquidating" and not "handouts." The Bankslanders had their own schooners and journeyed across from Banks Island to Aklavik or Tuktoyaktuk for their supplies. Under the provisions of the newly established Loan Fund, in 1953 eleven trappers and their families wintered on the island, and in 1954 seventeen individuals were again equipped to trap on Banks, earning around $50,000 (Canada, 1957a). Including family members, twenty-seven Bankslanders lived on the island in 1951–52, increasing to fifty-four in 1954–55 (Usher, 1970: 65).

The impetus for the Banks program, according to Cantley (1950a), was not simply to establish seasonal trapping on Banks but "to encourage these people to break away from the Delta entirely and to build up their own community on the island." He acknowledged that whether they "would be content to stay there indefinitely or not would depend largely on how attractive the proposition could be made to them." Cantley's advice was that the Department assist the trappers financially by setting up and operating a cooperative store on Banks Island.

When Jim Wright (1950), chief of the Arctic Division, wrote to R. H. Cheshire, general manager of the Company's fur-trade department, in 1950 about the plan for repopulating Banks Island, he advised that, if a post were to be established on the island, arrangements could be made "to transfer the Banks Island natives back there permanently." During the drop in fur prices in the late 1940s, the Bankslanders had moved to the Mackenzie Delta on the mainland for three years. Wright now emphasized that "it would be preferable . . . to endeavour to break their connection with the Delta entirely." The Banks resettlement scheme had two advantages: it colonized an unoccupied island, and it improved the participants' standard of living by eliminating their dependence on relief and encouraging them to be self-supporting. The Department thought the Inuit would have a much better chance of becoming self-sufficient on the island rather than on the mainland (ibid.).

Once an Inuit population had been re-established on Banks Island, the RCMP built a detachment there at Sachs Harbour in 1953, coinciding with the creation of the Loan Fund and the opening of detachments at Alexandra Fiord and Resolute Bay. Had the Department's initiatives failed to encourage the Bankslanders to reoccupy the island, or had the advances not been repaid, plans for further resettlement of the High Arctic Islands in 1953 might not have been pursued as keenly as they were. The successful Banks Island resettlement project established a prototype for colonization experiments, both by demonstrating that Inuit relocation could fulfill the sovereignty objective of territorial occupation (Usher, 1970: 56; Williamson and Foster, 1974: 13) and by institutionalizing Departmental support for these operations through the Eskimo Loan Fund.

· PART 2 ·

SOUTH OF EDEN

RELOCATION
OF THE INUKJUAMIUT

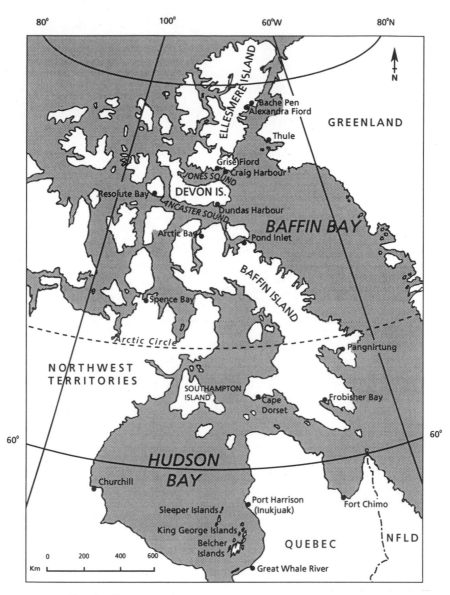

MAP 3.1 Canadian Eastern Arctic

3

RELOCATION TO THE HIGH ARCTIC

In June 1993, former senior Department officials testified before the Royal Commission on Aboriginal Peoples about their involvement with the government-sponsored relocation project set in motion forty years before in 1953–55. In the back of the hall, an Inuk was sitting with other Inuit women, listening intently to what was being said. Her name was Martha Flaherty, the newly elected president of the national Inuit women's organization, Pauktuutit. The officials were describing events that involved Martha and her family, who in 1955 were relocated from Port Harrison to Grise Fiord (see map 3.1). Martha's father was Joseph Flaherty, the Inuk son of filmmaker Robert Flaherty and Nyla, the co-star of the film *Nanook of the North.*

Just as Robert Flaherty tried to recapture the character and images of "traditional" Inuit life, so the Department in the early 1950s envisaged a relocation project that would rehabilitate and socially transform a group of Inuit so that they could live like the idealized Nanook. Ironically, Robert Flaherty's own son was selected by officials to be relocated to the High Arctic as part of this rehabilitation experiment. Joseph Flaherty and other Quebec families were transported to a land completely foreign to them, far to the north of the Arctic Circle, on Ellesmere and Cornwallis Islands. Why were Joseph Flaherty and the other Inuit specifically selected for relocation? and, What happened to these Inuit relocatees that warranted a Royal Commission investigation forty years later?

Officials Take Remedial Action

The first evidence of a plan to relocate Canadian Inuit to Ellesmere Island is found in a report drafted by Alex Stevenson (see fig. 3.1) when

FIGURE 3.1 Alex Stevenson, officer in charge of the
eastern Arctic patrol, aboard the CGS *C.D. Howe*, 1953.
Credit: Alex Stevenson/National Archives of Canada, PA-176800

he was serving as the Department's officer in charge of the annual eastern Arctic patrol in the summer of 1950. The patrol was a celebratory
occasion, for it was the maiden voyage of the government's new ship,
the *C.D. Howe*. Insp. Larsen was on board the vessel, and when they
reached the RCMP detachment at Dundas Harbour on Devon Island,
which was the northernmost point of the voyage, Larsen and Stevenson discussed the possibility of an Inuit relocation further north. Under
the heading "Establishing Eskimo Camps North of Lancaster Sound,"
Stevenson (1950: 7) noted that there were two North Baffin Inuit families employed at the RCMP Dundas Harbour detachment (open 1924–
33 and 1945–51) on Devon Island. Because the Force was planning to
reopen the Craig Harbour and Bache Peninsula detachments on Ellesmere Island soon, Stevenson suggested that at least four Inuit families
be moved to Devon and others be established on Ellesmere Island and
other High Arctic Islands. He reported that Insp. Larsen thought such a

plan was quite feasible and, provided the Inuit were willing to move, he could see no reason why it should not be a success. Stevenson suggested that once the Inuit had been relocated, the RCMP could be responsible for their welfare (ibid.). The project could serve two goals, proposed Stevenson: to "give our natives a chance to cover this country, and also if it is considered necessary help improve the position regarding sovereignty rights" (Grant, 1993: appendix 32).

When the RCMP detachment at Dundas Harbour was closed and the Craig Harbour detachment was reopened the following summer in 1951, Stevenson and Larsen were present at the ceremonies. Two Inuit special constables and their families, comprising sixteen people, were relocated from Dundas Harbour to Craig Harbour (as noted in table 2.2). When preparing to reopen the Bache Peninsula (Alexandra Fiord) detachment the following year, Larsen (1952a) sent a memo to Commissioner Nicholson entitled "Proposed Movement of Eskimo Families from Baffin Island to Ellesmere Island, N.W.T." Larsen recommended that "we should in addition to the two native families employed permanently by the Police, endeavour to recruit three or four good Eskimo families from Pond Inlet area to be transported up there for the purpose of trapping, hunting, etc., and thereby in a general way improve their economic circumstances."

With the exception of the RCMP Inuk special constable (S/Cst.) and his family living at the detachment at Craig Harbour, there were no Canadian Inuit living on Ellesmere Island or on any of the Queen Elizabeth Islands. Commissioner Nicholson (1952) responded to Larsen's request by contacting Major-General Hugh Young, deputy minister of the Department, with regard to the plan's implications for the movement and welfare of the Inuit.

At the same time that Larsen was planning a relocation from North Baffin Island to Ellesmere Island, the Department was discussing a relocation from Port Harrison to South Baffin Island. In his report on the 1952 eastern Arctic patrol, the Department's officer in charge, R. G. Johnston, described his attempt to encourage Inuit from the Port Harrison area to take part in a relocation scheme:

If it is desired to move any native families off the Quebec coast and north to Baffin Island, Inukpuk E9-904, Pellypushie E9-720, and eight other families of the Port Harrison area have signified their willingness to move. In order that we might encourage natives to move from Quebec to better hunting grounds it is suggested that these people be moved next summer on the "Howe." (Johnston, 1952)

The Department's plan to move Inuit families from Port Harrison to Baffin Island was an extension of the RCMP's instructions in 1951–52 to equip and relocate small groups of Inuit away from Port Harrison to the nearby King George Islands and the Sleeper Islands off the coast during the autumn months. According to the RCMP, this action had proved to be effective in aiding the hunters to obtain more game and making the families more self-reliant. A relocation to Baffin was a more extreme measure than "assisting" Inuit to hunt on the islands in Hudson Bay, but both were in keeping with officials' desires to "break up concentrations" of Inuit around settlements. There was a fundamental difference, however, in the case of the assisted movement now being considered. Whereas the earlier efforts by the RCMP were moves of a temporary nature to locations near Port Harrison, the Department's new plan—to move families from Port Harrison to Baffin Island—would entail relocations to more distant sites on a more permanent resettlement basis.

The RCMP proceeded to develop its own plan for the Inuit relocation project, and in September 1952 Insp. Larsen informed Commissioner Nicholson of his idea to move several Inuit families to Craig Harbour, Cape Sabine, and Dundas Harbour "where colonization by them appears to be suitable and feasible" (Larsen, 1952c). At the first meeting of the Special Committee on Eskimo Affairs, held on 16 October 1952 in Ottawa, a policy of relocation in accordance with Larsen's plan was discussed. Officials agreed that a project "of assisting natives to move from overpopulated areas" to Ellesmere Island should be investigated (Eskimo Affairs, 1952a: 4).

The connection with the relocation of Port Harrison Inuit to the High Arctic was established when Larsen's plan to move a group of Inuit from North Baffin to Ellesmere Island and the Department's plan of moving a group of families from Port Harrison to South Baffin Island were brought together in one relocation scheme. The coupling of the two schemes was a crucial moment in the genesis of the plan. Some observers have suggested that the Inukjuamiut were relocated to the High Arctic so that there would be no risk of the colonization scheme failing, because the "volunteers" would be physically unable to leave of their own accord (Inukjuamiut informants, personal communication). It is my contention that the link had simply been made for administrative convenience, thereby combining two northward moves into one cost-effective package. A memo that Stevenson wrote to Cantley on 8 December 1952 demonstrated the connection:

I understand that you are considering the transfer of about ten families from the Port Harrison area of Northern Quebec to Ellesmere Island where they can be looked after by the present R.C.M.P. Detachment at Craig Harbour and by the proposed detachment near Cape Herschel. In connection with the above I would suggest that one or two families from Northern Baffin Island be moved with the Port Harrison group. These natives would be familiar with conditions and could greatly assist the Port Harrison people, and would help to sustain the morale. (A. Stevenson, 1952)

The plan to relocate Inuit from northern Quebec to the High Arctic Islands was a bold initiative that had never been tried before by any agency, and it represented decisive remedial action. It was vital for the Department's external credibility at this time to be seen as finding solutions to the "Eskimo problem." A relocation on this scale presented an ideal opportunity for officials to demonstrate to the public that action was being taken. Viewed from the outside, the scheme to colonize the High Arctic Islands was impressive. It was certainly a cost-effective experiment. Since the *C.D. Howe* was scheduled to visit Craig Harbour anyway on its summer patrol, and the C.G.S. *d'Iberville* was expected to supply the Alexandra Fiord detachment, the cost of transporting the relocatees would be minimal. The new colonies themselves were designed to be self-supporting and self-contained under the field supervision of the RCMP.

By 18 December 1952, Cantley had formulated the Department's initiative for the "transfer of natives" from "overpopulated areas." He advanced a plan for the Inuit to "be made self-supporting" and suggested relocating about ten families from the Port Harrison area to Ellesmere Island aboard the ships the *C.D. Howe* and the *d'Iberville* in the summer of 1953 (Cantley, 1952b). Cantley also proposed to transfer (in the same ships) about ten Inuit families from northern Quebec and/or Cape Dorset to Resolute Bay on Cornwallis Island, provided arrangements could be made with the RCMP to station a constable there to look after them. He was hopeful that the Department of Transport (DOT) or the Royal Canadian Air Force (RCAF) might be able to employ some of the Inuit on a year-round basis as a maintenance crew on the base at Resolute Bay.

Acting on Cantley's suggestion of moving some of the Port Harrison families to Resolute Bay, Major-General Young asked Commissioner Nicholson if the RCMP would consider opening a detachment at Resolute. This memorandum of 20 February 1953 might suggest that the decision to reopen the RCMP detachment at Resolute Bay was prompted by the Department; however, R. A. J. Phillips, who at the time worked in the Privy Council Office, informed the clerk of the Privy Council (the most senior Canadian civil servant) on 29 December 1952 that there were tentative plans for the RCMP to reopen its Resolute Bay detachment (Canada, 1990a: 1196–1200). In his memorandum, Phillips expressed concern about the imbalance between a growing U.S. military presence and the small number of Canadian forces in the High Arctic

Islands. He noted that, in the entire Canadian Arctic archipelago, there were only four places with exclusively Canadian installations, so he was pleased that the RCMP was establishing a detachment at Cape Herschel (Alexandra Fiord) on Ellesmere Island the following year. For the same reason, Phillips favored the reopening of the RCMP Resolute detachment and recommended that the Department support this idea (ibid.: 1199). Young's replacement, Deputy Minister Gordon Robertson, later confirmed that "the location of the RCMP at Resolute was a demonstration of sovereignty" (Canada, 1993b: 132). At senior levels of government there was thus a direct link between the reopening of the Resolute Bay and Alexandra Fiord detachments and the interest in establishing operations that were wholly Canadian to demonstrate a greater Canadian presence in the High Arctic Islands. Young's letter two months later may simply have been intended to draw attention to the advantage to be gained for the Department from a situation of which he was perhaps already aware.

A precondition of the relocation experiment, as Young (1953c) noted, was police cooperation in assisting the relocatees to adjust to the new circumstances. Nicholson (1953) responded that he would be quite willing to select a good man and have him stationed there with the specific job of taking care of the natives. He asked whether the RCMP would be allowed to help in the matter of selecting natives for Resolute. Young (1953d) replied that he was pleased that the RCMP was prepared to open a detachment at Resolute Bay and that the Department would welcome the assistance of the RCMP in selecting the Inuit for relocation.

The "Migration" Selection Process: Recruits for Reform

Once the Department had delegated the task of selecting the relocatees to the RCMP, Insp. Larsen asked his officers at the detachments in Port Harrison, Pond Inlet, and Fort Chimo to prepare lists of families suitable to go north. Larsen appointed Constable Ross Gibson, a thirty-one-year-old junior officer, to the task of selecting the Port Harrison Inuit. During this period, one of the Department's "welfare teachers," Miss Margery Hinds, was based at Port Harrison. The photograph in figure 3.2 of Inuit children in the Port Harrison one-room schoolhouse was taken in 1950 by Margery Hinds. The girl on the far left of the picture, Ekoomak (Ekumiak Agatusuk), was one of the children relocated to Grise Fiord in 1953.

There were no special teaching materials for Inuit children, so the Department's policy was to supply the standard primary readers used

FIGURE 3.2 Ekoomak (Ekumiak Agatusuk) and other Inukjuamiut children attending school at Port Harrison, 1950. Credit: Collection Margery Hinds, courtesy of Avataq Cultural Institute, Inukjuak, Québec

in the south such as *Fun with Dick and Jane, Our New Friends*, and *Streets and Roads* (Jacobson, 1955). In addition to the daunting task of teaching Inuit children who lived in small hunting camps about "streets and roads" in English, the welfare teacher's job was to monitor the health and welfare of the Inuit families in the area (Hinds, 1958). Hinds collected information on the local Inuit and sent regular reports of her findings to the Department. Her reports provide important background information both about the relocation selection process and about the individuals concerned.

On 4 May 1953, Cst. Ross Gibson informed Miss Hinds that he was calling a meeting in Port Harrison that evening to discuss the question of moving some families to the North. According to Miss Hinds (1953a), Gibson said that "he was under no obligation to discuss the question with anyone" but that he thought people in the various departments might be interested and have suggestions to offer. All the Whites in the settlement were present at the meeting, including the nurse, Mrs. Reynolds, and the Company post manager, Mr. Reuben Ploughman (see fig. 3.3). Miss Hinds (1958: 161) thought the relocation project was "a very wise

FIGURE 3.3 Christmas party in Port Harrison, 1952. Cst. Ross Gibson (back row), nurse Margret Reynolds, teacher Margery Hinds (middle row from left), HBC trader Reuben Ploughman and his wife, Lily (bottom row).
Credit: Reuben Ploughman

plan," and she suggested that those who had proved themselves capable of living far from the trading post and who got along without much help from the government or the HBC were more likely to be successful relocatees (Hinds, 1953a).

There are indications, however, that the social-reform experiment was to some degree intended to get rid of the least valued members of society (Constantine, 1991: 64). Cst. Gibson (1990) apparently decided not to allow the welfare teacher or the other White officials, with the exception of Company manager Ploughman, to take part in the process. Against the advice of Miss Hinds, Gibson also decided not to choose families who had recently managed without government assistance. In a teletype message that Larsen apparently sent to his constables at Port Harrison, he requested that the heads of families to be relocated be "energetic hunters" (document provided in Grant, 1993). Larsen later recorded privately, however, that he had instructed Gibson to select a cross-section of average hunters and also to include "some which had shown little or no inclination to support themselves over the years" (Larsen, n.d.: 44). Gibson (1990) thus selected those families who in general had become most reliant on relief benefits and supplies from the Company post. He did so despite the welfare teacher's comment that she "did not consider any local Eskimos suitable for they had acquired un-Eskimo habits at the post" (Hinds, 1953a). Cpl. G. A. Mansell (1950) described these "un-Eskimo habits" in a report on Port Harrison, in which he also discussed some of the individuals later selected by Gibson: "[Inuk A] and [Inuk B] who with their families spent all their efforts in begging around the post; they were in to the post sometimes four or five times each week instead of remaining in their camp hunting. . . . These two families have now been put on permanent relief."

Similarly, in her report for July 1953, Miss Hinds described her visit to the camp of some of Gibson's relocatees. This camp included the families of [Inuk C], [Inuk D], [Inuk E], and [Inuk F]. Hinds stated that "they seemed to be among the most destitute in this camp. . . . [Inuk F]'s tent gave an impression of utter destitution" (Hinds, 1953b). Cst. Gibson (1956) himself described the relocatee [Inuk D] in a report: "While in Port Harrison [Inuk D] had poor equipment, three poor dogs, and lived entirely from his family allowance and asked from time to time for assistance." These quotations reflect the ethnocentric perspectives of their authors and indicate the nature of Gibson's selection criteria, but they do not reflect the way these Inuit saw themselves. For example, one of the Inukjuamiut elders who was not relocated, Lazarusie Epoo, remembered Paddy Aqiatusuk (referred to above by pseudonym) from before the move as "a very competent hunter [and] a very generous provider to many families and camp groups" (Canada, 1993a: 62). This man was the person Gibson ultimately selected to be the camp boss at Grise Fiord. In chapter 4, I will discuss further perceptions of Aqiatusuk and his symbolic role in the relocation.

In virtually all the Department and RCMP accounts, as well as in press releases, officials emphasized that the families were "volunteers." In November 1953, Cantley and Stevenson prepared a statement about the relocation for the journal *The Arctic Circular*. Their rhetoric suggests how they wanted the project to be perceived:

Food supplies were reported to be plentiful and there is every indication that this *migration* should prove a success. This *transfer* of Eskimos was organized by the Department of Resources and Development. . . . If the results this year warrant it, other natives can be moved to these *pioneer points* and to other points selected later. For the present, however, this migration is being considered as an *experiment* to determine if Eskimos can be *induced* to live on the northern islands. . . . All the Eskimos moved this past summer, did so *voluntarily*. (Cantley, 1953) (italics mine)

Cantley and Stevenson did not use the word "relocation," which might imply dislocation or intervention. Instead, the rather benign word "transfer" and the more distinctive word "migration" were used. "Migration" suggests a naturally occurring annual movement or possibly a permanent move. How significant was the use of this word in the context of a relocation project? Historically, Inuit have migrated for various reasons. The Inukjuamiut, like many Canadian Inuit in the 1950s, were a seminomadic people who moved cyclically in search of game between traditional summer and winter camps in a well-defined area of about fifty square miles (Willmott, 1961; E. A. Smith, 1991). Much has been written on the importance of the rotational patterns of Inuit migration (*aullaartut*) that took place within a specific territorial range for reasons of resource harvesting and fellowship (Birket-Smith, 1929a; Damas, 1963 and 1968; Freeman and others, 1976; Riches, 1982).

At times, however, Inuit have migrated away from areas they traditionally exploited, as Susan Rowley (1985b) has shown in her excellent ethnohistorical study of population movements in the Canadian Arctic (Susan Rowley is the daughter of Graham Rowley, a former senior government official to whom I occasionally refer). Rowley reviewed twenty-seven cases of Inuit migration and identified the causal factors as associated with environmental and social pressures. In the event of famine and scarcity of game, Inuit moved on in search of better areas. Rowley (1985b: 102–3) noted that starvation camps were almost never re-inhabited by the same group. Mobility also played an important role in conflict resolution (Condon, 1982: 157). Rowley (1985b: 103) cites fear of revenge as a primary social cause of migration. If a murder occurred, fear that the victim's family could seek revenge prompted the murderer and his family to flee the area (Rowley 1985a: 16). A person who committed an antisocial act, or series of acts, and who was viewed as a threat to the rest of the band might be banished from the area. Feuds between individuals or families might cause one group to leave their homeland altogether.

In the case of the relocation experiment organized by the Department in 1953, there appear to have been no factors within Inukjuamiut society that might have motivated any traditional migration response mechanisms. This project was externally conceived and introduced by the Department. The planners' standard use of the word "migration" to describe the relocation in press releases and in other documentation is of fundamental importance for understanding how the project was perceived. Because the scheme was described internally as a "rehabilitation project" (Fryer, 1954a), I would argue that one could interpret official use of the word "migration" as a metaphor for social reform (Constantine, 1991: 62) and as a term of self-justification. (These themes will be developed at greater length in chapter 8.) The official view was that when, as in Port Harrison, Inuit were seen to be "loitering" around a White settlement, one could reform them by removing them from their traditional homeland and moving them to an isolated, unoccupied site where they might be encouraged to behave in a Nanook-like, independent manner. It was assumed that once again they would rely on their own capabilities and wild game rather than on "White man's handouts." This ideology pervaded the two primary case studies and many of the other relocations to which I refer.

In the Department's press release quoted above, the description of the relocation project in naturalistic (and self-motivating) terms by calling it a migration is offset by the use of the words "pioneer points," "experiment," and "induced," which raise questions about the consensual nature of the project—perhaps why the authors emphasized that the participants had moved "voluntarily." The Inuit today think that "induced," or coerced, would be a more apt description of the recruitment process (Inukjuamiut informants, personal communication; Canada, 1993a). The nature of Inuit compliance with requests by the police and other Whites to volunteer for relocation is crucial to understanding the forty years of resentment that led the Inuit to present their case before the recent Royal Commission on Aboriginal Peoples. Jaybeddie Amagoalik (see fig. 4.2) recalled that, when the police approached their camp outside Port Harrison, they said: "You are going to go. You are going to leave." Jaybeddie asked the police: "What about our boat? What is going to happen to our boat?" The police told him: "We are going to give you all the equipment you need, including boats." "So, that's what we were told, but there was nothing" (Canada, 1993a: 232). As Anna Nungaq explained, "We had no idea of where we were going or why. We were very confused" (*Inuktitut*, 1981). Other Inuit agreed with her comments. John Amagoalik stated: "[My parents'] first reaction was no we cannot leave our home, we cannot leave our families. We just cannot agree to this. The RCMP went away but they came back, they came back two or three times as I remember and they were very, very persistent" (Canada, 1990b).

Although the Department was implying in its press release that these people were "venture migrants" on their way to the High Arctic, it might be more appropriate to characterize them as "indentured migrants." Although their ascribed status was that of volunteers, Inuit narratives portray the operation as a forced relocation (Canada, 1993a). They have subsequently referred to themselves as "exiles" (ibid.), a term I will explore in chapter 8. In recognition of their status as indentured migrants, the Inuit were offered a two-year contract in the new colonies with an option thereafter to return home with government assistance. It was a high-risk undertaking to be in a group of pioneer migrants, because the organizers could not predict the project's success or failure (Schuler, 1986: 129). The two-year clause thus represented a crucial safety valve for the Inuit. Unfortunately, the promise was only a verbal one, later forgotten, that served to obscure the precise nature of their status. The nature of the two-year promise will be discussed in chapter 4.

The Inuit relocatees remember when Cst. Gibson came to their camps looking for people to go north. Edith Patsauq recalled the incident:

My late husband and I were visited by a police officer and his interpreter. They sat themselves in front of us and for the first time we heard about the relocation issue. They said they had come to ask us if we will want to be relocated as well since our relatives had already agreed to go. Not being able to do without our relatives, we said we would go too, for he was also saying that we could return home after two years. (Makivik, 1986)

Gibson (1990) selected the relocatees because "these people were all welfare cases and were perhaps some of the poorest Eskimos in the Arctic." Highly illustrative of Gibson's selection criteria was his choice of two Inuit men. One man was accused of stealing from the Company store. In fact, he reportedly took back a carving he had made, for which he felt he had been underpaid; nevertheless, his name went down on Gibson's list for relocation. Another man, Johnny Inukpuk, was a highly respected hunter and was regarded by his peers as an *angajuqaaq*, a "superior person" (Inukjuamiut informants, personal communication). The Department's officer in charge of the eastern Arctic patrol in 1952 had put Johnny Inukpuk's name on the preliminary list of people selected for relocation to Baffin Island (the Department's first plan, which was changed later in 1952) (R. G. Johnston, 1952). When I asked Johnny Inukpuk why he was not put on the *C.D. Howe* for relocation in 1953, he said that, since he was considered one of the best trappers in Port Harrison, the Company trader may have asked that his name be removed from the list (Inukpuk, personal communication). A man who was considered undesirable was thus chosen, whereas another who had a good reputation was de-selected.

When reflecting on the consensual nature of the move, Larsen stated that "under no circumstances did I wish to have any Eskimos talked into, or be moved against their will, as far as we in the Police were concerned, it had to be an absolutely voluntary move by the Eskimo" (Larsen, n.d.: 948). Gibson (1990) still believes "the natives made their final decision—no one was pressured or promised anything by myself." Given the variables and complexities of explaining the experiment, Gibson's method of talking to the prospective relocatees may have been misinterpreted (Tudor, 1974: 25). The Inuit, however, remember things differently: "There was a lot of arm twisting. The RCMP was held in fear by our people. It was intimidating to my parents. To say that people were eager to move is nonsense" (Amagoalik, personal communication).

If it was intended as a voluntary project, why were police requests to join the relocation interpreted by the Inuit as commands? The Inuit who presented testimony at the Royal Commission hearings in April 1993 often spoke of the fear or awe (*ilira*) that they had of the Whites. The policemen, like other Whites, could be intimidating (*iliranartuq*) and frightening (*kappianaq*). Hugh Brody has written on the subject of *ilira* and has found in his discussions with elders that all relations with Whites could cause the Inuit fear and anxiety (Brody, 1975: 159–65; also Briggs, 1968: 32–33). "We describe someone who is intimidated as *ilirasukttuq*," explained one of the relocatees (Audlaluk, personal communication). The well-being of the Inuit, their access to store goods (including food, clothing, and essential equipment), their very survival depended on getting along with the Whites. Roughly two-thirds of Inuit income in the early 1950s in Port Harrison came from family allowance credits and government relief. Foodstuffs and supplies purchased with family allowances and relief reinforced the already existing dependency relationship of the Inuit. The Whites "were a crucial resource," observes Brody. "To risk offending them was to risk losing the supply" (Brody, 1993: 3). When considering the cultural context of Inuit relations with the RCMP, John Amagoalik (see fig. 4.2) explained, "you must . . . understand that in 1953 the white man was viewed as almost a God by our people. They were feared. I mean we were afraid of them. We were afraid to say no to anything they wanted" (Canada, 1990b). The combination of a dependency relationship with the Whites and Inuit fear of them produced a situation conducive to compliance with requests from the police for Inuit to join the relocation, as Brody (1993: 3) describes:

This relationship, and the feeling of *ilira* to which it gave rise, meant that whatever the Qallunaat [Whites] suggested or wanted was likely to be done. Inuit did not have the inner freedom and certainly had not developed the habit of asserting their own preferences in defiance of, or even as an alternative possibility to, the wishes of the Qadlunaat.

The relationship between a policeman (*puliisi*) and the Inuit was determined by the recognition that the police had absolute authority (Brody, 1975: 28). The Inuit referred to constables and other Whites by nicknames (*taiguusirttaq*) that resembled their physical characteristics. Some were called *Puliisialuk*, "big policeman," or *Puliisirajaak*, "skinny policeman," or in Ross Gibson's case *Auparttuq*, which means "red" because people said he had red cheeks and his face would flush red if he was upset. The stereotypical officer of the RCMP was a physically imposing man. Like Cst. Gibson, he was tall and stocky, and his persona demanded respect and reflected the authority of his role. The police were often seen by the Inuit as the highest-status Whites in the eastern Arctic (Freeman, 1971: 38).

The influence of the police became even greater after they had responsibility for overseeing the provision of family allowances and government relief. In the early 1950s, when Inuit income from trapping fox pelts was at an all-time low, the need to maintain good relations with the police was vital to a family's well-being. Freeman surmised that "the native population is unable to oppose the imposed autocracy [of the RCMP], and apparent passivity and acquiescence (tolerance) typify the community response to this form of patronage" (ibid.: 34). Although a standard Inuit response to this relationship might be *ajurnamat*, "it can not be helped" (or literally, "because it is not possible"), in private they might speak about individual policemen with contempt or sarcasm, as Freeman observed in Grise Fiord (ibid.: 54). For example, depending on the context, the suffix "*-aluk*" can either mean "big" or "forceful"; in a derogatory or playful sense the nickname *Puliisialuk* can become "the bad policeman" (ibid.; MacDonald, personal communication).

The patron/client relationship between the police and the Inuit (Freeman, 1971) was exemplified by the often subservient role of the Inuk RCMP special constable. Constables recorded in their reports that they led the long-distance reconnaissance dog-sled patrols, but it was their Inuit special constables, "the boys," who actually acted as their guides (ibid.: 39). In this White myth of independence, the Inuit guides became invisible counterparts to the constables in their travels through unfamiliar places (Clifford, 1992: 106). In fact, the special constable and his family would supply the detachment with water, look after and provide meat for the police dogteams, and carry out other manual chores as required by the detachment. Many officers had a limited understanding of Inuktitut and could not engage in a detailed discussion or consider possibilities raised by the Inuit; thus, the limited linguistic ability served to channel relations between Qallunaat and Inuit along narrow and authoritarian lines (Brody, 1993: 5). Constables accepted as a matter of course the view expressed by Larsen that "the Eskimos being a simple people [are] in the habit of doing almost anything any white man will tell them to do" (Larsen, 1951: 1). A local Inuk who had some knowledge of English, such as the special constable, was used at times by the police as an interpreter (*tusaaji*), but even with the assistance of an Inuk interpreter, discussions with the interviewee could be a perfunctory affair.

At the time when families yielded to the RCMP's demands for relocation recruits, their experience of earlier RCMP-assisted moves was limited to the seasonal, two-day trips during the summers of 1951–52 on the RCMP Peterhead boat to the King George and Sleeper Islands to hunt walrus (*aiviq*), which was used for dog food. After a few months, they were returned by police boat to Port Harrison. When officials promised the relocatees that they could return to Port Harrison after spending two years in the High Arctic, the Inuit naturally related this offer to their earlier experiences of assistance in returning from the offshore islands.

Several of the Inuit whom Cst. Gibson selected could have been regarded as inappropriate for the relocation. They included a woman, Sarah Amagoalik (see fig. 3.6), who was eight months pregnant (she gave birth to her son Paul aboard the ship), an eighty-year-old grandmother, Nellie Amagoalik, and a disabled person, Anna Nungaq, who had to be carried on board the *C.D. Howe*. Some of the elders Gibson chose were in their fifties, and there were twelve children ranging in age from three months to fifteen years. The welfare teacher's criticisms of the selection process were overlooked or dismissed, even though she made them in a report to the Department planners of the experiment in Ottawa. Government files do not show that Department officials or the RCMP made any comments about the individuals selected to participate in the relocation experiment who had handicaps and were physically unsuitable. Not surprisingly, in a later report from Resolute Bay about a second shipment of relocatees, Cst. Gibson advised that "it is felt this area is not the place for aged who would be a hindrance in making this program a success" (Gibson, 1955).

Cst. Gibson's disagreements with Miss Hinds during the selection process were indicative of the competition between the RCMP and the Department in the 1950s to control Inuit welfare (see chapter 2). The RCMP dominated the relocation process from the outset and was effective in maintaining virtual total control over the new colonies once they had been established. The Force did so despite subsequent attempts by the Department to exert some influence and intercede on behalf of the Inuit, as discussed in chapter 8.

Classification of Inuit for Relocation

Inuit relocation became one of the three policy options developed by the Department, as outlined in a classification system formulated in 1953 (Canada, 1953b). In this taxonomy, planned policy for Canada's Inuit was divided into three broad categories:

1. In areas where the natural resources would support the inhabitants, it was decided that their basic way of life was to be maintained.

2. In areas where permanent White settlements existed, the Inuit would be educated to adapt them to this new situation.

3. In areas that could not continue to support the present population, attempts would be made to move the Inuit to areas with greater natural resources.

Fort Chimo in northern Quebec was temporarily included in the relocation plans. During World War II, it had been the site of a U.S. air base that employed local Inuit as laborers. As such, Chimo fell within category 2, but because the base was now closed, the loss in wage employment had to be offset by comparatively large allocations of state benefits. The Chimo Inuit were thus considered for relocation under category 3. After receiving an RCMP list of potential relocatees from Fort Chimo, however, the Department reversed its earlier decision to add them to the Port Harrison Inuit for relocation to the High Arctic. Shortly before the move, Deputy Minister Hugh Young came to feel that the Fort Chimo Inuit had become too acculturated and might therefore be unsuitable for inclusion in the experiment. Young's concern was about whether they would be able to adapt themselves to conditions at such a place as Resolute Bay (Young, 1953e). Furthermore, he understood that few, if any of them, still had the knowledge to build snow houses and would therefore have to be housed and guaranteed full-time employment at the base at Resolute.

The concern about the assimilation of the Fort Chimo Inuit and their housing requirements was discussed in Cantley's 1950 economic survey. He noted that in the area around Fort Chimo "there is a growing inclination on the part of the natives to give up their rather nomadic ways" and to settle in a permanent location (Cantley, 1950b: 28). At Fort Chimo, where there were supplies of wood, the Inuit constructed houses and endeavored to set themselves up "in the manner of white men." Cantley advised, however, that in places where the natives had little regard for hygiene any attempt by them to build permanent dwellings should be discouraged (ibid.: 29).

In June, the month before the move, the Department informed

Larsen that the Inuit families selected from Fort Chimo were being dropped from the High Arctic relocation plan (LeCapelain, 1953). The Department decided to experiment with a different type of relocation and, in 1953, moved five of the Fort Chimo Inuit families to a site of wage employment, with housing, at a Canadian army base in Churchill, Manitoba.

According to the Department's own criteria, the Port Harrison Inuit should have been classified as category 2, since the village had been a permanent White settlement for forty years. After all, Port Harrison was one of the first Arctic communities to acquire a federal school. The Department, nevertheless, decided to include Port Harrison in category 3, using relocation as a means of depopulating the region. Unlike the Fort Chimo Inuit, whom the Department decided would have to be housed, the Port Harrison Inuit would not have to be provided with housing or wage employment.

In a letter to J. C. Lessard, deputy minister in the Department of Transport (DOT), Major-General Young (1953b) confirmed in June 1953 that plans for the relocation were now complete. He outlined the revised quotas to be filled, comprising seven families from Port Harrison and four from Pond Inlet. Young authorized that the Inuit be distributed in three groups—four families to Resolute Bay, four families to Craig Harbour, and three families to Cape Herschel (Alexandra Fiord). Soon afterwards, Joseph Idlout's family, from Pond Inlet, was dropped from the plan, which left ten families altogether. Idlout, the star of *Land of the Long Day*, had been due to join the relocation, but when the film's director, Doug Wilkinson, asked to spend an additional year with Idlout's camp, Idlout was able to postpone moving to Resolute Bay until the second relocation there in 1955.

The Relocation and Dividing of the Families

On 25 July 1953, the government's eastern Arctic patrol ship, the *C.D. Howe*, anchored off Port Harrison on the northwest coast of the Ungava Peninsula and picked up Gibson's seven Inuit families, consisting of thirty-four men, women, and children and their sled dogs and belongings. They were stowed in the bow of the ship, and mattresses for them to sleep on were placed on the steel deck. On 28 August the ship reached Pond Inlet on North Baffin Island, and another group of three Inuit families, comprising sixteen men, women, and children, were taken on board (appendix A). The following day, the ship arrived at the RCMP detachment at Craig Harbour on Ellesmere Island. Four of the Inuit fami-

FIGURE 3.4 The CGS *C.D. Howe* rendezvousing with the CGS *d'Iberville* at Craig Harbour, Ellesmere Island, 29 August 1953. Credit: Wilfred Doucette/National Film Board of Canada/National Archives of Canada, PA-176810

lies disembarked, including the Port Harrison families of Paddy, Elijah, Joadamie, and Phillipoosie, together with Samuel Anukudluk's family from Pond Inlet. The other families were separated and transferred to the icebreaker *d'Iberville* (see fig. 3.4). When Larsen saw the Inukjuamiut relocatees at Craig Harbour, he described them as "dirty, ragged, and unkempt, a very unlikely looking lot of colonists" (Larsen, n.d.: 45).

Problems soon developed. The ice conditions were sufficiently severe that the new icebreaker *d'Iberville* was damaged by an iceberg at Craig Harbour. Doug Wilkinson (1953), who filmed the relocation for the Film Board, recounted that he could see daylight through the two big gashes in his starboard cabin. The ship proceeded north to reach the new RCMP detachment four hundred kilometers away at Alexandra Fiord. At latitude 78° 35′ N, Alexandra Fiord was the northernmost RCMP detachment and had been established just a month before under the supervision of Supt. Larsen. Due to heavy pack ice and the captain's reluctance to risk more damage to his ship on its maiden voyage, the *d'Iberville* was unable to reach it. Instead, the ship returned to Craig Harbour, where on 4 September it dropped off two more Inuit families. This group comprised Thomasie Amagoalik and his family from Port Harrison and Akpaliapik's family from Pond Inlet.

The *d'Iberville* reached Resolute Bay on Cornwallis Island on 7 September and left Cst. Gibson there with nineteen Inuit. Cst. Gibson's mission was to establish an RCMP detachment at Resolute Bay and to ensure the success of the relocation. His charges comprised the three families of Simeonie Amagoalik (see fig. 3.6), Daniel Salluviniq, and Alex Patsauq from Port Harrison, and the family of Jaybeddie Amagoalik (no relation to Simeonie) from Pond Inlet.

Upon reaching Ellesmere Island after the six-week voyage aboard the *C.D. Howe*, the officials had separated the Port Harrison families on the ship without prior warning. Elijah Nutaraq, who was twenty-one years old at the time of the relocation in 1953, recalled that "I had assumed that we would all be together, so I was not happy when I learned that we were going to be such a small community" (*Makivik News*, 1989b). The division of the families made a lasting impression on John Amagoalik:

When we got near [Craig Harbour] the RCMP came to us and they told us: "half of you have to get off here." And we just went into a panic because they had prom-ised that they would not separate us. . . . I remember we were all on the deck of the ship, the *C.D. Howe*, and all the women started to cry. And when women start to cry, the dogs join in. It was eerie. We were dumped on the beach—and I mean literally dumped on the beach. (Canada, 1990b)

Government documents and statements made by officials support the Inuit contention that they were not told in advance that they would be split into different groups. A final ship's passenger log prepared by the Department lists the relocatees collectively under all three destinations and does not distinguish between them. While the families were aboard the *C.D. Howe*, RCAF Squadron Leader O'Neil asked a Department official how many families would be going to each of the three settlement areas (Canada, 1953b). Mr. Cantley replied "that this would be decided on the boat taking the Eskimo to their destination. It was not desirable to break up family groups if possible." His statement indicates that officials did not decide until the ship reached Ellesmere Island how the families were going to be split up. Ross Gibson (1990) explained that he "was not made aware of what was in the workings until we got to Craig Harbour, when Henry Larsen advised me of the decision to split the Eskimo people. Due to the time element I doubt that very much thought was given to the final outcome and how it would affect those people in-volved."

Gibson's statement thus confirms Inuit recollections that they had no prior knowledge that they were going to be divided into smaller groups.

In fact, the Inuit had no idea where they were, or where the three groups were being sent. As Anna Nungaq recalled: "When we were told we had to move, we automatically thought we were going to be neighbors with the people who were sent to Resolute Bay. Because we were related and had lived together all our lives, we thought we would be settled close to each other" (*Inuktitut*, 1981). The fact that the Inuit were not informed about the planned distribution to different colonies demonstrates that they were not fully consulted about the relocation beforehand. This point also indicates the form of "inducement" used by officials and referred to in the aforementioned Department press release (Cantley, 1953).

Controversy and External Perspectives

Even while the Inuit were en route to Craig Harbour and Resolute Bay, some officials, including Air Commodore Ripley, were voicing their objections to the plan. In July 1953, James Sharpe, deputy minister of the Department of National Defence, wrote to Major-General Young about the Inuit relocation to Resolute Bay, where the Canadian Air Force had a base: "It will be noted that the Air Officer Commanding is quite worried that the experiment will result in hardship on the Eskimo families concerned and that the RCAF will likely be faced with the problem of tendering care for which they are unprepared" (Sharpe, 1953).

In response to the concern expressed by the air force, Hugh Young quickly arranged an interdepartmental meeting to discuss the operation. The meeting took place in Ottawa on 10 August 1953, with four Department officials, including Ben Sivertz and James Cantley, participating in the discussion. The minutes of this meeting, to which I will refer a number of times, reveal the extent of the planners' experimental strategies for conducting the relocation. RCAF Squadron Leader O'Neil raised one of the air force's primary concerns, about the availability of natural resources on Cornwallis Island, and said he was afraid there was not sufficient wildlife in the Resolute area to provide for the proposed Eskimo population (Canada, 1953b). His question highlights the laboratory metaphor used by Bob Phillips (referred to in chapter 1). Cantley replied that they had reason to believe that there was sufficient marine life to support the Inuit families. "No one could say for sure that this was the case," said Cantley, "consequently, the experiment was being staged." His candid remark confirms that the relocation was seen as an *experimentum crucis*—a crucial trial (Cantor, 1989: 176)—designed to test the hypothesis that Inuit could repopulate the High Arctic Islands.

The Department had justified the move to the public by stating that families from an overpopulated area where resources were scarce needed to be moved to an area where resources would be plentiful; however, it carried out no wildlife studies in the area until the late 1950s. A pragmatic—and more responsible—approach to repopulating the area would have been to conduct wildlife studies there before introducing the human subjects of the experiment. Cantley's comment that the Inuit were being moved there to test the theory of plentiful game and a habitable environment demonstrated the appeal of experimentation, often the most persuasive strategy when arguing for a doctrine (Cantor, 1989: 161).

The rationale for moving Inuit from Port Harrison was that hunting was poor in the area. During the year 1951–52, when the relative paucity of economic resources in the Port Harrison district was being assessed by officials and used as a reason for experimenting with relocation, income from trapping was bound to be low because the fox population was at the bottom of the four-year fox cycle. In fact, 1953–54 was a peak year in the four-year cycle for trapping in the region of Port Harrison, when a record 4,920 foxes were traded (Willmott, 1961). As the records of the Company's Port Harrison post show (see fig. 2.4), from 1950 onwards, even during the bottom years of the fox cycle, the post was profitable.

Was there any possibility that the 1953–55 relocation from Port Harrison was a famine-induced "migration" of the kind that has occurred in many other parts of the world (see, for example, Mageean, 1991)? At the Royal Commission's hearings in June 1993, Ploughman, the HBC post manager stationed at Port Harrison at the time of the move, testified about the availability of food. He stated that, although there was very little caribou hunting for the three years that he was at Port Harrison, "nobody was starving" because there were other country food resources. "Starvation, as far as I am concerned," remarked Ploughman, "didn't even enter into the picture at all" (Canada, 1993b: 83). Despite the Department's public assurances that the relocation of the Inukjuamiut to the High Arctic was carried out on humanitarian grounds, therefore, any scarcity of resources in the Port Harrison area was exaggerated; indeed, it was not the planners' primary consideration. Instead, as Sivertz asserted at the meeting on 10 August, "the Eskimos' prime purpose in going to the High North was to see if it were possible for them to adapt themselves to conditions there and secure a reasonable living" (Canada, 1953b).

The question of sufficient resources in the areas of the new colonies became an important issue. Despite their initial setback in the summer of 1953, officials still wished to establish an Inuit colony at Alexandra

Fiord. Supt. Larsen (he was promoted from inspector to superintendent at the time of the relocation) sent a message to the detachment there in January 1954, asking them if they thought the Alexandra Fiord area could easily support four or five families (Larsen, 1954a). The Alexandra Fiord detachment responded that the district could not support that number of families; furthermore, the officers reported that no land game had been obtained or sighted. Stevenson (1954) subsequently sent a note to Cantley advising that "maybe we should just carry on for another year with the families at Craig and add to Resolute." Within a week of arriving at Craig Harbour, the relocatees were moved by the RCMP to Lindstrom Peninsula in Grise Fiord, one hundred kilometers away.

The Department pursued a combined economic policy in establishing the new colonies at Grise Fiord and Resolute Bay. At both sites, relief benefits were abolished except in extreme cases, and the Inuit were expected to become self-reliant on the basis of land and sea resources. Resolute Bay, however, was the center in the High Arctic Islands for military and government supply operations, and increasingly for resource exploration activity. One of the most important functions of the military air base at Resolute was to supply the five weather stations (Resolute, Mould Bay, Isachsen, Eureka, and Alert) jointly operated by Canada and the United States. In view of these activities, the Department envisaged a growing need at Resolute Bay for manual labor.

After their initial objections to and misgivings about the project, base officials and government agencies operating out of Resolute soon came to realize the advantages of having a native labor pool to draw upon. The Inuit could be employed part-time as equipment operators, refuse removers, cleaners, and general handymen. The Department proposed the second stage relocation to Resolute Bay in 1955 to meet a growing demand for casual labor in unloading supplies during airlifts and during the summer resupply (Eskimo Affairs, 1954). Yet the Inuit were still left to find their own shelter and to feed themselves from the land. Cst. Gibson concurred that the government had brought the Inuit families to Resolute Bay, "hoping they'd kill enough polar bear and seal to keep going. That way, men would be available to load aircraft and do other chores" (Brown, 1955). Grise Fiord did not offer the same opportunities for wage employment, and throughout the 1950s and 1960s, its economy continued to rely almost entirely on hunting and trapping. In 1955, only one Port Harrison family was moved to Grise Fiord: Joseph Flaherty, his wife, Rynee, and their children Martha, Mary, and Peter (see fig. 3.5). Having had no contact with his real father, Robert Flaherty, Joseph had been treated as an adopted son by Aqiatusuk. He had be-

FIGURE 3.5 Joseph Flaherty and his wife, Rynee, and daughters Martha and Mary, Grise Fiord, 1959. Credit: Jaybeddie Amagoalik

FIGURE 3.6 Johnnie Echalook's camp near Port Harrison, 1950. Credit: Collection Margery Hinds, courtesy of Avataq Cultural Institute, Inukjuak, Quebec

come concerned about the older man and his family since they had been moved to Grise Fiord two years earlier.

Because resources at Alexandra Fiord appeared to be poor and it now seemed that the families originally designated to go there would have to remain at Grise Fiord, the plans were changed to keep the Inuit population level at Grise Fiord the same. In the summer of 1955, one of the Pond Inlet families at Grise Fiord was transferred to the Alexandra Fiord detachment, where the father served as an RCMP special constable, and a family from Port Harrison was sent up to take their place at Grise Fiord. Three more families from Port Harrison were relocated to Resolute Bay, as Alex Stevenson had advised. They were all related to families who had been moved to Resolute Bay two years earlier: Levi Nungak was Daniel Salluviniq's brother; Johnnie Echalook and his wife Minnie Allakarial-lak's daughter Sarah (married to Simeonie Amagoalik) had already been relocated; Andrew Iqaluk was Minnie's brother. Johnnie Echalook, who was a catechist, was the head of a large family (see fig. 3.6). They were joined in Resolute Bay by Joseph Idlout's extended family from Pond Inlet (appendix A).

The Department was proud of the relocation experiment and ensured comprehensive coverage in the press. It was only fitting that the *C.D. Howe,* which had carried the Inuit families north, should appear in full color on the front cover of the June 1953 issue of the nationally distributed magazine of the HBC, *The Beaver.* Canadian newspapers accepted official statements and press releases on the relocation without question. *The Vancouver Province* (30 July 1953) stated that the Inuit were to be resettled in better hunting areas. *The Kitchener Record* (30 July 1953) noted that the Department was "undertaking a project of Eskimo resettlement which may be the forerunner of larger population movements." The *Record* continued: "If they are successful in fending for themselves, other families may be moved north from the game-depleted southern Arctic."

Positive media coverage continued. By October 1954, the *Montreal Gazette* was reporting that the Inuit were pleased with their new surroundings. Under the headline, "New Homes for Eskimos Said Success," the article claimed that the six families at the new settlement of Grise Fiord "have expressed a desire to remain there, although they do not see the sun from mid-November to mid-February" (*Montreal Gazette,* 1954). The article also quoted Cst. Clay Fryer's buoyant remarks that the "Port Harrison natives could hardly be recognized as the same ones who had first landed at Craig Harbour. They all looked happier, healthier, having visibly put on weight."

Thule Ruins and Site Selection

Both the Department and the RCMP called the 1953 relocation to Grise Fiord and Resolute Bay a "rehabilitation experiment" numerous times in memos and reports. What form of rehabilitation did the relocation take? Larsen's utopian notion of creating ideal Inuit settlements in the High Arctic embraced an element of history and perhaps folklore. When selecting the locations for the Resolute and Grise camps, he chose sites where there was clear archaeological evidence of previous habitation (Larsen, n.d.: 1007; Maxwell, 1985). Both of the new colonies on Ellesmere and Cornwallis Islands were right next to the archaeological remains of Thule Eskimo encampments over five hundred years old. Detailed knowledge of these sites had been published for the first time in the year before the relocation plan was developed.

The ruins on Cornwallis Island had just been excavated and documented by a joint archaeological expedition organized by the Smithsonian Institution and the National Museum of Canada, which reported on the finds in their annual reports for 1949–50 and 1950–51. In fact, the archaeologists were continuing their work in the summer of 1953, immediately before the relocatees' arrival (Collins, 1955: 22). Dr. Collins commented that it was because of the recent establishment of the weather station and air base facilities at Resolute Bay that the scientists were able to conduct their research in the area (Collins, 1951: 49). Collins and his colleagues found a number of Thule village sites on the island, none of which had been properly examined. He noted that a sizeable Inuit population had inhabited the island for a number of years in the past, but that they no longer lived there. Indeed, he speculated initially that the houses were in such good condition, containing over a thousand samples of tools and other implements, that they could not be more than a few centuries old (ibid.: 52).

I believe that Larsen's fascination with repopulating the High Arctic Islands and the interest in the Department were directly influenced by the recent archaeological studies in the area. In fact, the National Museum of Canada, which had organized the expeditions and reported on the finds, was a branch of the Department (the Department of Resources and Development). The articles Collins published included a number of photographs of the ruins and provided information that suggested that the islands were potentially rich in game. In one excavated stone house at Resolute, Collins found "masses of blubber held in the stone bins [which] meant that food was abundant" (Collins, 1952: 50). From the animal bones he found at the old sites, Collins posited that the principal foods of the former inhabitants were seal, bowhead whale, and walrus; the team found little evidence of musk-ox, caribou, or birds. Collins noted that very little was known of the natural history of Cornwallis Island (Collins, 1951: 52).

The site Larsen selected for the relocatees was a raised beach beside a row of nine stone and whalebone houses that they called *qarmartalik,* "old ruins." These were part of the largest collection of permanent house sites on the island. The Thule Inuit had left the area during either the first phase of the Little Ice Age, about 1450 to 1520, or the third phase, around 1600 to 1750. Occupation of the region occurred, as elsewhere throughout the Arctic, during periods of population expansion and contraction, influenced by changing climatic conditions. As winters became intolerably cold, the caribou, musk-ox, and other game migrated southwards, the people followed, and the land was left uninhabited (Mary-Rousselière, 1991: 160). Nevertheless, Larsen felt that if their "ancestors" had been able to survive here at one time, perhaps the relocatees could do so as well.

When Larsen was planning his heroic colonization scheme, one wonders if he had in mind the folklore saga of Qitdlarssuaq. This migration is the only one recorded in which a group of Inuit moved a great distance from one polar region to another (Rasmussen, 1908: 23), with some similarity to the 1953 relocation from northern Quebec to the High Arctic. Around 1840, an Inuk called Qitdlarssuaq committed a murder, and to escape the revenge of the victim's relatives he and his family fled from the region of Broughton Island northwards up the coast of Baffin Island (Mary-Rousselière, 1991). Qitdlarssuaq was a shaman, and he had visions of polar Inuit living somewhere far to the north. Ultimately he was joined by about fifty followers, and together they migrated across Lancaster Sound to Devon Island. After some time, they crossed Jones Sound to Ellesmere Island and then crossed Smith Sound to Anoritoq in Greenland, where they did in fact meet up with the polar Inuit living there, twenty-three years after beginning their journey. Qitdlarssuaq came into contact with various explorers, and aspects of his journey were documented (and recounted most recently in Guy Mary-Rousselière's superb book; see also Petersen, 1962; S. Rowley, 1985b). The visions of Qitdlarssuaq and Larsen have interesting parallels—both were searching for a northerly new world, guiding a group of Inuit on an odyssey to Ellesmere Island, and leaving behind a troubled situation. Larsen, coincidentally, was concerned about the loss of Inuit shamans and instructed Gibson to provide strong leadership and give the relocatees spiritual guidance (Larsen, 1952d; Gibson, 1990). The fate of Qitdlarssuaq's followers did not bode well, for most of them later died of starvation on Ellesmere Island. The Inukjuamiut who were transplanted to Ellesmere and Cornwallis Islands were worried that a similar fate might befall them, as I shall discuss in chapter 4.

Social Reform and Survival

A few months after the arrival of the Inuit at Grise Fiord, Cst. Fryer wrote an article on the relocation for the Force's in-house publication *RCMP Quarterly*. Entitled "Eskimo Rehabilitation Program at Craig Harbour," the article exemplifies official attempts to persuade people of the success of this social experiment. Cst. Fryer was serving at the Craig Harbour detachment during 1953–54 with Cpl. Glenn Sargent. Fryer explained his understanding of the rationale for the move, stating that relocation was designed to rehabilitate the Port Harrison Inuit. With this plan, he stated, "the Eskimo could follow the native way of life and become less dependent on the white man" (Fryer, 1954a: 139). Fryer's remark encapsulated the social-reformist spirit of the project.

Gibson instructed the Inuit at Resolute that the military base was out-

FIGURE 3.7 RCMP detachment at Grise Fiord, Ellesmere Island, 1957. Credit: National
Archives of Canada, PA-61670

of-bounds, as was the base dump. There was to be complete segregation
of the Whites at the base and the Inuit camp. Larsen agreed that such
a practice was necessary if they were to keep the Inuit pure, otherwise,
"had Gibson allowed everybody to run about as they liked, those Eskimos would have been ruined the first winter" (Larsen, n.d.: 48). He was
particularly concerned about "indiscriminate association" between the
Whites and the Inuit women. Base personnel were informed that they
were not to approach the Inuit camp, and any request to do so had to be
approved by the constable (Gibson, personal communication). Gibson
pinned a note on the bulletin board in the base recreation room, though,
stating that he would give guided tours of the Inuit camp so that people
could take pictures of the relocatees (Larsen, n.d.: 47). The Inuit called
the base *aupartualuk*, meaning "the big red one" because of its red buildings. Gibson, nicknamed *Auparttuq*, "red," thus lived in quarters at the
aupartualuk.

The practice of isolating the relocatees from the store was also followed by the constables at Grise Fiord. They moved the relocatees to
Grise Fiord, while they stayed in Craig Harbour where the RCMP detachment and store remained until 1956 when the officers also moved to
Grise Fiord (see fig. 3.7). This action was in part a precautionary reha-

bilitation measure so that the Inuit would not become too dependent on the detachment and store. Similarly, in the Scoresby Sund colonization of 1924, referred to in chapter 2, Mikkelsen (1927: 218) and the settlement planners decided to scatter the huts for the "prospective colonists" along the coastline, thereby counteracting "the intelligible but regrettable desire of a people . . . to gather around the store, whereby their economic status suffers." When the Russians relocated Eskimo families to Ostrov Vrangelya in 1926 (see chapter 2), the project manager, Ushakov, was told that the natives should not be encouraged to become too reliant on the trading store; he was instructed: "Never allow the development of a parasitic attitude among the settlers" (Barr, 1977: 12). Gibson pursued the same strategy at Port Harrison in order to keep the Inuit away from the town and out hunting on the land.

Larsen (1952b) insisted that the RCMP was the most logical agency to control and maintain supervision of Inuit welfare. He believed in the malleability of human beings and thought that under the rehabilitative ideal of RCMP supervision the Inuit could be reformed (Allen, 1981: 18), but the isolation component of the rehabilitation project was vital. At Port Harrison, the Inuit had become accustomed to interacting with the various Whites who lived there, including the trader (*niuviqti*), the teacher (*ilisaiji*), the minister (*ajuqiqtuiji*), the nurse (*aanniasiuqti*), and the police (*puliisi*). One advantage of the presence of so many Whites was that the actions of one official were mediated and validated by the presence of the others. At Resolute and Grise, the Inuit were alone with the *puliisi*, and except for the day when the annual supply ship called at the settlement, the police had sole authority in the colonies. In effect, police supervision of Inuit welfare as envisaged by Larsen turned the new colonies into reformatory camps. Cst. Fryer (1954b) at Craig Harbour outlined the need for a rehabilitation program by reporting that the "first impression given to the members of this detachment by the Port Harrison natives, was that they were a depressed, lifeless group of individuals, who were looking for too many handouts from the white man."

During the experiment, the officers sought to persuade the Inuit to live off the land, without aid from the government. According to Gibson (1990), Larsen's instructions were "above all else keep them in their native clothing and foot gear." Such plans were difficult to put into effect, however. In August 1956, it was reported that Cst. Gibson had tried to keep them wearing sealskin boots, but there was a demand for rubber boots, partly for the children in the spring (J. C. Jackson, 1956). Larsen was distressed that the natives were increasingly becoming more poorly clad in store-bought clothes, which he felt were inadequate for the northern climate compared with the traditional skin clothing. Larsen

(1951: 2) was bothered that the Inuit were no longer using native-made clothing or seal skin. As James Cantley pointed out, Larsen had over-looked the fact that in the eastern Arctic many Inuit had limited access to caribou skins (because of a reduction in caribou populations) with which to make winter clothing.

Sealskin clothing was considered by the Inuit to be unsuitable for win-ter use, Cantley said, which explained why this form of traditional cloth-ing was not worn as much as in the past. Under these circumstances, remarked Cantley (1951), the Inuit had no recourse but to get what clothing they could from the trade stores. Such were the conflicting atti-tudes of the RCMP and the Department. After visiting the Inuit settle-ment at Resolute Bay, J. C. Jackson, the Department's officer in charge of the eastern Arctic patrol in 1956, advised his superiors that, since these people had earned their own money, a delaying action was about all that could be done to provide them with rubber boots and other "civilized ap-parel" (Jackson, 1956). Jackson noted that, indeed, much of the men's clothing comprised items discarded by the air force personnel stationed at the base.

A party of senior officials, including two air force commodores and Ben Sivertz, visited Resolute Bay a few days after the Inuit arrived on 7 September 1953. In a report on the trip, the arrival of the Inuit was discussed, together with the initial problems associated with their en-campment at Resolute:

The reasons for moving this family are grounded in an attempt to keep the Eskimo in his native state and to preserve that culture as primitive as it is. How-ever, moving the Eskimos to an area where they come into intimate contact with White men destroys the basis of this reasoning while leaving them untrained to cope with the problems presented by this contact. (Stead, 1953: 6)

The report's author commented on the view widely held at the time that Inuit relations with military and transient civilian personnel should be closely monitored and discouraged. He suggested that, by placing Inuit near the Resolute base, the project's objective of preserving "native-ness" was being jeopardized. The report therefore advised that legisla-tion be considered to make Inuit settlements out-of-bounds to non-Inuit. Given what one might characterize as a "keep the Eskimo an Eskimo" approach to social development at Resolute Bay and Grise Fiord, it is interesting to note the somewhat paradoxical statement by Jean Lesage (1955), minister of the Department at the time of the second reloca-tion to the High Arctic in 1955: "The preservation of the Eskimo in his primitive state is not a real alternative. . . . It would involve segregation and isolation [and] denial of the most humane services." In this case, the social policy the Department was advocating in public did not accord with what it was putting into practice.

C. J. Marshall of the Department's Advisory Committee on Northern Development (ACND) visited Cst. Gibson and the Inuit camp at Resolute Bay within a few months of the move. In a confidential report, Marshall (1953) expressed his dissatisfaction with the relocation and outlined the operation's mismanagement. He noted, for example, that when the relocatees arrived at Resolute Bay they had no stockpile of meat for the winter. Hunting every day since they arrived, he stated, leaves them insufficient time to repair their gear and prepare for the winter. Hunting difficulties were exacerbated because, when they arrived at Resolute Bay, the Inuit had only one kayak between them (Larsen, n.d.: 47). Marshall also reported that their tents were in bad condition and no new tents or repair material had been provided. Some vital supplies were lacking, and others were unnecessary, such as the twenty-four pairs of extra-large men's work pants—for there were only four men in the group. Larsen observed that the relocatees lacked adequate skins for clothing.

Marshall (1953) examined the goods in the Inuit store at Resolute and stated that, for the prices charged, some of the items were of extremely poor quality. He also reported the critical number of important items missing from the shipment. These included rifles, tent material, lumber, duffle cloth, oil lamps, fish hooks, and first-aid supplies. When Cst. Gibson went over the supplies, he found a shortage of $1,124 worth of goods. By Marshall's calculation, it appeared that about 40 percent of the supplies intended for the Inuit store at Resolute Bay had not been landed. Marshall added that everyone wanted the experiment at Resolute to be a success but that the task had been made more difficult because of "hasty planning" during the early stages of the experiment.

Although the families were clearly unprepared for the drastic change in environment, the public was told a different story. Apparently, part of the experimenters' task was to persuade others of the viability of the project (Cantor, 1989: 161) and, in an article, Cst. Fryer presented his view: "It would be difficult to find a group of Eskimos anywhere in the North that could claim to be as well off as the Grise Fiord camp. . . . Eskimo conditions could hardly be better. The Port Harrison natives have adapted themselves well, following the example set by the Pond Inlet group" (Fryer, 1954a). According to the discourse of experiment, Fryer's optimistic comment is consistent with the view that the experimenter is never alone with nature, for there is always an audience, real or implied, that must be addressed and persuaded (Gooding and others, 1989: xiv).

Although the officers informed the public and their superiors that the Inuit were "happy" in their "new homes," the Inuit have presented a different picture. Their narratives reveal that they felt far from content during those early years; they were struggling to survive and found it difficult to adapt to the severe environmental conditions. Martha Flaherty (1986), who was relocated to Grise Fiord, remembers that her father

used to go hunting in −40° to −60° weather in the dark for days at times without eating. . . . I don't think I even had a childhood between the ages of 7 to 12 because I had to hunt with my father for food, in very cold weather, with absolutely no daylight. . . . Sometimes I used to cry knowing how cold it was going to be, but then my father would just say, "Do you want us to starve?"

When conducting an experiment, the scientist makes observations and records the data, and that is precisely what the constables in the colonies were doing. The settlements were designed to be "self-contained," and because of their isolation and the minimal outside influence, metaphorically they were ideal field laboratories. The policemen were trained in surveillance techniques, which they applied to the experiment by observing the responses of the relocatees to their new environment and by filing monthly reports noting the process of adjustment. Two years after the relocation, Cst. Gibson (1955) could thus report to his superiors: "The native camp at Resolute Bay continues to survive." In order to survive, however, the relocatees had to hunt regardless of the weather conditions. John Amagoalik remembered "being very excited when any military airplane arrived in Resolute, because we knew that the people on those airplanes had box lunches, food. We used to rush to the dump five miles away in the middle of winter to go to the dump and get those boxes of half-finished sandwiches" (Canada, 1990b). Lizzie Amagoalik recalled that they

were always hungry. We had to look through the white man's garbage for food for our children. We had to take clothes that had been thrown away, for our children. When the policemen found out that we were living off their garbage, they got very angry at us and told us to stop. We asked, "How are we going to eat?" (*Makivik News*, 1989a)

Supplementing the Inuit diet of country food with leftovers from the White man's dump became a contentious issue between the RCMP officers and officials at the Department. This situation undermined a basic tenet of the rehabilitation project—that if relief was abolished the poor would become self-reliant (H. Johnston, 1972: 11). Cst. Gibson was intent on adhering to the guidelines established for the rehabilitation project and insisted that the group should comply with isolation measures. Gibson (1954) therefore reported: "Strict instructions were given the natives that they were not to carry away any articles found in the dump." Department planner Ben Sivertz (1958c) cautioned his deputy minister about the implications "of the growing problem of Eskimos scrounging from garbage dumps." He was particularly concerned about the public's perception of such activity, since "it is the sort of thing which can give rise to embarrassing publicity. . . . It is our view that, if Eskimos are really destitute, they must, as a temporary measure, be provided with relief and proper food. We must not be put in the position of providing garbage as relief rations for Canadian citizens, which is exactly what is happening in some places." Yet, this same situation persisted in 1964 when Cst. Lucko at the Resolute Bay detachment commented on the source of building materials the Inuit were using. As before, they needed to resort to "what they obtained for themselves from the local dump" (Lucko, 1964).

A Lack of Services

At Port Harrison, there was a variety of services, including a trading store, school, medical station, and church (see map 1.1, drafted for the Department in 1953). By contrast, the new High Arctic colonies were characterized by a lack of those same services. At Craig Harbour and Resolute Bay, the RCMP set up a single government store; Gibson improvised by fashioning the store from the U.S. Weather Bureau's old, five-seat outhouse (Gibson, personal communication). Supplies were shipped north once a year on the *C.D. Howe*. Because of the colonies' isolation, though, sources of supplies for the new stores were greatly restricted, whereas Port Harrison was closer to southern supply sources. Former Grise Fiord Constable Bob Pilot also recalled that Department officials in Ottawa used to cut back arbitrarily on the annual order of supplies the RCMP had requested for the Inuit store (Pilot, personal communication).

Health care was lacking during the early period of the relocation. Markoosie Patsauq was twelve years old at the time of the move, and his brother John Amagoalik was five. Both recall how sick Markoosie was before they boarded the *C.D. Howe* in Port Harrison. "I was spitting up blood," said Markoosie Patsauq (personal communication). He had tuberculosis, but his illness was not diagnosed. In his report, the chief medical officer aboard the *C.D. Howe*, Dr. Simpson (1953), noted that the thirty-four Inuit from Port Harrison to be transferred to Ellesmere and Cornwallis Islands were examined; however, the X-ray machine used routinely to check the Inuit was not on board the ship when medical staff examined the families at Port Harrison (Hinds, 1953b). Within his first year at Resolute Bay, Markoosie's condition deteriorated to the point where he could no longer stand up and was confined to his family's tent. Despite the Inuit camp's proximity to the air base at Resolute, Markoosie was not evacuated until the summer of 1954, aboard the *C.D. Howe.*

RCMP officers in charge of Resolute Bay and Grise Fiord were responsible for providing health care but had limited knowledge as lay dispensers and equally limited resources. Grise Fiord's isolated location and severe winter weather could make emergency airlifts difficult. In one emergency, for example, on 4 November 1960, the RCMP at Grise Fiord radioed Resolute Bay that there was an epidemic in the settlement (Sivertz, 1960a). A radio blackout in bad weather conditions prevented the message from reaching Resolute Bay, but the United States air force base at Thule, Greenland, picked up the message and relayed it. They also tried, on their own initiative, to air-drop medical people at Grise Fiord but were unsuccessful. Indian and Northern Health Services arranged for a doctor to fly from Ottawa to Resolute Bay on an RCAF plane. Five days later, the doctor reached Resolute Bay and discovered that one child, Elisapee, had already died. That same day, the doctor finally arrived by chartered plane at Grise Fiord and diagnosed six children as seriously ill with whooping cough, complicated by a secondary infection of bronchopneumonia.

Such was the interagency conflict between the RCMP and the Department that, in an attempt to preserve its exclusive control of Grise Fiord, the RCMP actually tried to block later efforts by the Department to provide professional health care for the community. In 1964, Chief Supt. C. B. Macdonell (1964) reaffirmed this position: "I might say that the placing of a nurse at Grise Fiord would now negate the necessity of our having a detachment there at all." He ended with the warning: "Content of this memorandum is not to be passed along to anyone outside the Force for obvious reasons." As the Canadian outpost most distant from Ottawa, Grise Fiord's isolation ensured that, even in the mid-1960s when the RCMP's sovereignty role in the area was no longer so important, the agency could attempt to legitimize its continued presence in the community through its control of Inuit welfare.

4

THE PROCESS OF ADAPTATION

A White woman, Freddie Knight, who grew up in Port Harrison, spoke fluent Inuktitut, and knew the relocatees, had the opportunity of seeing them again and talking with them when the *C.D. Howe* stopped at the Baffin settlement of Cape Dorset en route for the High Arctic in 1953. She recalled that many of them appeared to be pleased at having been selected for the project. They felt, she said, like "chosen people"—chosen because they were special (Knight, personal communication). This view is striking because it contrasts ironically with Gibson's selection criteria. However naïve they were about the reasons for being chosen, though, their expectations were soon to be tested dramatically. The relocation of Inuit from the southern Arctic to Resolute Bay and Grise Fiord involved an inevitable period of adjustment to a new environment. As far as the officials were concerned, the physical hardships the relocatees had to overcome to survive were a part of the rehabilitation process. In this chapter, I explore the diverse Inuit and White perceptions of this transitional period.

The "Garden of Eden"

The world was all before them, where to choose
Their place of rest, and Providence their guide:
They hand in hand with wandering steps and slow
Through Eden took their solitary way.

—John Milton, *Paradise Lost* (1667, bk. xii, l.646–49)

One of the two police officers with the detachment at Craig Harbour in 1953–56 was Cpl. Glenn Sargent, whom Larsen described as a stocky,

FIGURE 4.1 (from left) Cpl. Glenn Sargent, Cst. Bob Pilot, S/Cst. Kyak, and Joseph Flaherty, Devon Island, 1958. Credit: Bob Pilot

powerful fellow (Larsen, n.d.: 45). The Inuit called him *angajuqaaq*, "the boss" (see fig. 4.1). One year after the arrival of the Inuit, Sargent (1954) informed his superiors that, for the Port Harrison newcomers, "Craig Harbour and the surrounding country is their *Garden of Eden*" (emphasis his). One of the most enduring metaphors is the creation of a garden in the wilderness; here, it was paired with the Jeffersonian precept that cultivating a garden is an ennobling experience (Short, 1991: 13, 103). Through the act of harvesting their new Arctic garden, it was hoped the Inuit would rehabilitate themselves. Sargent (1954) thought that southern Ellesmere Island was abundant in game, and he reported that the Inuit were happily and successfully hunting, trapping, and improving their condition. Indeed, the Inuit also thought they were going to be sent to such a place. Minnie Allakariallak (see fig. 3.6), whose husband Johnnie Echalook was a lay preacher, arrived in Resolute Bay in 1955 feeling that "God has placed us here, and we were imagining a place where there's plenty of vegetation" (Canada, 1993a: 39). She soon discovered that "the Garden's" vegetation was far less than that in the area of Inukjuak. The idea that place could transform a people, however, was an integral component of the experiment.

The area chosen for relocation made the rehabilitation experience exceptionally difficult. The climatic differences between Port Harrison and Grise Fiord and Resolute Bay are extreme. Port Harrison is at latitude 58° 27′ N in the southern Arctic, whereas Resolute Bay is at 74° 42′ N and Grise Fiord at 76° 25′ N in the High Arctic. Port Harrison is nine hundred kilometers south of the Arctic Circle and thus never experiences continual winter darkness, whereas at Grise Fiord and Resolute Bay there is no daylight from late October until mid-February. During the dark period, the snow surface reflects the moonlight and provides limited visibility. The relocatees also had to adjust to four months of continual daylight, from the end of April to the end of August. Temperatures are much colder, and winter conditions are more severe and of longer duration in Resolute Bay and Grise Fiord than in Port Harrison.

Despite newspaper stories of "new homes" for families in the High Arctic (*Montreal Gazette*, 1954), housing remained a serious problem for the Inuit. The homes for most relocatees were old tents. Supt. Larsen (n.d.: 1007) himself recorded that, when the Inuit arrived at Grise Fiord, their tents were threadbare, and, in his inspection report of the Resolute Bay camp, C. J. Marshall (1953) noted that many of the relocatees' tents were in poor condition. In northern Quebec, the Inuit were able to build an igloo (*illu*) around November, whereas the Inukjuamiut soon discovered that, despite colder temperatures in Grise Fiord and Resolute Bay, snowfall was sparse, and they might not be able to construct igloos until January. During the month of December, snowfall averages only 1 inch in Resolute Bay and 2.8 inches in Grise Fiord, whereas Port Harrison receives an average of 9.3 inches. Individuals such as Riewe (1991: 297) have commented on the difficulties of finding sufficient snow with which to build igloos in the area of Grise Fiord: either there was simply not enough, or it had fallen elsewhere. During the project's first winter, Cst. Gibson (1953) at Resolute Bay reported in mid-October 1953 that the Inuit were still living in tents; but temperatures were low and snow was drifting, and he thought that igloos would be built within the next few days. Cpl. Sargent (1953) at Craig Harbour, in his report on 31 December 1953, conceded that "at present all families are living in tents due to lack of suitable snow for snow houses." Freeman (1971: 40) has commented that at Grise Fiord the Inukjuamiut were unfamiliar when they arrived with the method of building the sod and stone dwelling (*qammak*) necessary for winter habitation. Elijah Nutaraq recounted his adjustment to the colder climate:

We had to live in tents all winter because there was not enough snow to build a snow house. I remember waking up every morning rolled up like a ball because it was so cold! Today, I am glad I did not have a wife then—it would have been very difficult for a young couple's relationship to survive in that severe climate. (*Makivik News*, 1989b)

Ross Gibson (1983) admitted that "the cold was something the Quebec Eskimos had never endured the like of." Gibson's observation reflects the theory that a scientific experiment invokes nature as an independent judge (Gooding and others, 1989: xv). Gibson's comments and those of the relocatees leave the impression that the environmental conditions, in themselves, would have caused the relocation experiment to fail. Gibson (1983) declared: "I am sure they would have all gone home right then if they could." The confinement of the relocatees on their isolated island meant that they were unable to act on their instinctive response to the experiment and return to the familiar climate of their homeland. They wanted to be in Inukjuak (Port Harrison), "in our land" (*nunattinni*). The restrictions placed on their movements will be discussed later in this chapter.

In 1952 Larsen had advised that, wherever the Inuit continued to live as hunters and trappers, officials should assist them by building permanent wooden dwellings (Larsen, 1952b). Joseph Flaherty and his family had been given a wooden house (*illujuaq*) in Port Harrison because he was employed by the radiosonde station. Yet no wooden dwellings were built for the relocatees until they started building shacks for themselves at Resolute Bay in 1954 and at Grise Fiord after 1956, using packing cases discarded from the annual sea-lift (see fig. 4.2). James Cantley offered a reason for discouraging the practice of building shacks, noting that, compared with igloos, the wooden structures were not as effectively heated by seal-oil lamps. A primary disadvantage of the wooden shacks, according to Cantley (1950b: 29), was that the health of the natives was undermined and they became progressively less able to withstand the rigors of the climate.

In fact, not providing houses for the relocatees was consistent with the project's rehabilitation ideology, which discouraged the adoption of nontraditional practices. As mentioned earlier, the Fort Chimo Inuit were dropped from the relocation experiment because officials concluded that they would have to provide housing for them in the High Arctic. When in 1959 the RCMP submitted a low-cost housing plan for Grise Fiord, Alex Stevenson (1959) was not supportive and advised that "the existence is marginal here and it may be more practicable to use this settlement for experimental purposes." His decision illustrates the extent to which the laboratory metaphor was being perpetuated.

During the planning stage of the experiment, Alex Stevenson had expressed his concern about the relocatees' ability to cope with the three-

FIGURE 4.2 (from left) Sarah Salluviniq, Jaybeddie Amagoalik, Mawa Iqaluk, Anknowya, George Echalook, and John Amagoalik, Resolute Bay, 1956. Credit: Jaybeddie Amagoalik

month dark period. "As you are well aware," he wrote to James Cantley, "the Port Harrison natives will have to contend with the dark period which they are not familiar with and although the terrain is similar to the Quebec Coast, I know that from past experience with the Dorset natives that the dark period causes some discontentment" (Stevenson, 1952). Larsen later recorded his thoughts about the experiment: "I wondered if I had done the right thing in advocating this move," he wrote, "but when at their respective destinations I saw the Eskimos, both men and women, setting to with a will, erecting their old and threadbare tents, . . . I knew I had nothing to fear, as the Eskimo men came forward to shake hands in gratitude for having brought them to this rich looking land" (Larsen, n.d: 1007). Exposure to continual darkness and daylight can cause temporal disorientation, sleep disturbance, mood changes, and mental exhaustion (Condon, 1983: 131). Although this was the first time that Inuit from the southern Arctic regions had been brought north to be exposed to these extreme conditions, apparently the planners did not foresee the physical constraints and psychological effects that the long months of darkness would have on the families.

Department officials have maintained that the Inuit were told in advance about the conditions in the High Arctic, but the high mountains

behind Grise Fiord (see fig. 3.7), the dark period, and the colder temperatures clearly came as a shock. "The first two or three years were
terrible for us," recalled John Amagoalik, "especially the dark season"
(Amagoalik, personal communication). The Pond Inlet Inuit referred to
the dark season as *tauvijjuaq* (J. MacDonald, 1993). Initially, the Inukjuamiut did not have a word for the dark season, since they had never
experienced it before, but used the phrase *kausuittualuk* to describe it as
"the big dark period." Elijah Nutaraq explained: "I assumed that the far
north had the same terrain as the Inukjuak area. It turned out that the
land was not the same, and that the sun behaved differently at those lati-
tudes. . . . It got darker and darker and eventually disappeared for good
in November. . . . We couldn't get used to the never-ending darkness"
(*Makivik News*, 1989b).

While Cst. Gibson was observing Inuit responses to the dark period,
he too was having difficulty acclimatizing. "I found during the dark season it was quite depressing for me under such circumstances," noted
Gibson (1990). Nonetheless, in an article written in 1954, Cst. Fryer
attempted to persuade his audience that the dark period had not inter-
fered with Inuit activities (Fryer, 1954a). His remarks illustrate the extent to which an experiment's results can differ from its published report
(Cantor, 1989: 160). This dichotomy between the private views expressed
by officials and the contradictory views presented in the written record
highlights the need always to question the motivation behind statements
in "official" reports. The disparity between the accounts published by officials like Fryer and the Inuit descriptions of the impact of their new environment on the group is confirmed in this case by the name they have
now officially selected for Resolute Bay: *Qausuittuq* (place of darkness).

Even finding sources of drinking water (*imiq*) was initially a problem
for the relocatees (Freeman, 1971; Nutaraq, personal communication).
The Port Harrison region has streams, rivers, and lakes that provide
drinking water year-round. Land-sited water is more difficult to obtain
in the Grise Fiord and Resolute Bay areas, and the families had to obtain fresh water from ice floating in the sea. Elijah Nutaraq recalled that
Grise Fiord "did not have much greenery, and there were no lakes or
rivers to draw water from. We had to get ice from icebergs for drinking
water" (*Makivik News*, 1989b). The annual precipitation is much lower in
the High Arctic and at Grise Fiord and Resolute Bay averages only 5.28
inches, whereas at Port Harrison the average is 13.60 inches. Sargent's
biblical metaphor was particularly inappropriate for the unpopulated,
polar-desert (*inuillaq*) environment of the High Arctic, whose strikingly
un-Edenic characteristics include not only low levels of precipitation but
also a lack of the willow scrub and other vegetation found near Port Har-

rison (Riewe, 1991). There is a small, land-locked lake near the camp at Resolute, but it was discovered that the fish were full of parasites. After sending a sample away to a laboratory, Gibson told the Inuit not to fish from the lake.

White and Inuit perceptions of a given place — the way they viewed the landscape — were reflected in their descriptions of life in the High Arctic. In northern Quebec, as throughout the Arctic, the process of place-naming has a cultural function for the Inuit. Naming the landscape has been important for subsistence activities, human activity, and fellowship (Nuttall, 1992: 51). Whereas the White explorers often named places after people on their expedition, benefactors, or sovereigns, Inuit place-names often reflected specific physical features and hunting experiences. Ancestral land use and occupancy were bound up with the Inuit sense of identity (Brody, 1976: 185). Inuit associations with the landscape not only endowed the landscape with meaning, they were vital for survival. Knowing the place-names was equivalent to knowing the good places to hunt and trap.

Whites have often described the Arctic tundra as barren and feature-less, but the Inuit did not see it that way. In the Port Harrison area, a fine web of place-names had been woven over generations by Inukjuamiut hunters. For a young man, an important feature of learning to hunt was learning the place-names of the land your band depended on for their livelihood. The memory that individuals and the community maintained of the landscape (and seascape) provided orientational knowledge for hunting and foraging activity as well as a binding sense of collective association with a particular area. Places "resonate with community consciousness" (Nuttall, 1992: 57); but the relocatees now found themselves in an "unoccupied" (*nunagijaunngittuq*) and unknown High Arctic landscape.

Even though landscapes pre-exist all human consciousness (Vitebsky, 1992), it is human experience that invests a landscape with cultural meaning (Helms, 1988: 20). "By the act of naming, undifferentiated space is symbolically transformed into place and gradually endowed with value — a space with a history" (P. Jackson, 1989: 168; Tuan, 1977: 6). Place-names or toponyms serve as a cultural imprint on the landscape (Müller-Wille, 1983: 132). Recent studies have resulted in the compilation of a place-name inventory in northern Quebec and confirm that the Inukjuamiut's cultural landscape is a finely woven tapestry of toponyms built up over many years (e.g., Avataq, 1981; Müller-Wille and Weber, 1983). Some Inuit place-names describe physical features and standard landmarks, such as *Nuvukataaq* ("long point" of land), *Kuuraapik* (small river), and *Kangirsinialuk* (big bay). Names can have symbolic as well as purely descriptive content (Robinson, 1989: 160). Other Inuit place-names indicate historical events and foraging experiences, such as *Kaavvik* (rapids called "place of starvation"), *Aananniavik* (brook trout fishing place), *Isanniavik* (moulting bird hunting place), *Sijjaaluit* (a valley called "many big fox dens"), and *Sirmisarniavik* (place to collect moss for sled runners). In what is a culturally valued environment, Inuit toponyms play a crucial role for subsistence activities and fellowship (Lee, 1982; Nuttall, 1992).

The dense, overlapping physical information and the cultural nuances of the place-names allow individuals with this knowledge to travel on the land and sea and to orientate themselves, irrespective of the climatic conditions. Culture evolves, in part, in response to a need to exploit the environment for reasons of survival and material amelioration (Norton, 1989: 167). Toponymic knowledge of a region is a necessary survival strategy, but, as Nuttall has shown, the Inuit cultural landscape is embedded with layers of meaning, personal stories, and myths (Nuttall, 1992: 54–58) (a subject that has stimulated substantial research in other cultural settings; for example, Basso, 1984). "Place is an organized world of meaning" (Tuan, 1977: 179), and relocation to the High Arctic severed the Inuit from their profound associational knowledge of the landscape. This act resulted in a loss of hunting knowledge and a loss of cultural and intellectual security. Although Larsen felt that the Inuit were being relocated to "a virgin land" in the High Arctic (Larsen, n.d.: 998), what he believed was a positive attribute was paradoxically a negative factor for the Inuit. As one of the relocatees observed, "I was moved to a land I did not know" (*nuna qaujimanngitara*) (Nutaraq, personal communication). It was as if an inverted "rite of passage" had occurred, and knowledgeable hunters were overnight transformed into neophytes (Gennep, 1960). They were projected into a new landscape beyond their familiar spatial boundaries.

Because they were moved to a "land without names," the relocatees had to learn a new mental topography or "memoryscape," as Nuttall (1992: 51) has described it. This process entailed not only finding "good places to hunt" (*umajursiuviksiavak*) but also developing hunting skills appropriate to the different ice, terrain, and conditions of continual darkness. Travel in the Grise Fiord area is severely restricted by the surrounding mountains, glaciers, icecaps, and polynyas (open stretches of water surrounded by ice). In his Inuit land-use study of the Grise Fiord region, Riewe (1991: 297) found that 75 percent of the territory was impassable by a dog team, whereas the flat topography of the Port Harrison area is more accessible.

The relocatees also had to adapt to a more limited diet than the one to which they were accustomed. The Inuit were told by the officials that there would be an abundance of game in the North; as the Port Harrison store manager Reuben Ploughman recounted, "they thought they were going to the land of milk and honey and things just weren't that way" (Canada, 1993b: 85). Yet the government had carried out no wildlife resource studies before the relocation. Buster Welch, a professor of zoology who has studied the wildlife in the Resolute area over the last twenty-five years, has stated bluntly: "For land animals Resolute is about the worst place you can get" (Welch, personal communication). Riewe (1991: 296) has described the Grise Fiord area as "probably the least productive land in North America." In fact, in the case of Alexandra Fiord, the officials were proved wrong, and game resources were deemed to be poor. Ross Gibson informed the Royal Commission in June 1993 that it was fortunate they were not relocated to Alexandra Fiord, because "certainly we would have been much more isolated and our chances of survival were far less than they were at Resolute Bay or Grise Fiord" (Canada, 1993b: 219).

Table 4.1 reproduces, with a few changes, Smith's comprehensive list of game resources in the Port Harrison area (Smith, 1991: 81), for it is important to demonstrate the variety of foods the Inuit were accustomed to harvesting before their relocation to the High Arctic. This list also serves to counter official assertions that there was a paucity of game in the Port Harrison region in the 1950s. It is true that caribou were scarce near the coast in the 1950s, and the Inukjuamiut had to travel several weeks inland to find a herd (Willmott, 1961: 8). Studies of the caribou indicated a period of low population densities in the first half of this century (Banfield and Tener, 1958), which some Inuit have attributed to a seventy-year cycle. Indeed, after a period of about seventy years, the numbers of caribou along the Ungava coast have increased again; when I was in Inukjuak (Port Harrison) in 1992, I was able to observe caribou herds grazing beside the community. When there was a cyclical fluctuation in the availability of caribou or harp seal, other game would supplement the Inuit diet.

The area around Port Harrison was "a land which was very satisfying" (*nuna nipuinnarviugujuktuviniq*); but at Grise Fiord and Resolute Bay, there were few birds, caribou, or fish. Larsen (n.d.: 46) later acknowledged that "southern Ellesmere Island is mostly a barren country unable to sustain great numbers of land animals." Riewe (1991: 297) found that 94 percent of the Inuit diet in Grise Fiord was comprised of meat obtained from the sea. Ringed seal became their staple food, followed by harp seal, char, walrus, polar bear, beluga, bearded seal, and narwhal (Riewe, 1977). Relatively few caribou were obtained. Moreover, the

TABLE 4.1: Animal species harvested
in the Port Harrison area

English name	Latin name	Inukjuamiut dialect
Marine mammals		
Ringed seal	*Phoca hispida*	*natsiq*
Bearded seal	*Erignathus barbatus*	*ujjuk*
Harp seal	*Phoca groenlandica*	*qairulik*
Walrus	*Odobenus rosmarus*	*aiviq*
Beluga whale	*Delphinapterus leucas*	*qilalugaq*
Polar bear	*Ursus maritimus*	*nanuq*
Land mammals		
Caribou	*Rangifer tarandus*	*tuttu*
Arctic fox	*Alopex lagopus*	*tiriganniaq*
Tundra wolf	*Canis lupus*	*amaruq*
Arctic hare	*Lepus arcticus*	*ukaliq*
Bird species		
Canada goose	*Branta canadensis*	*nirliq*
Snow goose	*Anser caerulescens*	*kanguq*
Eider duck	*Somateria mollissima*	*mitiq*
Mallard duck	*Clangula hyemalis*	*aggiakannaq*
Red merganser	*Mergus serrator*	*pangajuk*
Black guillemot	*Cepphus grylle*	*pitsiulaaq*
Great loon	*Gavia immer*	*tuullik*
Arctic loon	*Gavia arctica*	*qallulik*
Seagull	*Larus argentatus*	*naujaq*
Ptarmigan	*Lagopus lagopus*	*agiggiq*
Snowy owl	*Nyctea nyctea*	*uppik*
Fish species		
Arctic char	*Salvelinus alpinus*	*iqaluppik*
Lake trout	*Salvelinus namaycush*	*isarulitaq*
Speckled trout	*Salvelinus fontinalis*	*aana*
Whitefish	*Coregonus clupeiformis*	*kapisalik*
Polar cod	*Boreogadus saida*	*uugaq*
Sculpin	*Oncocottus hexacornis*	*kanajuq*
Mussel	*Mytilus edulis*	*uviluq*

Sources: Dorais, 1990; E. A. Smith, 1991: 81.

Queen Elizabeth Islands were within the Arctic Islands Preserve, created in 1926, and special game regulations applied. The RCMP thus forbade the Inuit to hunt musk-ox (*umingmak*) and strictly regulated the killing of caribou. "There were a lot of muskoxen, but we were forbidden to kill them," said Elijah Nutaraq (*Makivik News*, 1989b). In fact, the RCMP in part justified its detachments at Alexandra Fiord and Craig Harbour because the officers could ensure that Greenlanders from the Thule district did not come over to Ellesmere and hunt musk-oxen, as they had done in the past. Elijah Nutaraq remembered that initially they "survived on seal and polar bear meat."

Guards and Guides

The Department supported the inclusion of the Pond Inlet families in the relocation plans because they were more accustomed to conditions in the High Arctic, and officials assumed that they would help the Port Harrison Inuit adjust to the new environment. Together with the police officers, the Pond Inlet hunters had the role of guides to the Port Harrison Inuit. Supt. Larsen (1952d) wanted young officers who would be willing to devote their entire service to the Inuit cause. He informed Cst. Ross Gibson that it was his responsibility to ensure the project's success (Gibson, personal communication). With sympathetic guidance, Larsen believed the police could provide the leadership he felt the Inuit needed (Larsen, 1952d).

Gibson took it upon himself to provide leadership, expecting complete obedience from the Inuit under his care. "They certainly didn't [tell] me that they resented my authority," recalled Gibson, but he accepted that there was "a cultural barrier there between myself and the Eskimo" (Canada, 1993b: 204, 217). The officers felt that only with firm disciplinary measures would the rehabilitation programs succeed. Anthropologist Milton Freeman (1968: 113) found this form of "imposed autocracy" still in evidence at Grise Fiord in the mid-1960s. Unlike the constables at most other Arctic detachments, Gibson conducted no dog-sled patrols, because he kept no dog team. He lived at the base and oversaw the Inuit camp. "I had no work," Gibson told the Royal Commission in June 1993. "I worked for them really" (Canada, 1993b: 204). Gibson restated his total commitment to the project's success. "If we had perished, I would have perished with them because I couldn't have done anything else. I was part of the project. It was my responsibility" (ibid.: 219).

The relationships the Pond Inlet "instructors" established with the Port Harrison groups and the RCMP were harder to define because they were more complex. When Joseph Idlout, the film star of *Land of the Long Day*, arrived at Resolute Bay in 1955 with his large extended family, he reportedly informed Ross Gibson: "I'm going to be the boss now." Gibson was taken aback by this attempt to alter the hegemonic structure of the community by questioning his authority as the head "guide." He retorted: "Oh no Idlout, if anyone around here is going to be the boss, old Ross will be the boss!" (Gibson, personal communication). The Inuit had a mocking phrase for the constable, saying he was *angajuqaa-raaluujurijuq* (one who thinks he is the big boss). For Joseph Idlout, who was a proud *isumataq* (wise man) and well respected by the Whites on North Baffin Island (Wilkinson, 1956), this situation was quite awkward.

(Idlout had also been awarded the Coronation Medal by the government in 1953.) During the next two years, until Gibson finished his tour of duty at Resolute Bay, the two men had a difficult relationship (Gibson, personal communication). Idlout himself remained at Resolute Bay until his tragic death, referred to in the epilogue.

In his article on the relocation, Cst. Fryer at Craig Harbour described the situation as he saw it in 1954: "Relations between the Port Harrison and Pond Inlet natives are good. Differences in dialect and routine haven't formed any barriers" (Fryer, 1954a). Fryer's assessment is surprising, however, for social relations between the Pond Inlet and Port Harrison families were not as supportive as officials might have wished. The Canadian anthropologist Milton Freeman conducted fieldwork in Grise Fiord in the late 1960s. Even then he found that, rather than the cooperation that the officials had hoped for, intergroup relations could reflect "indifference, ridicule and even hostility" (Freeman, 1969: 774).

Owing to the difference in their dialects, they initially had trouble understanding each other (Freeman, 1984: 680). Dialectal differences could give rise to humorous situations, one person recounted, as when two hunters, one from Port Harrison and the other from Pond Inlet, went out hunting together for the first time (Audlaluk, personal communication). When they spotted a polar bear, the Pond Inlet hunter said to the other man that they should move forward "right now" (*manna*). The other man did not move, and the first hunter repeated, *manna, manna*. The Port Harrison hunter still hesitated, for in the Inukjuamiut dialect *manna* means "later on"; "now" is *tagataga*.

The social incompatibility of the two groups was lasting. At Grise Fiord, the groups split into two camps so that in 1962 the Pond Inlet family dwellings were on the east side of the RCMP detachment, and the Port Harrison families were on the west side (Freeman, 1969: 774). At Resolute Bay, the two Inuit groups had similar problems cooperating, as Cst. Jenkin noted in his report of December 1959. There was only one morale problem that could develop into a serious situation at Resolute Bay, observed Jenkin—the jealousy between the group from Port Harrison and the smaller number from Pond Inlet. Openly, they got along together well, but "the dislike, jealousy, or whatever it might be called, is plainly present" (Jenkin, 1959).

Cpl. V. R. Vitt (1968) at Grise Fiord reported in December 1968 that the social division between the Port Harrison and Pond Inlet groups continued unabated and remained the greatest obstacle to the improvement of community morale. In creating these artificial Inuit communities, Supt. Larsen failed to foresee the long-term social implications of placing two groups from different cultural backgrounds together in confined colonies. Ultimately, Akpaliapik, Anukudluk, and Amagoalik, the heads of the three Pond Inlet families who were moved to Resolute and Grise in 1953, returned to Pond Inlet.

Looking for Eve

Such was that happy Garden-state,
While Man there walk'd without a Mate

— Andrew Marvell, *The Garden* (1681, st. 8)

Despite Cpl. Sargent's (1954) optimistic statement that Craig Harbour was a Garden of Eden for the Inuit, finding marriage partners became a major complication for the experiment. The relocated Inuit were comprised of extended families, and intermarriage within a family group was not desirable. Intermarriage with the Pond Inlet group would have been socially problematic, and the small populations of the colonies reduced the likelihood of finding suitable spouses (Freeman, 1969: 776). This eventuality had not occurred to the planners of the experiment, and no forethought had been given to the effects of limiting the group's reproductive capacity. The necessity of finding unattached females was a common problem in other migration schemes (Constantine, 1991: 65). In his annual report for 1955, Cpl. Sargent (1955) at Grise Fiord recorded that three young men had approached him about finding wives. Sargent recommended that one of the men, whom he did not consider to be a good provider, should be discouraged, but that the other two be assisted in obtaining wives "before they caused trouble." The officer in charge of the 1958 eastern Arctic patrol noted in his report that Cst. Bob Pilot at Grise Fiord (see fig. 4.1) had also been approached by a young man there who had requested help in finding a wife. Accepting his responsibility as a "guide," Pilot took the man with him to Resolute Bay but had difficulties arranging a match (Gould, 1958a: 4). Some of the experiment's defects became apparent when RCMP officers took on the role of matchmakers and marriage counselors for the Inuit.

Supt. Larsen wrote to Commissioner Nicholson in 1956 offering a solution to the problem of finding spouses. He suggested that "a few young boys or girls might have to be added to the settlement from year to year as they become of marriageable age" (Larsen, 1956b). This proposal might have yielded fruit had it not been for the reluctance of single girls, when approached by the RCMP, to agree to moving north for this purpose. Cpl. Decker, the senior officer at Port Harrison in 1955, and his wife, the settlement nurse, informed Bob Phillips (1955: 43) that "they

were in favour of migrations not for economic but for eugenic reasons"
because of what they saw as endemic in-breeding amongst the Inuit.
Phillips continued, "obviously we cannot place people purely on grounds
of eugenics for the desire of the Eskimos will naturally be to establish communities of their friends." He recommended that forethought
should be given to the genetic composition of new Inuit colonies, suggesting "some rather flexible formula along the lines, for instance, that
in planning any migration we would aim that in five years that no more
than 25 percent of the new community would have come from one area."

Eventually, some of the Pond Inlet Inuit were allowed to return home
permanently, precisely because they could find no partners in the two
colonies. Some of the Inukjuamiut managed to find partners within their
extended families. Because of the low population density, it was perhaps
unavoidable (Riches, 1982: 119), though certainly not ideal (Graburn,
1969: 65). The long-term social implications of the way the artificial
colony at Grise Fiord was populated are revealed in an RCMP report that
stated that even by 1965 "there are not really sufficient of either sex in the
same age group to allow much, if any, choice of a partner" (Vitt, 1965).

Relocating the Carvers

Phillipoosie Novalinga was one of the Port Harrison elders to be relocated to Grise Fiord in 1953. As a teenager, he appeared in Flaherty's
film *Nanook of the North* and later became a hunter and a gifted carver
(fig. 4.3). One major error of the relocation was in the displacement of
a number of stonecarvers. In his article in the *RCMP Quarterly*, Cst. Fryer
made the curiously revealing observation that, given their ability to carve
ivory and stone, the Inukjuamiut would never be in need even in a poor
trapping year since they had a source of income that would buy necessities from the store (Fryer, 1954a). If that was the case, then why were
they moved from Port Harrison? Both the welfare teacher at Port Harrison, Margery Hinds (1953b), and Alex Stevenson (1953) commented
on the fact that a number of the Inuit to be moved were excellent stonecarvers. James Houston of the Canadian Handicrafts Guild discovered
that Port Harrison was one of the finest areas in the Arctic for the quality
of its soapstone (*kullisaraq*), and in 1949 he successfully established a
local handicrafts industry based on soapstone carvings (Houston, personal communication). Soapstone, or steatite, is a soft mineral found in
the Port Harrison area and in other places throughout the Arctic. The
Inuit had traditionally used soapstone to make seal-oil lamps and bowls.
Houston (1977) offered them an average of five dollars per carving for

FIGURE 4.3 Phillipoosie Novalinga at Grise Fiord, 1957. Credit: Bob Pilot

small sculptures of animals and people. Houston's offer was attractive because, at the time, the Inuit were receiving only fifty cents for a sealskin and three dollars for a fox pelt due to the severely depressed fur market. The soapstone carvings themselves were just as attractive as furs to southern Canadians. The three hundred carvings Houston collected at Port Harrison in 1949 were sold in three days by the Canadian Handicrafts Guild in a Montreal showing. Interest in Inuit soapstone carvings spread quickly across Canada, the United States, and Europe (Graburn, 1976). As a result, income from carvings grew rapidly in Port Harrison in the early 1950s (see table 4.2). Though handicrafts represented only some 8.4 percent of Inuit income in 1951, carving soon became extremely profitable for the Inukjuamiut, as discussed in chapter 8.

During the 1953 relocation, some of the best carvers were removed from Port Harrison, which is why overall income from handicrafts in Port Harrison did not rise by as great a percentage in 1953 as in the previous years (see table 4.2). The planners, however, had not established that soapstone was available in the new colonies, and the lack of soapstone at Grise Fiord and Resolute Bay became a source of discontent to the Inuit. RCMP officers ordered supplies from Port Harrison to be delivered on the *C.D. Howe*'s annual visit, but often the shipments did not arrive or were of inferior quality. Although a profitable market developed for handicrafts, carvings, rugs, and clothing at the Resolute Bay

TABLE 4.2: Estimated earnings from
handicrafts, Port Harrison, 1949–53

Year	Amount
1949	$1,500
1950	6,500
1951	8,900
1952	11,900
1953	12,500

Source: Houston, 1954

base, J. C. Jackson (1956) reported that "Gibson has been loath to encourage this activity too much as it could result in less hunting and prove
a detriment." The relocatees were thus dissuaded from earning a viable
income from carving both because soapstone supplies were insufficient
and because some of the officers insisted the Inuit adhere to a traditional
hunting culture.

Paddy Aqiatusuk was designated by the RCMP as the camp boss of the
group at Grise Fiord. He was also one of the finest carvers in Port Harrison. One of the first loans from the Eskimo Loan Fund was made out in
his name, or, rather, to "Fatty," — a nickname the Whites had given him —
and was used for the provisioning of the store at Craig Harbour. (The
use of his name on the loan was cosmetic, for the RCMP had complete
control over it.) He was also referred to in RCMP reports as "Fatty," and
Cst. Fryer (1954a) described him as "the old fogey" who wanted to return home. Paddy did not survive the first year; he died of a heart attack
in July 1954 (see fig. 4.4). His son Larry Audlaluk recalls that, when they
arrived in the High Arctic and his father saw the place where they were
supposed to live, he became troubled about their relocation and about
the hardships they would have to endure during the first winter (Audlaluk, personal communication; Freeman, 1969: 774). The week before
his death, he climbed to the top of the 2,400-foot mountain behind the
Grise Fiord camp to try to see a way home to Port Harrison, but *ajurnamat,* "it was not possible." The sense of isolation he experienced had
been intended to contribute to his moral re-education, to encourage him
to cast off his "bum" status (Ignatieff, 1978: 102). Such was his reputation as an artist at Port Harrison, however, that his death was reported in
the Milestones column of *Time* magazine in October 1954. In fact, Paddy
Aqiatusuk is probably the only Inuk to have had a *Time* obituary.

FIGURE 4.4 Larry Audlaluk at the grave of his father, Paddy Aqiatusuk, Grise Fiord, 1991. Credit: Alan Marcus

Right of Return

For the Inuit transported to Ellesmere and Cornwallis Islands in 1953–55, geographical isolation from their homelands was complete. They were separated from their kinship groups to the south, and the Inuit at Grise Fiord were even separated from their relations at Resolute Bay. The relocatees were wholly dependent on their government guides for repatriation. Because the relocatees had difficulties adjusting to the new environment, they told their "guides" they wanted to return (*utiruma-lirniq*) to their homeland. They often spoke of being homesick (*anar-rasiktuq*). "I think all people, all human beings, have distinct attachment to the place where they grew up and were raised," observed Samwillie Eliasialuk (Canada, 1993a: 47). In fact, the officials had promised the passengers that they could return to their original homes after two years if they wished.

To inform the public about its relocation plans for the second shipment of Inuit from Port Harrison in 1955 to Grise Fiord and Resolute Bay, the Department issued an enthusiastic press release (italics mine):

It will be moving day this summer for 35 Eskimos in Canada's Arctic. And they are moving further north.

The "moving van" for the Eskimos will be the Arctic Patrol vessel "C.D. Howe."
. . . This is a *purely voluntary migration*, the continuation of a policy started two
years ago by the Department of Northern Affairs and National Resources. . . .
The programme has been an unqualified success, and the Eskimos have been
enthusiastic about *their new homes* farther to the north. Although they are *free to
return* if they wish, the response so far has been to urge their friends and relatives from the "south" to join them. (Canada, 1955a)

Not only was the relocation supposedly "a purely voluntary migration," but the Inuit were "free to return if they wish." The question of
whether the Inuit were actually free to return home and whether a promise was made to return them within two years if they wished to leave
the colonies has featured prominently in discussions the Inuit have held
with the government regarding repatriation. Until recently, the government has disputed that a two-year promise of return was ever given. In
1984 the Department commissioned a report to investigate the alleged
promise. Marc Hammond (1984), the author of the report, concluded
that the Pond Inlet Inuit moved in 1953 "received such a promise in no
uncertain terms." The Port Harrison Inuit moved in 1953 "quite likely
received such a promise, but if they did not, it is clear that they were
not discouraged from thinking that they did." Hammond added that the
Pond Inlet and Port Harrison Inuit who were moved in the second-stage
relocation in 1955 probably moved with the same understanding as did
those moved in 1953.

In a more recent investigation, the Department's "Hickling Report"
addressed the question of when the Inuit first asked to return to Port
Harrison for a visit. It stated that "the earliest example of such a request, that we could find, occurred around 1960" (Hickling Corporation, 1990: 55). Curiously, Department planner Alex Stevenson (1977)
remarked that there "were rumours from time to time in the first seven
years that there were some dissatisfied or were homesick but this was
never confirmed nor were there any approaches on record having been
made to officials of the Federal or Territorial Governments."

There is ample evidence, however, that early on the Inuit wanted to
move back to Port Harrison and their old camps (*nunaliviniq*). J. C.
Jackson, the Department's officer in charge of the eastern Arctic patrol
in 1956, notified his superiors that at Resolute Bay on 21 August he
had held a meeting attended by all of the Inuit men, Supt. Larsen, Cst.
Gibson, and an interpreter. The presence of two strong figures, Johnnie
Echalook and Joseph Idlout, both of whom had arrived in Resolute in
1955, may have strengthened the group's resolve to make a number of
their complaints known to the officials from the eastern Arctic patrol.
The role of a lay preacher, such as Echalook, and that of an *isumataq*

like Idlout were highly respected in Inuit society (Matthiasson, 1992: 121). Jackson's report on this meeting with the Inuit is crucial since the meeting took place just three years after the move, when the Inuit would have expected the "two-year promise" to have fallen due. "The question of returning to Port Harrison for a visit was raised," noted Jackson, and "there seems to be some thought that this was in the original agreement" (Jackson, 1956). In response to their request, Jackson stated:

I pointed out that transportation difficulties might require that visits be for a year and that it would be expensive to transport a family there and back. . . . I do not know what the agreement may have been when the move was first made, but aside from any definite promises, if there were any, I would be inclined to suggest that if any family goes back for a visit, the family should pay part or all of the transportation cost and be able to guarantee to be self-supporting during the visit.

Officials appear to have been not only unsympathetic to requests to return home, they also made it seem almost impossible for the Inuit to do so. The Inuit had no means of funding their return to Port Harrison, and there was no commercial transport available; so they were completely in the hands of the Department. Jackson's account was confirmed three months later, in November 1956, when Cst. Gibson at Resolute Bay reported that the Inuit "from time to time express their desire to return to friends and relations at Port Harrison" (Gibson, 1956). This report was sent to Commissioner Nicholson, and a copy was sent to the Department's director of northern administration, Frank Cunningham.

In October 1956, Ben Sivertz, chief of the Arctic Division, sent a memorandum to his superior, Frank Cunningham, about the settlements at Resolute and Grise Fiord. Sivertz wrote:

It should be remembered that we are feeling our way in these projects. So far things have gone well,—better than we could properly have hoped. After two years the people seem content to stay on, whereas they only agreed to go in the first place on condition that we promise to return them to their former homes after "two or three years" (Sivertz, 1956a; cited in Marcus, 1990).

The planners in Ottawa knew that Inuit wished to return, and, as Sivertz's memo to Cunningham indicates, privately they acknowledged the Department's two-year promise of return. They nevertheless ignored the Inuit requests. In fact, Larsen had informed his constables in Port Harrison and Pond Inlet by teletype messages on 14 April 1953 that the Inuit selected for the project should be told that they "will be brought back home at end of one year if they so desire" (cited in Grant, 1993: appendix, 71).

At the same time as the relocatees at Resolute Bay and Grise Fiord were asking to return home, some of the Fort Chimo Inuit who had been relocated to Churchill in 1953 were making similar requests. Two years after their relocation, sixteen of the thirty Inuit informed the Department's Northern Service Officer at Churchill, Bill Kerr, that they wanted to be returned home. The Department's most fluent speaker of Inuktitut, Leo Manning, asked them why they wanted to go. Manning told Phillips (1955), who reported to the deputy minister, that the Inuit expressed "an undefinable longing to return to familiar grounds far distant from this strange place whose material rewards could not outweigh its alien ways."

Deputy Minister Young communicated with C. M. Drury, deputy minister of the Department of National Defence. "I agree that it would be the responsibility of the Department of Resources and Development," Young (1953b) assured him, "to return to his original settlement any Eskimo who proved unsatisfactory or who did not wish to remain at Churchill." Indeed, a number of Chimo Inuit were returned home by the Department. Because the Inukjuamiut had been placed in colonies as remote as Grise Fiord and Resolute Bay, however, the Department did not follow the same policy of right of return for them.

This result was a repeat of the events of 1934–36 when the Department had authorized the Hudson's Bay Company to relocate fifty-three Baffin Inuit to Dundas Harbour on Devon Island in an attempt to establish the northernmost permanent colony in the High Arctic. The Inuit only agreed to go on the condition that, if they were unhappy on Devon Island, the Company would return them to their homeland after two years (Russell, 1978: 41). After one year, the Inuit told the Company manager supervising the operation, Chesley Russell, that they wanted to go home. The following year, the Company ship *Nascopie* came to evacuate the group as agreed; however, the Company's officials told the Inuit that they would not be able to take them home and instead transported them to Arctic Bay where a new post was opened. They were moved again in 1937 to Fort Ross, and then again ten years later to Spence Bay. Jenness (1964: 61) referred to them as "the homeless Ishmaelites." Russell recorded that both he and the Inuit were "bitterly disappointed" that the promise had not been kept. Insp. Henry Larsen visited the relocatees at Fort Ross in January 1942 while on patrol on the *St. Roch*. He reported that although a good number of the original number had died, the remaining twenty-four Inuit wanted to return to their homeland (Larsen, 1942). Everyone he spoke to "expressed an ardent desire to be taken back to Cape Dorset, Baffin Island as their present location did not agree with them." The 1953 relocation to Resolute Bay and Grise Fiord was a near reenactment of the 1934 Devon Island relocation experiment. In both cases, the Inuit were told of better hunting conditions and promised that they could return home in two years. In neither case did officials abide by the original terms of the agreement.

From discussions with the Inukjuamiut relocated in 1953 to Resolute Bay and Grise Fiord, it is apparent that many of them thought the relocation was planned as an extended hunting and trapping expedition and not as a permanent separation from their homeland. One relocatee said that, when the Whites had talked to the Inuit about going north, "they made him believe" (*uppirnaqsititsugu*) they would return home to Port Harrison (Eliasialuk, personal communication). Markoosie Patsauq recounted that when Gibson came and talked to his father about a land rich in game, his father got very excited about trapping lots of foxes. Most importantly, Markoosie said that his father hoped to get a lot of foxes "so that he might have enough money after we returned to Inukjuak to buy a boat" (Patsauq, personal communication). He thought they were only going for two years and had every intention of returning home. Perhaps surprisingly, Supt. Larsen later described the establishment of the "little trial colonies" at Resolute Bay and Grise Fiord as a temporary measure. Inuit could be moved to the new locations on a temporary basis, he thought, until areas to the south had been developed to such an extent that the Inuit could make a living again or obtain employment and thus "regain their self respect" (Larsen, n.d.: 998–99).

The relocation to Grise Fiord and Resolute Bay had the effect of separating families permanently from their relations. They were separated from a collection of camps that had strong bonds of kinship, and the families were placed in distant colonies from which they were unable to communicate with their relatives down south. The Inuit asked themselves *qanurli taga*, "what now?" "what can we do now?" (Nungaq, personal communication). Cst. Gibson was uneasy about the effect the lack of communication would have on the families. He notified Supt. Larsen that he was going to try to arrange for the relocatees to speak over the radio to their people at Port Harrison, feeling that this measure would "keep the people more settled at this point" (Larsen, 1953). Anna Nungaq insisted that she never heard from her relatives at all. She recalled getting one letter after being there many years. There was no means of communication and therefore no contact with relatives (*Inuktitut*, 1981). The relocatees experienced a profound sense of loneliness (*hujuujaqnaqtuq*) for their relatives (Canada, 1993a). (For a good discussion of Inuit feelings of loneliness and isolation, see Briggs, 1970: 202–8.) The Port Harrison trader, Reuben Ploughman, confirmed Anna's recollection. He told the Royal Commission that from the time they went north until he left Port Harrison two years later, "I don't think any mail had come out from those places" (Canada, 1993b: 85). Gibson confirmed that he did not think the Inuit received any mail from their relations in Port Harrison during his four years at Resolute Bay (ibid.: 206).

In the 1950s, it would have been difficult for the families to return to Port Harrison to visit or to live. Grise Fiord and Resolute Bay were supplied once a year by the government ship the *C.D. Howe.* "It was a one-way ticket," said former constable Bob Pilot (personal communication). The *C.D. Howe* stopped at Port Harrison on the way north, but not on the return trip. Not only was it impracticable for the families to make their own way home, it was also actively discouraged by the officials. "When discussing moving back to Inukjuak with the police, they used to try to convince me not to go," recalled Samwillie Eliasialuk (Makivik, 1986).

According to Samwillie, the constables tried to discourage him from leaving Grise Fiord by telling him that he would be leaving his mother's grave behind and that the economic situation in Port Harrison was poor. Death did play a role in the relocatees' desire to leave Grise Fiord. After Aqiatusuk died within the first year, the others felt insecure and unhappy about staying (Inukjuamiut informants, personal communication). In 1958, when a one-month-old baby (Johnassie) died, followed by Thomasie's two sons, Allie (twelve years old) and Salluviniq (nine years old), who drowned in an accident, Cst. Bob Pilot reported that "morale was at a very low ebb at the native camp" (Pilot, 1958). He noted that the Inuit still held to their superstitions, and several men stated that "they wished to move from this area." Pilot also noted that they were unhappy that the store was out of basic provisions such as flour, oats, milk, and tobacco. Cpl. Sargent confirmed that "all of the Eskimos had talked to him about leaving Grise Fiord because of the food shortages" (Gould, 1958a: 7). When the officer in charge of the 1958 eastern Arctic patrol was informed of this situation upon visiting Grise Fiord, he duly reported it to his superiors at the Department. He added that he, too, had spoken with one of the Inuit, Thomasie, who had said that, if the police did not stock more food this winter at the store, they would all wish to leave Grise Fiord next year (ibid.: 6).

Unable to return to Port Harrison, some Inuit tried to move between Resolute Bay and Grise Fiord to join their relatives. The RCMP at times discouraged this practice. In 1959 Elijah and his wife and mother asked to move from Grise Fiord to Resolute Bay to join Elijah's brother Samwillie, who had gone to Resolute Bay in search of a wife (Pilot, 1959). In his report, Cst. Pilot at Grise Fiord recorded that he was against such a move since it was known that others from this area would like to live at Resolute also, and if one moved, more would follow. He then listed the names of other Inuit who had asked to leave the settlement for Resolute Bay. Cst. Pilot discussed the matter with his colleague at the

Resolute Bay detachment, Cst. Jenkin, and asked that he report to head-quarters and request that the Department write to the Inuit concerned and discourage the move. In his report, Jenkin (1960) warned that, if these families were not successfully discouraged from moving to Resolute, three other families would move with them.

Isolated from their families and social groups and unable to return to Port Harrison, some Inuit wrote to their relations asking them to move north to join them in the colonies. Having failed to assess the game resources in the Queen Elizabeth Islands, the Department became concerned after 1955 about overpopulating the region and, therefore, placed a restriction on further Inuit relocation to the colonies. Cst. Jenkin at Resolute Bay reported in 1960 that there were growing difficulties in enforcing this policy. He wrote that two other families had been corresponding with relatives from Port Harrison about resettling at Resolute (ibid.). The Inuit claim that some of their letters to relatives were destroyed. John Amagoalik remembered that they found their letters thrown in the dump (Canada, 1990b). To dissuade the families at Resolute from encouraging relatives to come north, Cst. Jenkin (1960) warned them that they would lose many of their present advantages such as free electricity, a fair amount of employment, and good hunting and trapping. Aided by the sheer distance from Port Harrison and the overall isolation of the colonies, the RCMP and the Department were successful for a number of years in their attempts to limit immigration and keep southern Inuit from joining their relations. The sense of confinement the relocatees experienced on Cornwallis and Ellesmere was conveyed by their vivid descriptions of isolation (Canada, 1993a). One is reminded of the original meaning of the word "paradise" (*pairidaeza*): an enclosed garden. The Inuit soon discovered there was no way of leaving Sargent's "Garden of Eden."

· PART 3 ·

THE FLIGHT FROM EDEN
RELOCATION OF THE AHIARMIUT

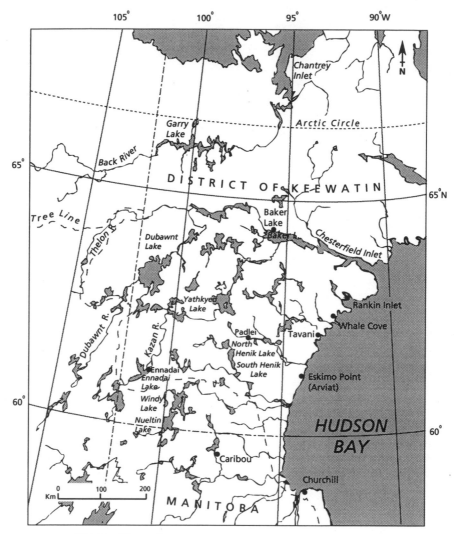

MAP 5.1 District of Keewatin

· 5 ·

"ESKIMOS FLY TO NEW HUNTING GROUNDS"

The Ahiarmiut of Ennadai Lake

The relocation of the Inukjuamiut in 1953–55 was seen as a proto-type for future relocations, in which Inuit would be moved away from White settlements to unoccupied, "wilderness" areas. Using the Inukjuamiut move as a successful example of this policy, the Depart-ment pursued a second Inuit relocation in 1957 when it moved the entire band of Ahiarmiut by plane from their homeland at Ennadai Lake to a northern site called Henik Lake, which had been pre-selected by officials (see map 5.1 and appendix B). These two case studies have intersecting histories and many aspects in common. The two groups were perhaps the best-known Inuit in Canada: the Inukjuamiut had been exhibited in *Nanook of the North,* and the Ahiarmiut were featured in Mowat's *People of the Deer.* The two relocations were well-documented events and were the Department's highest-profile operations for resettling Inuit in wilderness sites. Many of the same officials, including Larsen, Sivertz, Cunningham, Stevenson, and Robertson, were involved in both projects. The essential difference between the two relocations was that the 1953 Inukjuamiut move ushered in a bold, new relocation policy, and the 1957 Ahiarmiut move brought it to a sudden conclusion. The operation ended in the deaths of a number of the relocatees and resulted in a famous murder trial, which I shall discuss in chapter 6.

This chapter reconstructs the events that led to the 1957 relocation and identifies the causal factors. It argues that the relocations can be seen as acts of social reform in response to White concern about Inuit reliance on "handouts" (relief and social benefits) and about what was perceived as the growing tendency of Inuit to cluster around settle-

FIGURE 5.1 Akjar with her baby Igyekah, and Ookanak, Ennadai Lake, 1955.
Credit: Geert van den Steenhoven

ments. The planners described the relocations as "voluntary migrations"
designed to reaffirm the value of self-reliance and discourage reliance
on the state. Although officials may have viewed the utopian schemes as
altruistic attempts to return the Inuit to a reconstituted Edenic state, evidence suggests that the Inuit saw the operations as enforced migrations
to places that were not of their choosing.

The Ahiarmiut were considered by the Whites to be among the most
"primitive" Inuit in the Canadian Arctic (*Life*, 1956). They were a band
of Caribou Inuit who lived on the Keewatin barrens (see fig. 5.1). They
depended almost entirely on the caribou (*tuktu*) for their sustenance and
often hunted them with a spear (*iputujuq*) when not using a rifle. The
Ahiarmiut had migrated to the Keewatin interior from the coast some-
time in the midnineteenth century. They were thus called "Ahiarmiut"
(inland people) by those Inuit who lived on the coast. They have called
themselves the Ahiarmiut for as long as people can remember, though
originally they may have identified themselves by the -*miut* phrase *Tahi-
riarmiut* (people of the lakes) (Csonka, personal communication). The
size of the population has been contested in the literature (Mowat, 1952;
Porsild, 1952b; Burch, 1986), but before 1920 they may have numbered
approximately four hundred people; in the 1920s–40s, starvation and

epidemics reduced the band to less than sixty people (Csonka, 1991). By 1955, there were only fifty-two Ahiarmiut left, and they lived in the area of Ennadai Lake, 460 kilometers northwest of Churchill, Manitoba. The nearest permanently inhabited point was the HBC trading post at Padlei, 225 kilometers northeast of Ennadai. This area was occupied by a band of Caribou Inuit known as the Paallirmiut. To the south of the Ahiarmiut were the Chipewyan Indians of the northern forest.

The terrain around Ennadai Lake is low, with rolling hills and many lakes and rivers. The treeline is about twenty-five kilometers south of Ennadai Lake, but in the area there are a few small spruce and willow trees that the Inuit used as fuel for heating and for the partial construction of their dwellings. The Ahiarmiut migrated between seasonal camps, living in the south near Nueltin Lake, in the east at Kasba Lake or Windy Lake (where they encountered Farley Mowat in 1947), and at numerous river points throughout their territory. In 1949 the Canadian Army Signal Corps built a radio station at Ennadai Lake, which was taken over by the Department of Transport Air Radio Branch in 1954. No other government, mission, or trading representatives were resident in the area. "Ennadai Lake" is actually a Chipewyan place-name meaning "the lake of the enemies." The Ahiarmiut referred to the lake as *Qamanirjuaq* (big lake), though in the past they also reportedly called it *Qikiqtarahattuq* (lake of many islands). Like the Inukjuamiut and other Inuit bands, the Ahiarmiut had assigned a dense web of place-names to the region in which they hunted and foraged. The peninsula that protruded into Ennadai Lake, which the Whites had appropriated for their radio station, the Ahiarmiut called *Atiqturniarvik* (Csonka and Ahiarmiut informants, personal communication).

During the winter, the Ahiarmiut lived in dwellings with walls made of snow blocks and capped with a roof of caribou skins, supported by wooden tent poles. Inside were one or two sleeping platforms about two feet above floor level. In the center of the dwelling, a stove (usually made from a ten-gallon fuel drum) was raised on a stone platform, with a chimney poking through the roof. Willow twigs and moss provided fuel for the stove. The dwellings were comfortable, and during the winter the indoor temperature could average 55°–65°F. In the summer, the families would live in conical, poled tents made of caribou skins and canvas (see fig. 5.2). Cooking was performed outside over an open fire, protected by a windbreak of spruce boughs.

As long as caribou meat was available, the adults ate almost nothing else. Ptarmigan, water fowl, fish, and berries supplemented their diet, depending on the season. The caribou migration usually passed the Ennadai Lake region in May, traveling in a northwesterly direction. The

FIGURE 5.2 Owlijoot's camp, Ennadai Lake, 1955. Credit: Geert van den Steenhoven

second annual migration occurred in September and October, when the caribou traveled in a southeasterly direction. The Ahiarmiut used firearms, though they were reportedly often short of ammunition (Rudnicki and Stevenson, 1958). During the autumn migration, they would employ their traditional hunting strategy of approaching the caribou when they were swimming across narrow crossing points at lakes, spearing them from their kayaks. The men would go hunting daily on foot or by kayak (*qajaq*); every adult owned a kayak, which was slender and covered with caribou skin (see fig. 5.3). The band killed an estimated one thousand caribou a year (Houston, 1955). The caribou were so numerous on their migrations in 1954–55 that one official reported: "In the average year the danger of excessive killing is greater than the possibility of obtaining too few caribou for the group requirement" (ibid.: 3). Some of the caribou were cached when killed, but many were simply gutted and left on the ground. The hunters would return to the carcasses during the winter as necessary. The skins were used for clothing and housing, but most were left on the carcasses. The winter dress, including parkas, pants, stockings, and boots, was made from caribou skins. Summer dress included imported southern clothing obtained by trade from the radio station.

FIGURE 5.3 Owlijoot constructing a kayak, Ennadai Lake, 1955.
Credit: Geert van den Steenhoven

Two researchers who worked independently came to live with the Ahiarmiut during the spring and summer of 1955 and reported on their socioeconomic condition. One of the men was James Houston, a Northern Service Officer (NSO) with the Department who had worked with the Inuit in the eastern Arctic to develop a profitable handicrafts cottage industry. The other man was Geert van den Steenhoven, a Dutch legal anthropologist, who spent several months living with the Ahiarmiut while preparing a study on them for the Department. Their reports, referred to later in the chapter, offer useful external perspectives of the band just two years before their relocation by the government in 1957.

In 1955 the Ahiarmiut band was comprised of thirteen families, divided roughly into two groups: one loosely under the leadership of Owlijoot (see fig. 5.3), an *isumataq*, or respected elder, and the other under Pongalak (see fig. 5.4), who was a shaman (*angatkuq*). They lived in camps within a radius of twenty-four kilometers of the radio station. Owlijoot's camp was sited five kilometers from the station in May 1955, and in August the group moved to a lake eleven kilometers from the station. After the establishment of the radio station, the Ahiarmiut made minor seasonal moves of perhaps eight kilometers between their winter and summer camps (Houston, 1955: 2). Steenhoven lived with Owlijoot's camp in the summer of 1955. He described the camp as cheerful

FIGURE 5.4 Pongalak, his wife Ootnooyuk, son Kiyai, grandson, and daughter-in-law Alikaswa, Ennadai Lake, 1955. Credit: Geert van den Steenhoven

and peaceful, with caribou herds around almost all the time he was there (Steenhoven, 1962: 12). Owlijoot (forty-three years old), Hallow (thirty-five years old), and Owlijoot's stepson Anowtelik (twenty-three years old) were described by Steenhoven (personal communication) and Houston (1955: 5) as being among the best Ahiarmiut hunters. Houston recorded that the Ahiarmiut had the appearance of good health and vigor.

The Ahiarmiut's encounter strategy with the station personnel was to approach them after the buildings had been constructed and the Whites were established in their dwellings (for a fascinating historical account of Inuit encounter strategies, see Bravo, 1992). In August 1949, the station's log recorded the "first Eskimos visit station—six people, led by Ohoto, asking if they could earn some money—came walking and left same day—came from a place two sleeps to the north" (Steenhoven, 1955). The Ahiarmiut settled nearby, probably because the personnel were friendly and because of the opportunity to obtain goods and make use of items discarded by the station. In addition, they were given jobs moving fuel drums, hauling water, and other chores in exchange for rations. Houston (1955: 9) noted that the army and DOT personnel at the radio station admitted that the Inuit had been of great assistance to them. He wrote that they had shown the Whites how to live in the country and how to dress for cold weather, and that they provided a much-needed interest beyond the cramped life within the station.

The new radio station at Ennadai had a direct impact on the lives of the Ahiarmiut and, as I shall explain, led ultimately to a series of relocations. The station was established by the Royal Canadian Army Service Corps over a four-year period as part of "Operation Ennadai." Following a series of trials in 1947–48, a "trail-breaker party" of heavily laden tractors made the round trip over frozen lake ice in January 1949 from Churchill to Ennadai in forty-six days, through temperatures of –62°F. Additional tractor trains brought in 187 tons of supplies to Ennadai in 1949–50, and Lancaster aircraft dropped spare parts en route (Berry, 1951). A landing strip was constructed at Ennadai, allowing the station to be supplied by air once it was operational. The four to five personnel manning the station were also flown in and out on a regular rotational basis by aircraft from Churchill.

Although in the mid-1950s the Ahiarmiut were under the jurisdiction of the Department's NSO and the RCMP detachment in Churchill, the officer in charge (OIC) of the Ennadai radio station, of his own volition, collected their fox skins, forwarded the products by air to Churchill, and arranged for the distribution of goods, of provisions in lieu of family allowances, and of relief rations if necessary. The OIC arranged for the weekly distribution of goods amongst the Inuit at what were called "tea days." The effect of this practice was to limit the Inuit to housing locations no further than one day's travel from the station, whereas in fact they would have preferred to live at sites somewhat further from the station where fishing was known to be better (Steenhoven, 1962: 11).

The Ahiarmiut first began trading with Brochet in the Chipewyan territory in 1868, probably through Chipewyan intermediaries (Csonka, 1991: 455). Between 1906 and 1941, the Hudson's Bay Company, Revillon Frères, and a number of independent traders operated posts in the Ennadai Lake–Windy Lake–Nueltin Lake area (Harper, 1964; Usher, 1971). During the 1930s, when the price of fox fur fell, many of the traders left, and the Company closed its Nueltin Lake post permanently in 1941. One family of White trappers continued to trade with the Ahiarmiut until 1949, when they too left the area due to the collapse of the fur market (Harper, 1964: 15, 63). When the radio station was constructed in the same year, therefore, the Ahiarmiut viewed its personnel potentially as substitute traders, although the staff was probably unaware of this perception or of the Ahiarmiut's history of trading with Whites.

Relocation to Nueltin Lake

The encounter between the Ahiarmiut and the radio station personnel soon set in motion a series of events. In 1949, when the radio station was opened, officials initially took a dim view of Inuit interest in camping nearby. Pointing out that fish and caribou were plentiful in the adjacent district, one report suggested that "the Eskimos preferred the occasionally received 'hand-out' from the personnel of the Radio Station to fending for themselves farther afield" (Sivertz, 1959e). This statement suggests that Department officials, at least, saw the Ahiarmiut as a nuisance to the Ennadai personnel.

An official indicated the social hazards by remarking that "concentrating at this point, subtle degeneration set in and they became more and more reluctant to move from the site" (Sivertz, 1959b: 2). At the same time, the Department learned of possible starvation amongst other Caribou Inuit, though not the Ahiarmiut. The threat of starvation coupled with the Ahiarmiut's growing dependency on the radio station was perceived by the Department as problematic. In retrospect, Sivertz felt that the Ahiarmiut themselves "were unaware of the demoralizing consequences to those who lose their initiative and become dependent on relief."

Shortly after the Ennadai radio station was built, Sigurdson and Martin, a private firm of merchants from Churchill, sent a message to the RCMP at Eskimo Point: "Re: Natives Ennadai Lake. We are in position to feed and put to work all who can reach new post. Suggest your department fly them down immediately" (Rowley, 1956a). The firm had just opened a private trading post at Nueltin Lake and intended to develop a fishery. This sudden offer presented the Department with a timely solution to "the Ahiarmiut problem." The Department responded favorably to the plan, on the condition that the Department be responsible for transporting the Inuit from Ennadai to Nueltin, after which the firm would supervise them. The radio station log noted in April 1950: "Found true—preparations for evacuation to Nueltin, since natives starving" (Steenhoven, 1955).

On 2–3 May 1950, at a cost of $1,270, the Department relocated the entire Ahiarmiut group of forty-seven people by air from Ennadai Lake to Nueltin Lake, one hundred kilometers to the southeast, to work in the commercial fishery scheme of Nueltin Lake Fish Products (Sivertz, 1959b). Despite the fact that no other Inuit lived near the lake, the company had advised the Department that the lake was capable of providing a livelihood for every Inuk from Baker Lake southwards. Three months after the relocation, an evangelical missionary, Mr. Ledyard, contacted officials to inform them that he had recently visited Nueltin Lake. He reported that the Ahiarmiut had poor skin clothing and that they were not fishing but did have a few nets in the lake and were obtaining enough fish for their needs (Larsen, 1959). An RCMP report noted that Ledyard had advised the police that the Ahiarmiut did not like Nueltin Lake, saying that it was strange to them, and that they were talking of returning to the Ennadai Lake area (ibid.).

By December 1950, the Inuit had drifted back to Ennadai of their own accord. Pongalak, one of the two headmen, returned to the Ennadai radio station within weeks of being moved and appeared to the staff to be "very disgruntled, . . . claiming it to be a terrible place for hunting. He insisted there were so many trees around that it was extremely difficult to be at home and impossible to kill any game. [He] intends to remain here" (Steenhoven, 1955). Meanwhile, the company had found it did not have the capital to finance the operation after being refused a government loan and therefore dropped the project. Between May and October, a number of conflicting reports were received about the welfare of the Ahiarmiut, but officials commented that "one thing seemed clear— they were really no better off than they had been in their former home and they were not particularly happy in their new environment" (Rowley, 1956a). Not only were the Ahiarmiut dissatisfied with the change in habitat, but their trading relationship with the Nueltin merchant was less favorable than the one they had had with the radio personnel. They therefore returned to Ennadai.

A Departmental report later revealed that consensual arrangements for the relocation were compromised by the fact that officials overlooked the need for an interpreter to explain to the Inuit why they were being moved and the nature of the work the company expected them to do (Sivertz, 1959b). Sivertz acknowledged that "this unfortunate omission was our fault and a considerable factor in the project's failure." Indeed, one Inuk was recorded as having said that he thought the Whites were going to fish for them at Nueltin Lake. The Department accepted that the lack of success was not surprising, for the Ahiarmiut did not take to fishing and did not have any boats or other equipment for proper fishing (Rowley, 1956a). A senior Department official later advised that "if we added any further explanation it might only tend to draw attention to the incident, which I do not think would be useful" (ibid.). The outcome of this relocation experiment demonstrated that an attempt to turn caribou hunters into commercial fishermen by moving them to a location not of their choosing, and with little or no support, stood little chance of fulfilling White expectations.

Officials did not achieve consensus with the Inuit when planning the project. The Department developed a plan, and the Inuit acquiesced, not because they understood or agreed with the need for or aims of the experiment but because they were doing what the Whites wanted them to do. Unlike the Inukjuamiut relocatees in 1953, who had no means of escape, the Ahiarmiut could return to their homeland of their own volition soon after being relocated to Nueltin Lake. They were able to do so because they had been transported across a contiguous area of land and a distance of only one hundred kilometers, whereas the Inukjuamiut had been relocated over 2,200 kilometers from their homeland. The geographical factor thus provided the Ahiarmiut with a safety valve that the Inukjuamiut did not have.

Back at Ennadai Lake

The following year, relief rations were airlifted to Ennadai Lake, and conditions were deemed by officials to have improved. The nomadic nature of Ahiarmiut life troubled officials, who felt that "the same uncertain and precarious elements of caribou migrations" were not to be relied upon (Sivertz, 1959b). Over the next five years, however, conditions improved to the extent that, by the time of Houston's and Steenhoven's visits in the early spring and late summer of 1955, the Ahiarmiut were reported to be prospering. Even in May 1954 the RCMP officers who visited the Ahiarmiut found them to be doing well, and the dogs appeared to be well fed and cared for (Laliberte, 1955). They had harvested between one thousand and twelve hundred caribou since the fall and were now camped twenty-four kilometers from the station at a good fishing site. In December 1954, the RCMP in Churchill recorded that, since no family allowances had been expended since October, the Ahiarmiut had fairly large credits in that account. They also had sent eighty foxes to be picked up, reported the RCMP, so they were in good financial shape provided that the goods could be transported in to them (Rothery, 1955a). The Inuit also benefited from the fact that Mr. Taylor, the current OIC at the radio station, apparently took a very real interest in their welfare and gave them every assistance possible. The radio station provided medical treatment when necessary and issued weekly supplies in lieu of family allowance credits and in exchange for furs trapped. At the end of the year, however, the OIC was to be replaced by a new officer who might not be as favorably disposed to taking on the responsibilities of a trader and the duties of the Department. Houston (1955: 9) reported that the selection of a new OIC "with a sympathetic outlook" was crucial in determining whether the station would have a "good or evil [impact] on these native people."

The fact that the Ahiarmiut did not live near a trading post was regarded by the Department as a liability, placing a greater onus on the Department and the radio station personnel to act as unofficial traders and to supervise the group. NSO Bill Kerr discussed with OIC Taylor the feasibility of maintaining a supply of trade goods at Ennadai so that the Inuit could take advantage of their substantial outstanding credits. Kerr explained that the main idea behind this scheme was that the Inuit might have more incentive to trap or to produce articles like mitts or slippers for trade if they could bring them in and realize an immediate return (Rothery, 1955b). He noted it was sometimes months before they received anything for their labors.

The attitude of the transient station personnel toward the Inuit was crucial. In the previous year, the DOT had complained to the Department about the burden of supervising the Ahiarmiut at its Ennadai station. In October 1954, DOT Deputy Minister Baldwin (1954) wrote to DNANR Deputy Minister Robertson with the information that the Ennadai staff had been discharging duties that normally would be assumed by a nursing station. For example, when there was an outbreak of influenza amongst the Inuit, the radio station OIC was immediately able to telegraph the RCMP in Churchill with a detailed account of the illnesses, noting that penicillin had been administered and requesting that a doctor and more medicine be sent in. Two days later, a doctor arrived at Ennadai by plane from Churchill with an army major, supplies, and medicine (Rothery, 1955b). Despite the ability to respond promptly to medical emergencies, Baldwin reminded Robertson that the army felt there was too much work involved in handling the numerous details of Inuit welfare at Ennadai, since the station had been established primarily for meteorological and communications work. He therefore requested that the Department arrange to station an agent or RCMP constable at Ennadai "to handle the Eskimo problem there" (Baldwin, 1954).

Plans for a Second Ahiarmiut Relocation

Between 1950 and 1955, field officials saw the Ahiarmiut as being productive in terms of fur trapping and hunting caribou. The RCMP and the radio station personnel worked closely together to assist the Inuit. For example, in January 1955, when the station OIC had a stockpile of fifty white fox fur skins that had been brought in by the Ahiarmiut, he contacted the RCMP at Churchill, who then arranged for trade supplies to be flown in and for the furs to be flown out on an RCAF plane. Then officials in Churchill asked three local traders for bids on the fifty fox furs.

The Hudson's Bay Company and two independent traders made their bids, and in this instance officials accepted the offer of one of the independent traders (Rothery, 1955a). Two weeks later, on 29 January 1955, the RCMP plane again brought out a large quantity of furs: seventy-three white fox, thirty-one red fox, ten cross-fox, four blue fox, one silver fox, five wolverine, and one wolf. Four traders made bids, and officials accepted the offer made by the Hudson's Bay Company (Laliberte, 1955). On 7 February 1955, another shipment of thirty fox furs was brought out from Ennadai. Three local traders made their offers, and officials accepted the higher bid of an independent trader. Significantly, the RCMP reported that, while the Ahiarmiut were "in a good position financially, our only difficulty [is] in getting supplies to them." In Churchill, a backlog of supplies built up that had been charged against outstanding credits for the Inuit, but they were awaiting freight space aboard an RCMP or RCAF plane bound for Ennadai. At this point, the Inuit had $1,658 in fur credits and $3,570 in family allowance credits.

The RCMP and the Department became concerned about providing for Inuit needs at Ennadai, not wanting to depend too greatly on the cooperation and goodwill of the DOT station. Meanwhile, the Hudson's Bay Company was annoyed that the Department was selling Inuit furs directly to the highest bidder. In 1953 the Department and the RCMP had established several government stores in the High Arctic Islands, financed by the Eskimo Loan Fund (see chapter 2). Although the Company had not been interested in working with the Department to set up those trading operations, it increasingly saw the government's Ennadai trade as circumventing the Company's virtual monopoly. The Ennadai trade procedures were thought to be further evidence that the government might be contemplating the creation of a Crown trading operation, as proposed by Larsen and others (see chapter 1). The Company thus viewed the government-assisted trade with the Ahiarmiut as the specter of a nationalized fur trade. To prevent this independent activity from becoming institutionalized, a senior Company director, Peter Nichols, discussed the situation with the Department in June 1955. Nichols suggested that his Padlei post manager, Henry Voisey, could provide trading services for the Inuit if they lived closer to his post. The director of northern affairs, Frank Cunningham, saw the administrative convenience of Nichols's offer, which would allow the Department to rid itself of the time-consuming responsibilities of assisting the Ahiarmiut and supporting the RCMP trading operation. Cunningham (1955) therefore informed Supt. Larsen that, as a result of his discussions with the Company, the Department had "come to the conclusion that the most satisfactory solution would be to persuade this small group to move nearer to Padlei where they would have access to trading facilities."

Taking the lead, Cunningham suggested to Supt. Larsen that it would be desirable if representatives of the three organizations concerned— the Department, the RCMP, and the Company—discussed the matter jointly with the Inuit. The Ahiarmiut would be told that they could no longer expect the government to provide them with free transportation, storage, or handling. Cunningham confided to Larsen that, if the free servicing of Ennadai was not discontinued, the government would be subjected to increasing criticism from air carriers and traders (ibid.). He clarified the relocation project's benefits to the Department:

I realize that the alternative I propose may not be satisfactory to the Eskimos, but in this case I don't think the government should give undue consideration to the imagined convenience of this small and perverse group of ex-Padleimiuts who have apparently become used to and fond of free help from the Ennadai radio station.

Cunningham's statement is of profound importance for understanding how senior officials within the Department perceived the Ahiarmiut and how they justified the need for relocation. Officials who were based at or who visited Ennadai, such as the radio station OIC Taylor, Houston, Steenhoven, and the RCMP, had filed reports stating that the Ahiarmiut were prospering, and the RCMP noted that they had substantial fur and family allowance credits. At the same time, Cunningham, a senior Department official in Ottawa, described the Ahiarmiut as being a "perverse" people. By referring to them as "ex-Padleimiuts," he was indicating that they actually belonged in the Padlei district anyway (this may also have been an indirect reference to Birket-Smith, 1929a: 168), and that in his opinion they had no historical right to live at Ennadai. By the Ahiarmiut's own reckoning, however, Ennadai Lake was their homeland. Cunningham (1954a) nevertheless made the preemptive decision to inform his deputy minister that the new NSO being posted to Churchill, Bill Kerr, would proceed to Ennadai "to determine what arrangements can be made with these people to transfer to a more accessible area where they can be looked after more effectively than at Ennadai Lake." Kerr was to be assigned direct responsibility for the Ahiarmiut. Cunningham noted that the former radio station personnel had been willing to cooperate in supervision of the Inuit whereas the new personnel were not so inclined.

Despite the fact that Ennadai Lake was the homeland of the Ahiarmiut, Cunningham advised Robertson that there was no advantage in having them remain at Ennadai Lake and that they would be "much less of a problem" if they could be "persuaded" to move to a location near Padlei or Eskimo Point, where there were trading posts and where they could be visited by the RCMP. Robertson (1954a) concurred that he, too, felt it was not justifiable to assign an official to look after such a comparatively small group of people.

Supt. Larsen (1955b) informed his fellow officer commanding "D" Division in Winnipeg that Kerr would be responsible for recommendations on the move and for the relocation itself. Larsen (1955a), however, explained to Commissioner Nicholson:

> I had some doubts in asking the O.C. "D" Division to have Sgt. Rothery of his Churchill Detachment assist Northern Service Officer, Mr. Kerr, in persuading these Eskimos to make the move, but under the circumstances felt that I had no alternative but to make that request as a form of assistance to the Dept. of Northern Affairs, who are assuming responsibility for the move.

Larsen pointed out that, although the Ahiarmiut would be under the supervision, to some extent, of the HBC post manager at Padlei, hunting conditions there were no better, if as good, as they were in the Ennadai Lake area. He told him candidly that he wondered if the proposed move of the Ahiarmiut to the Padlei district was likely to be successful and whether they would be any better off economically at Padlei. Larsen also recalled a matter that was being overlooked in discussions about the impending relocation—the move to Nueltin Lake five years before. He reminded Nicholson: "That venture did not turn out well" (ibid.).

Three months later, the Department sent James Houston to Ennadai to spend a month investigating the circumstances of Inuit dependence on station personnel as described in Baldwin's memo. Houston suggested that "the most obvious answer" to the major problem of a lack of trading facilities for the Ennadai people would be for them to move to the Hudson's Bay store at Padlei, some 240 kilometers away. He reported, however, that "this they will not do since they have feuds or old debts in Padlei and will not go there" (Houston, 1955: 9). Houston therefore advised that they remain, since they had fairly large trapping and family allowance credits and lived in an area easily accessible from Churchill for medical treatment. They could be encouraged to cache more meat, Houston wrote, and "fish wisely," reaffirming that in his view the Ennadai Lake region was splendid for caribou and that vast quantities of fish could be obtained when necessary.

Within weeks, Cunningham had passed on information to Robertson that the Ahiarmiut had already obtained large catches of fish and six hundred caribou from the fall migration. In July 1955, NSO Bill Kerr visited Ennadai Lake accompanied by RCMP Sgt. Rothery from Churchill. On this trip, Sgt. Rothery brought rifles, tea, tobacco, and other goods for the Inuit as payment in kind for the fox furs that they had sent out with him earlier in the year. Contrary to Baldwin's assertion nine months earlier (that the Inuit were an unwanted burden on the station's personnel), Kerr found that the new staff were happy to provide support. He noted that the radio station OIC (Taylor) had allotted each of the Inuit men space in one of his outbuildings, and that each man had deposited possessions there. Taylor had adopted the custom of inviting the Inuit, who were scattered within a five-mile radius of the lake, to visit the station each Saturday and to take from his stock sufficient provisions for the families for the following week. Imported buffalo meat, kept in cold storage, had been issued to the Inuit when caribou had not been available. Kerr (1955) reported that "the natives were in apparently good health and their dogs were tied up and in excellent condition."

Kerr told the Ahiarmiut of the uncertainty of supplies being brought to them by government plane in the future and said the government would help them move and see that they were properly settled. Kerr discussed his relocation plan with Taylor and Rothery, and Taylor felt "the Natives would be discontented if moved to Padlei and would invariably drift back in a short time." Taylor asked the Inuit if they would like to move, "but they were unanimous in declaring that they did not want to leave Ennadai Lake which had always been their country." Larsen (1955c) duly informed Cunningham that, in view of the Ahiarmiut's response, they should be allowed to remain at Ennadai Lake; using force or trying to pressure them to make the move was out of the question he said.

Contrary to statements made by Cunningham and Sivertz that the Ahiarmiut were a people looking for handouts, Kerr noted that they "ask for nothing that they themselves can not pay for." Kerr (1955) concluded his review of the situation at Ennadai by stating: "I cannot help but admire these Eskimo who want to live their own mode of life and are confident of surviving on their own hunting ability rather than on Relief Rations. The Police, the present staff of the Ennadai Radio Station and myself all think they should be encouraged to continue as they are."

Before and After *Life*

Geert van den Steenhoven arrived in August 1955 to live with the Ahiarmiut for six weeks; he was soon joined by a journalist and photographer from *Life* magazine. Because there had been so much public interest in *People of the Deer*, the Ahiarmiut had been selected by the magazine as the subjects of a lengthy picture article. They were chosen as the most representative of "primitive" Canadian Eskimos. The cover of the 27 February 1956 issue of *Life* featured a tender picture of Anowtelik and his wife and newborn son (Anowtelik has been described at length by Harper,

1964: 17–26). The picture and the accompanying article presented the Ahiarmiut as a people bound to ancient traditions, hunters at harmony with their environment, living on the fringe of Western civilization in a bountiful Arctic Eden. Although they had inherited the "noble savage" mantle from *Nanook of the North*, there was no doubting this publication's contemporary wrapping. The cover ironically juxtaposes the headlines "Stone Age Survivors" and the latest "Long-Range Missiles in Color"— two readily identifiable symbols of the 1950s Arctic milieu.

The popular magazine's iconographic representation of the Ahiarmiut as the archetypal Caribou Inuit was significant for several reasons. Although the inland Keewatin Inuit were first mentioned in the anthropological literature in 1888 by Franz Boas, it was not until members of the Fifth Thule Expedition encountered them in 1922 that Birket-Smith (1929a) and Rasmussen (1930) gave them the name "Caribou Eskimos." Birket-Smith (1929b) speculated that these people were the original Eskimos, building on earlier hypotheses about the origin of the Inuit in the interior of North America, more specifically, the interior of the area west of Hudson Bay (Rink, 1875; Boas, 1888b; Hatt, 1916; Steensby, 1917). At the time of the *Life* article, the White perception was still largely determined by the mythical notion that the Caribou Inuit were "the sole survivors of the original stage of Eskimo development" (Arima, 1984: 458). This view had already been disputed (Mathiassen, 1930), and later research was still contradictory about the origins of the Caribou Inuit (Harp, 1962; Taylor, 1965; Burch, 1978 and 1986).

In the summer of 1955, everyone who visited the Ahiarmiut reported on their fine and healthy condition. By the time the *Life* article was published the following year, however, external perceptions of the Ahiarmiut had changed dramatically. Steenhoven recorded that caribou were plentiful during his stay in August and September, however the large herds of caribou failed to appear in the vicinity of Ennadai on the annual migration. Whereas the Inuit would previously have gone further afield to hunt the caribou, they now lived in closer proximity to the station, in part at the request of the OIC. This sedentism had the effect of limiting the range of their hunting activities. That autumn, the herds appear to have followed a somewhat different migration course, passing some distance from Ennadai. Official reports of the fall caribou hunt varied from "good" to "just short of a failure" (Kerr, 1956). A report dated 31 January 1956 stated that the situation at Ennadai Lake was normal and the Inuit were in good health (Sivertz, 1959e); however, the Inuit were able to cache only enough meat to last them to the end of January 1956.

By February 1956, circumstances had deteriorated considerably. Meat supplies had been exhausted, and the Ahiarmiut had lost seventy of their seventy-five dogs due to starvation (Kerr, 1956). The loss of dogs meant that the Inuit were not able to get to their trap lines easily, and they were man-hauling sleds from a site five kilometers away to gather wood for fuel (Richards, 1956a). An RCMP officer from Churchill visited Ennadai Lake in February to bring the Inuit supplies. He thought that they "depended far too much on handouts from DOT personnel" and that the new OIC allowed the Inuit "too much freedom" (Rothery, 1956). After reviewing the situation, NSO Kerr mentioned that the Inuit had become "shiftless," and he felt it was imperative that a competent person be employed to supervise and direct their activities (Richards, 1956a).

Once again the idea of relocating the Inuit away from the station was revived. Kerr (1956) noted that Henry Voisey, the HBC trader at Padlei, wished to have the Ahiarmiut moved to Padlei and had picked out a district some eighty kilometers from his post. Voisey, who had spent the past fourteen years at Padlei, stated that he had never seen a game failure in that region, that caribou were obtainable, and that there was good trapping. On the basis of this information and Kerr's own eyewitness account of the Ahiarmiut's situation at Ennadai that winter, Kerr informed his division chief of his conclusions:

After speaking with Mr. Voisey, I am inclined to believe a move to Padlei district is the only solution for the Ennadai Eskimo problem. I had previously been inclined to leave them where they were, as they appeared self-sufficient but I have changed my mind after seeing them this year and realized the extent of their indolence.

Richards (1956a) concurred with Kerr's view, stating that "there is uniform agreement that these natives should be moved to a location where wildlife is more abundant and they must be given proper supervision to encourage them to become reestablished elsewhere." The RCMP constable at Eskimo Point who had jurisdiction over the Padlei area, Bill Gallagher, was apparently in agreement with the relocation plan. In December 1955 he stated in a report that the Padlei area was abundant in game and in his opinion was slightly underpopulated in relation to available resources.

Because of the prolonged interagency discussions about the move and the unavailability of a police plane to transport the Ahiarmiut to the Padlei area, it was decided that it was too late in the season to carry out the relocation (Nicholas, 1956). The project was therefore abandoned until the following year. That autumn, the caribou migration was again assessed by officials as insufficient to provide enough meat for the Ahiarmiut to live on (Sivertz, 1959e). Because the Ahiarmiut now had few dogs, their range of hunting and trapping was limited. When Kerr and

RCMP Sgt. Nicholas flew to Ennadai with supplies in February 1957. Nicholas (1957) deplored the fact that the Inuit were "hanging around the D.O.T. Station in an attempt to beg for food or scrounge anything worthwhile." The circumstances at Ennadai, though, were not as dire as the officials thought. Nicholas noted that the family allowance credits had not been used during the last year because there had been sufficient fur credits to enable Kerr to purchase supplies. The foodstuffs distributed to the Inuit in February thus were not a form of relief but were goods purchased from the proceeds of Inuit trapping.

The Department was eager to proceed with plans for the relocation to avoid situations similar to those that hampered the operation the previous year (Sivertz, 1956b). Kerr and the RCMP officers in Churchill decided to bring forward the proposed relocation date to May, and Robertson (1957) notified Commissioner Nicholson of the change in schedule. The Hudson's Bay Company had already supplied their Padlei post in 1956 with additional trade goods to provide for the expected Ahiarmiut (Sivertz, 1956b). The 1957 relocation seemed inevitable, yet there were warning signs that a move to Padlei at this time might be a mistake.

Relocation from Ennadai Lake to Henik Lake

Cpl. Gallagher (1957a) at the Eskimo Point RCMP detachment reported a steady decline since the early autumn of 1956 in the economic conditions of the Inuit living in the E1 district. He stated that the economic conditions in the Eskimo Point and Padlei areas were the worst they had been for some years. Further epidemics and a change in caribou migration paths were to blame for the situation. Curiously, Gallagher still maintained that the district could support a larger population. Supt. Larsen, however, dismissed Gallagher's opinion and informed the Department that he did not agree with it, citing the large amounts of relief being disbursed to the Inuit in that area. Larsen (1957) argued that "if other Eskimos were moved to the area there would be a heavy drain on country resources, which would cause the present economic conditions of the Eskimos in the areas mentioned to deteriorate." The Department nevertheless pressed on with their plans for relocation of the Ahiarmiut.

In February 1957, Robertson (1957) wrote to Commissioner Nicholson about Kerr's request that the Inuit be moved in May and asked him to confirm RCMP cooperation. Nicholson (1957b) agreed that he had instructed his officers commanding "G" and "Air" Divisions to provide the cooperation necessary to facilitate the relocation. On 9 May 1957, NSO Bill Kerr, Cst. Mascotto from Eskimo Point detachment, HBC

Padlei trader Henry Voisey, and Department field officer Lewis Voisey (a cousin) arrived by plane at Oftedal Lake (thirteen kilometers southwest of North Henik Lake), where they had selected a new campsite for the Ahiarmiut. Tents and supplies were purchased from the Padlei post with Inuit family allowance credits. Kerr and Lewis Voisey, acting as interpreter, flew to Ennadai Lake, and the following day, in bad weather, the RCMP plane made four flights to transport the Ahiarmiut families to the site at Oftedal Lake. A total of fifty-nine Inuit and their six dogs were moved. Unfortunately, there was not enough space in the plane for the Inuit canoes, which they depended upon for hunting caribou (Mascotto, 1957).

On 24 May 1957, the Department's Information Division issued a press release about the Ennadai move entitled "Eskimos Fly to New Hunting Grounds." The document announced: "A community of some of Canada's most primitive citizens has moved—but they did it the modern way. Eskimo hunters and huskies left their ancient ways for a day to travel in the comfort of an aircraft to new hunting grounds" (Canada, 1957b).

Referring to the relocatees as "settlers," the press release uncharacteristically named the individual in charge of the operation. It stated that, with the cooperation of the RCMP and the Hudson's Bay Company, the move was made under the supervision of Northern Service Officer Bill Kerr. Furthermore, the press release established the connection between the relocation of the Ahiarmiut and the paradigmatic High Arctic experiment, discussed in chapters 3 and 4:

This is not the first time that Eskimo hunters and their families have volunteered to leave their homes because game was scarce. For the same reason, Eskimos from the east coast of Hudson Bay were moved to Cornwallis and Ellesmere Islands in 1953. If the success of these earlier settlers is any guide, the Ennadai Eskimos can hope to find relative prosperity in their new surroundings. (ibid.)

This linkage between the two relocations was made for a reason. The Department wanted to describe the relocations publicly as consensual projects and to portray the Inuit as "volunteers" who moved because game was scarce in their home district. No mention was made publicly of the other aims that featured in internal reports, such as "rehabilitating" the Inuit from "loitering" around settlements (Gallagher, 1957b). The Department wanted to give the impression that the move was essentially self-motivated, as discussed in chapter 8, and that officials were merely providing the technical assistance, in the form of a plane, to support the Inuit in their endeavor.

Difficulties Develop at Henik Lake

Shortly after the relocation of the Ahiarmiut, reports of trouble began to circulate. One of the two camp leaders, Pongalak (see fig. 5.4), died, aged fifty-seven, of suspected malnutrition. Pongalak died within a month of relocation, an event that echoes the death of the camp boss Aqiatusuk eight months after he was moved to Grise Fiord. In each case, the death of a headman of the group not long after resettlement contributed to an uneasiness about the new location and a wish to leave.

In June 1958, the Ahiarmiut were reported to have broken into a storehouse at the Sherritt Gordon Mining Camp at Bray Lake, thirteen kilometers from their campsite. The theft was reported to the RCMP Eskimo Point detachment by the geologist in charge of the mining camp, who apparently felt that the Inuit "had become a nuisance by hanging around the prospector's camp" (Sivertz, 1959c). Police reports cited theft and general vandalism of the premises, which were unoccupied at the time. Officials could find no explanation for the vandalism, though Steenhoven (1962: 74–75) has suggested that the destruction of another person's cache can be an act of vengeance. If the Inuit did vandalize the cache, which they have denied (Ahiarmiut informants, personal communication), it could have come from frustration about their resettlement.

The police flew in to Henik Lake on 2 August and arrested Iootna (twenty-one years old), who came from the Padlei area. Five days later, they arrested two Ahiarmiut hunters, Mounik (twenty-three years old) and Oohootok (thirty-seven years old). The three were flown back to Eskimo Point to await trial on charges of breaking the "White man's laws" (*Qallunaat piqujangit*), namely, "breaking, entering and theft." The police reported that, although the three who were seized

> were the ring leaders and broke into the camp in the first instance, all the Eskimos at Oftedal Lake were connected with the offence and to prosecute all the offenders would have necessitated moving the entire colony at Oftedal Lake to Eskimo Point to adequately care for the dependents of the offenders and prevent undue hardship. This was the reason why only the ring leaders were prosecuted as it was necessary to make these people aware of their wrong doing in a hope that it would be a deterrent to further occurrences of this nature. (Larsen, 1959: 5)

The RCMP responded to the break-in by selecting three men to incarcerate as a warning to the other Inuit. As punishment for breaking into the mine shed to obtain sufficient food supplies for the group, the three men were held at the Eskimo Point detachment. In September 1957, while the men were waiting for the Territorial Court to arrive, Cpl. Gallagher ordered them to break rocks. Perhaps Gallagher felt that this form of penal activity would be therapeutic for the offenders (Allen,

1981: 46), but in the absence of effective supervision, there was an accident. Oohootok was injured when a rock splinter entered his eye, blinding him permanently.

On 20 September, a trial was held at Eskimo Point, presided over by the judge of the Northwest Territories, Justice Sissons. Through the defense counsel, who had been appointed by the state, the men pleaded not guilty. The act of breaking the lock on the door was a breach in social relations with the Whites, however obscure the significance of this deed may have been to the hungry Inuit (Brody, 1975: 28). In Western culture, the lock represents a defined private space, and shared ideas about private property and authority are not to be violated (a rule is a rule only if everyone abides by it). From discussions I had with the Ahiarmiut about the incident, I received the impression that they considered the lock an insignificant impediment to obtaining from the shack the provisions they needed. To them, the lock was just part of the door, something that kept animals out (Ahiarmiut informants, personal communication). Nootaraloo (wife of Owlijoot) informed me that she told her eldest son Mounik to get the food from the shack because the children were starving. This view and the three men's lack of guilt according to the rules of their own society are further explained by a passage from Birket-Smith's study of the Caribou Inuit: "During a famine all right of possession to food is abandoned; all hunting spoils are common property and anyone who is hungry may simply take from another family's meat cache what he needs without thus making himself a thief" (Birket-Smith, 1929a: 263).

For the Whites, however, the crossing of the threshold to obtain food was rendered illegal by the presence of the lock. The three Inuit were thus found guilty of breaking, entering, and theft under section 292 (1)(b) of the Criminal Code. Mounik and Iootna were sentenced to two months in police custody at Eskimo Point, and Oohootok was sentenced to time already served (RCMP, 1957). Due to his eye injury, he was not returned to Henik Lake but was hospitalized in Churchill and then brought to Eskimo Point.

The effect of removing three of the hunters from the group just three months after their relocation was profound (Csonka, 1993) and demonstrates how an injurious situation can develop from the imposition of a foreign code of rules (Rasmussen, 1931: 21). Disciplinary punishment is intended to be "corrective," but as a result of the hunters' incarceration the whole group suffered punishment (Foucault, 1977: 179). Not only were there fewer men to trap and hunt but the absence of those three further undermined the social stability of the group. Because the three hunters were removed at the beginning of August and two of them were held until 20 November and the third man indefinitely, these men were not able to assist the other hunters of the band during the crucial autumn caribou migration. Their absence placed a greater burden on Owlijoot and the other men who had to provide food for Mounik's wife Ookanak (see fig. 5.1) and her young son, and for Oohootok's wife and two children. In their report, the officers admitted that:

It did appear that a food shortage among the Oftedal Lake Eskimos was the main reason for the B.E. & thefts, however, if this was so, it would indicate a gross mismanagement of food on the part of the Eskimos, as they had all received an adequate relief and family allowance issue on approximately May 15th, 1957, at the time of their transfer from Ennadai Lake to Oftedal Lake. (Larsen, 1959: 5)

The officials were critical of the Inuit for not adhering to the plan organized for their subsistence activities; but the Western concept of formalized planning is at odds with the flexibility and sensitivity necessary for hunting and foraging (Brody, 1981: 37). The plan also designated Lewis Voisey (twenty-three years old), who worked as a technical officer for the Department, to live with the Ahiarmiut and help them cache fish for the winter, but after just a month he was called away by officials on 21 September 1957 to work on a wolf-control program. Voisey made his living as a trapper, hunter, and interpreter. Doug Wilkinson, the director of the film *Land of the Long Day* (discussed in chapter 1), was now working as an NSO for the Department and was based at Baker Lake in the Keewatin District. On 25 September he advised the Department that, until the time of Voisey's departure, the Ahiarmiut had made no large kills of caribou and no winter caribou caches had been put up. He reported that Voisey had not been too hopeful about the adequacy of the future food supply for the group. Wilkinson (1957) ended his report with the prophetic warning: "I would venture the prediction that they will not be able to get through the winter without assistance."

In November 1957, Henry Voisey at Padlei reported to the RCMP that a further break-in had occurred at the mining camp. Apparently the deterrent arrest of Mounik, Iootna, and Oohootok had not stopped the others from trying to obtain food. Cpl. Gallagher (1957b) informed Supt. Larsen that the Ahiarmiut had to be kept under very close and strict supervision, which he said was quite difficult because of the location of the Inuit camp. In response to the reports of trouble, Insp. Fitzsimmons (1957) of the Criminal Investigation Branch suggested to Commissioner Nicholson that the Ahiarmiut had not adjusted to their new circumstances since their move from Ennadai Lake.

The Henik Lake site had been selected because Department officials insisted that this location would enable "closer observation" of the Inuit by Company and government personnel, who could deal more cheaply here with any emergency situation that might arise (Richards, 1956a). Yet Cpl. Gallagher (1957b) pointed out in his December 1957 report that he had been unable to provide sufficient support or to patrol Henik Lake because of its geographical isolation. Gallagher hoped such a patrol could be carried out in February 1958. After obtaining the agreement of Bill Kerr, Gallagher therefore proposed that the Ahiarmiut be relocated again, this time to Tavani, 145 kilometers up the coast from Eskimo Point. Gallagher suggested that Tavani was a better location because there were few vacant buildings, "thereby removing the temptation to commit theft." Commissioner Nicholson (1957a) wrote to Deputy Minister Robertson on 19 December 1957 that the Ahiarmiut have "been unable to adjust themselves to their new location." Nicholson stated that the group required constant supervision, and he recommended that they be moved to Tavani.

Relocation Aftermath, Henik Lake, 1958

For the previous six years, Department and RCMP officials, together with representatives of the Hudson's Bay Company, had discussed the virtues of relocating the Ahiarmiut to Henik Lake; yet after just six months, officials acknowledged that there was every indication that this relocation had been a mistake and that the Inuit should be moved again. On 7 January 1958, Cst. Laliberte (1958) at Eskimo Point reported that, on a patrol to Henik and Oftedal Lakes, he found the Inuit living in two large camps with smaller ones spread out along the rivers and lakes. The larger camp of thirty people was situated beside a river that was frozen to the bottom and therefore void of fish. When the officer asked about their fishing equipment, the reply was that their nets were torn and no longer fit to use. Their clothing was poor due to lack of caribou skins. Caribou had been scarce, but some fox had been caught. Food resources were not sufficient to support more than the six dogs they still had. Cst. Laliberte advised his superiors that "considerable thought should be given to this band of Eskimos."

The Ahiarmiut at Henik Lake were not alone in the difficulties they faced. Laliberte noted that the health and welfare of the Inuit in the E1 district had deteriorated over the last year (ibid.). Morale was low, health was below standard as a result of epidemics, trapping was poor, and many of the dogs had died of starvation because of a lack of caribou meat. The complete failure of caribou in this area for two years in a row meant that many Inuit were going hungry and were unable to clothe themselves adequately. Officials resorted to criticizing the Ahiarmiut and other Inuit in the district. Cpl. Gallagher (1958a) felt that the Caribou Inuit appeared to have no initiative in obtaining sufficient fish, ptarmigan, or seal. He thought they regarded caribou as their only suitable food, and other foods were "below their dignity." Gallagher assumed the Inuit "would rather sit and starve" while awaiting the return of the caribou.

Graham Rowley, secretary of the Department's Advisory Committee on Northern Development (ACND), sensed that the situation was becoming serious for the Ahiarmiut. Rowley reported directly to Deputy Minister Robertson, who asked Rowley for his views on the matter. In a confidential memo to Robertson on 29 January 1958, Rowley (1958b) expressed his reservations about the relocation and its consequences: "I am concerned that this group, which is now much further away from help than before, may get into serious difficulties early this spring, possibly while trying to return to Ennadai. You might like to suggest to Mr. Sivertz that a particularly close tab should be kept on them."

Rowley's point about the group's isolation was to prove vital in the coming weeks. At Ennadai Lake, the Ahiarmiut lived near the radio station, which had hourly contact with Churchill, whereas at Henik Lake they were three to five days' travel from the Padlei post. The relocation's object of establishing a "disciplinary space" between the Ahiarmiut and White assistance was now revealed as defective (Foucault, 1977: 143). Furthermore, Rowley told Robertson: "The recent move seems to have been from one depressed area to another. It was, however, from an area they liked to one of which they had unhappy memories, and one which they themselves believed to be less rich. It had therefore little or no chance to succeed" (Rowley, 1958c).

Drawing upon the study of the Ahiarmiut Steenhoven had prepared for the Department in 1955, Rowley noted that they liked the Ennadai region and did not want to leave it. It therefore appeared unlikely that the move was really accepted by them. He informed Robertson that it was comparatively easy to get a temporary acquiescence from the Inuit to any suggestion put to them, "and especially from this group who go to great lengths to avoid any form of conflict" (conflict avoidance was characteristic of Inuit relations with Whites; see, e.g., Brody, 1975: 152–53). Yet Phillips (1958a) opposed Rowley's solution for the group, and on 15 January he told Sivertz:

I cannot agree with this solution. Our entire policy of Arctic development must rest upon sound economic foundations. I think that it would be folly to encourage people to move to an area where we know that there is not a solid economic basis for their future lives. . . . We are not yet in a position to make any recommendations but unless you direct otherwise, we shall confine the possibilities to areas where we think that the people have a reasonable chance of making a future for themselves on the basis of adequate resources or other forms of income.

FIGURE 5.5 Angnukoak (Ungmak), Shikoak (Hickewa), and Ootuk next to the radio station, Ennadai Lake, 1955. Credit: Geert van den Steenhoven

Four weeks after this letter and in the midst of winter, with officials in Ottawa unsure of what course to take, tragic news reached the HBC post at Padlei. On 12 February the post trader, Henry Voisey, sent a radiogram to the RCMP detachment at Eskimo Point to report the murders of two Inuit at Henik Lake and the deaths of others in the area. On 14–16 February, the surviving Ahiarmiut were evacuated by RCMP plane to Eskimo Point under the supervision of NSO Kerr. Faced with a deteriorating situation, Deputy Minister Gordon Robertson finally responded on 18 February 1958 to the letter Nicholson had written two months earlier informing him of the hardships facing the Ahiarmiut at Henik Lake. Robertson (1958a) assured Nicholson: "Something must be done, but as yet we have not been able to reach a firm conclusion on the best course to follow."

The authorities soon discovered that seven of the Ahiarmiut had died within the space of a week (Sivertz, 1959b). On 7 February near Henik Lake, E1-627 Igyaka (a four-year-old girl) died of malnutrition; the following day, E1-471 Hallow (a forty-four-year-old man) was shot and killed, and E1-467 Ootuk (a forty-two-year-old man) was stabbed and killed (see fig. 5.5). On 10 February, E1-462 Angatayok (a fourteen-year-old boy) and E1-462 Kiyai (a twenty-four-year-old man) died of ex-

posure in a blizzard en route from Henik Lake to Padlei (see fig. 5.4).
On 11 February, E1-451 Ungmak (a forty-year-old man) died of exposure
and exhaustion en route to Padlei (see fig. 5.5), and on 16 February,
E1-614 Nesha (a four-year-old girl) died of exposure en route to Padlei.
A relocation begun as an "experiment" had ended in tragedy, but the
Ahiarmiut were not the only Caribou Inuit to perish that winter. Officials were alarmed to learn that nineteen Inuit had starved to death at
Garry Lake, and six more at Chantrey Lake. The Keewatin deaths produced two quick responses from the government: a decision to evacuate
the Caribou Inuit into settlements to prevent further starvation; and a
series of Department, police, and judicial investigations that resulted in
the murder trial of *Regina vs Kikkik*, which is discussed in chapter 6.

· 6 ·

RELOCATION ON TRIAL

A Postmortem on the Ahiarmiut Relocation

The bodies of the Ahiarmiut who had died of starvation and exposure were recovered by the RCMP and brought to Eskimo Point. Two weeks later, several of the corpses were flown down to the University of Alberta Hospital morgue in Edmonton, where a postmortem examination was carried out at the request of the Crown prosecutor of the Northwest Territories. The autopsy reports provide a detailed scientific analysis of the state of the corpses and the probable causes of death. The doctor examined the body of the four-year-old girl, Nesha, and recorded the weight of her heart as thirty grams, noting that it was "cone-shaped" and that the "outer covering is smooth and glistening" (Stirrat, 1958). He recorded that her left kidney weighed fifty grams, and the right kidney, forty grams. Each organ was removed and weighed, and its color and content were described. The doctor surmised that, in the absence of any evidence of active disease or injury, the probable immediate cause of death in this case was exposure to cold. He also noted that the child had not eaten for a considerable time.

There was a clinical preciseness about the autopsy report: the doctor was able scientifically to decipher a medical "truth" about the state of the bodies. When the Department sent an investigation team to Eskimo Point to establish what caused the deaths, their attempts to uncover the truth were much more difficult and open to interpretation. The RCMP also conducted investigations into the deaths and their connection with the relocation. What "truths" did these investigators uncover? Where did the responsibility for the deaths lie? As a result of three of the deaths, a murder trial was held in Rankin Inlet. The six-member jury, the lawyers, and the judge listened to the testimony of the Inuit, the RCMP officers, and others. The trial was the culmination of the Ahiarmiut's relocation from Ennadai Lake.

After the tragic outcome of the government's relocation of the Ahiarmiut, there were no further relocation experiments that moved Inuit to wilderness sites (Diubaldo, 1989: 176). This chapter analyzes the different assumptions and conclusions in this case: those reached by the doctor, the government investigators, senior officials, the police, the judge, and the jury. These recorded opinions will be compared with information found in newly released documents on the case together with interviews with the Ahiarmiut survivors and most of the principal Whites involved to obtain a more complete autopsy of the factors that led to the deaths and the contributory importance of the relocation.

The Slayings and Kikkik's Statement

In February 1958, Ootuk, his wife Howmik, and their three children were camped in an igloo at North Henik Lake. Ootuk was an *angatkuq* (shaman) who had been taught his craft by Pongalak, the other Ahiarmiut shaman, who died in May 1957 shortly after the group's relocation to Henik Lake. Ootuk and his family were camped about twenty-six meters from Hallow's igloo, where Hallow lived with his wife Kikkik and their five children. Hallow was considered one of the best Ahiarmiut hunters. The families were related: Ootuk's wife, Howmik, was Hallow's sister. During the winter, the two families were living separately from the other Ahiarmiut, who had spread out and were living in three or four camps of several families each. According to Kikkik, no other Inuit were camped near them all autumn and winter (Canada, 1958a: 4–5). Yahah, Hallow's brother, was camped closest to them, about eleven kilometers away (Canada, 1958b: 47). On 8 February, Ootuk killed Hallow, and then Ootuk was killed by Kikkik. Why would these killings occur when the families had kinship ties and had depended on each other for survival? After the slayings, Kikkik left the camp with her five children in an attempt to reach the HBC post at Padlei. After seven days on the trail to Padlei, Kikkik left two of her children, of whom one (Nesha) died and the other (Annacatha) was later rescued by the police. Were the deaths of Ootuk, Hallow, and Nesha connected with the group's relocation to North Henik Lake?

When Kikkik and her children were rescued by the police, they were without food, and according to Cpl. Gallagher, Kikkik was relieved to

FIGURE 6.1 Cst. Bill Gallagher, Eskimo Point, 1957. Credit: Geert van den Steenhoven

have been found (ibid.: 48). Kikkik and her children were evacuated by police plane to Eskimo Point on 16 February. On 20–21 February, Cpl. Gallagher (fig. 6.1, nicknamed *qautuuq*, "big forehead"), who was officer in charge of the Eskimo Point detachment, formally questioned Kikkik about the circumstances of the deaths. The interview, which took place in the kitchen of the RCMP detachment at Eskimo Point, was conducted in Inuktitut, the Inuk S/Cst. Jimmy Gibbons acting as interpreter. Each day's questioning lasted about six hours, and during the questioning only Gallagher and Gibbons were present.

At the trial, Gallagher was questioned under oath by Justice Sissons about the taking of Kikkik's statement. Gallagher swore that no inducement or threats were used and that Kikkik had made a voluntary statement. Before questioning Kikkik, Gallagher said that he gave her the customary police warning: "You need not say anything. You have nothing to hope from any promise, whether or not you say anything, and nothing to fear from any threat, but anything you do say may be used as evidence at your trial" (ibid.: 26). The warning was translated for her by Gibbons. NSO Bill Kerr also swore under oath at the trial that he had overheard the warning given and that Kikkik had agreed to make a voluntary statement. According to Gallagher, when she gave her statement,

Kikkik "showed little, if any, emotion. She seemed to be very rational; in fact, I would go so far as to say the accused seemed quite content. . . . I used the expression 'content' because I think she was thankful about having been located [picked up by the police]. She did not seem to be upset or nervous or irrational." The following excerpts are from Kikkik's statement (Gallagher, 1958b: 1):

Q. Since your marriage to Hallow had he and Ootuk camped together?
A. Not all the time but lots of times.
Q. Had you at any time known of trouble between Hallow and Ootuk?
A. No; I never knew of any trouble . . .
Q. What were the relationships and conditions between your and Ootuk's family? Just prior to Hallow's death?
A. Good.
Q. Will you tell me everything that happened on the day your husband died, to the smallest detail?
A. Yes: Early in the morning Hallow got up and we had no food, he went jigging and caught two fish, he returned to the igloo and started to eat. Just before Hallow started to eat Ootuk came to visit us and ate with us. While eating Ootuk and Hallow discussed going for Family Allowance to Padlei, they did not talk anymore and Hallow left to go jigging. Ootuk stayed in the igloo. Ootuk said that he would like to gather up the caribou hide as it would be good to eat. I said that I have no more caribou hide. Ootuk tried to eat a small piece of caribou hide which were scraps from the boots I was sewing.

When Ootuk finished eating the hide he said "I would like to look for ptarmigan" and Ootuk went out. I told my daughter Ailoyoak, "you go out and see where Ootuk went." I asked her this because it was a very stormy day and I knew it was no good to hunt ptarmigan and I wanted to know which way he went. My daughter Ailoyoak went out and came back right away and Ailoyoak said that Ootuk is walking downwind towards the edge of the lake.

Ootuk went to the lake, where he found Hallow jigging for fish. He shot Hallow in the back of the head and then went back to Kikkik's igloo, where he tried to shoot her. The bullet missed her; Kikkik managed to overpower Ootuk and killed him with a knife. Kikkik then went to the lake with her daughter Ailoyoak and brought Hallow's body back to the igloo. It was then dark, and the family went to sleep. Kikkik informed Cpl. Gallagher:

When I woke up in the morning I awakened all of my family and told them to get ready to go. I was afraid my children would starve as we had no food and I wanted to move to a better fishing lake. As soon as the children were up we made tea and started to break camp. I took the tent roof off of the igloo and I cut the tent in half and placed one-half on my husband's body and placed the other half on the sled. (ibid.: 3)

Kikkik had no dogs, so she placed the two younger children on the sled and pulled it herself, carrying her baby on her back. The two older children walked. After six days' traveling, Kikkik told the police that Nesha and Annacatha died during the night and that she had buried them "on the skin bed and put one skin blanket over them. I had no rocks so I covered them with snow and small trees and a tent pole." At this point, Kikkik was told that it would be better to tell the truth about her children, whom she had abandoned. The following questions were asked:

Q.   Were Nesha and Annacatha alive when buried?

A.   Yes, both of them.

Q.   Why did you bury them alive?

A.   They could not walk, I had dragged them a long way, they were heavy.

Q.   Why was it that when you were found that same afternoon that you did not tell the police about Annacatha and Nesha as there was still every possibility that they could have been saved?

A.   I was afraid to say.

The questioning came to an end. According to Cpl. Gallagher, after Kikkik made the statement it was read back to her, and she signed it with a cross. Kikkik had made no attempt to disguise the circumstances that led her to kill Ootuk, and there was no hesitation in her description of Ootuk's death (Canada, 1958b: 50).

On the same day, 20 February, at Eskimo Point, NSO Bill Kerr served as coroner at the inquest into the death of Hallow. At the inquest, Kikkik was questioned by Kerr, and she replied that when Ootuk came to their igloo he wanted Hallow to go with him to the Padlei post, but Hallow said it was too stormy. Hallow then left the igloo to go jigging for fish in the lake, and that was the last time she saw her husband alive (Canada, 1958a: 2). Yahah (Anayoenak) testified at the inquest that, in the early afternoon of 9 February, Kikkik arrived at his camp. She told him that Ootuk had shot Hallow and that she had stabbed Ootuk. Yahah said: "She did not say why Ootuk had shot Hallow. I do not know why Ootuk and Hallow should be mad at each other. Kikkik cried when she told me the story. Everyone slept at my camp that night and the next day we all left and camped nearer Padlei Post that evening" (ibid.: 5). Ailoyoak, aged twelve, Kikkik's eldest daughter, was also asked to testify at the inquest. She described the moment when her mother told her to go and look for her father at the jigging hole:

I went to the jigging hole and found my father with his hands and feet in the water. There was a lot of blood and I knew that Hallow my father was dead. I did not touch him. I ran back to where my mother Kikkik was holding Ootuk on the snow. I was crying and I told my mother Kikkik that my father was dead. My mother told Ootuk "You have killed my husband." . . . (ibid.: 7)

The Preliminary Hearing

Kikkik was told by officials that she had broken the White man's laws, *Qallunaat piqujangit*. The preliminary hearing of the criminal charges against Kikkik was held on 28 February at Eskimo Point before Justice of the Peace Doug Wilkinson (the filmmaker of *Land of the Long Day* and now a Department official). The Crown prosecutor was John Parker from Yellowknife (not to be confused with another John Parker who became commissioner of the Northwest Territories in Yellowknife). Kikkik was not represented by counsel, though NSO Bill Kerr was present "in an advisory capacity to the accused" (Canada, 1958b). Inuk S/Cst. Jimmy Gibbons was sworn in as the court interpreter. The first charge was unlawfully causing the death of her four-year-old daughter Nesha through criminal negligence, contrary to section 192 of the Criminal Code of Canada. The next charge was killing Ootuk, contrary to section 206 of the Criminal Code. The prosecutor called Cpl. Gallagher, S/Cst. Gibbons, Howmik, Yahah, and Kikkik's daughter Ailoyoak and son Karlak as witnesses for the Crown. After each witness had been questioned by the prosecutor, Kikkik was asked if she wanted to cross-examine; for the record it was noted that each time she declined.

At the preliminary hearing, the court heard that, on the evening of 13 February 1957, Corporal Gallagher at Eskimo Point received a radiogram about the deaths from Henry Voisey, the Company trader at Padlei. Gallagher immediately requested an RCMP aircraft from Churchill. The plane arrived on the morning of 14 February, and the two RCMP pilots (Staff-Sgt. Haemlin and Sgt. Ross of the Air Division), Cst. Laliberte of Eskimo Point detachment, Cpl. Gallagher, and S/Cst. Gibbons flew to Padlei. There they picked up Voisey and proceeded to North Henik Lake, where they discovered the body of Ootuk, covered by snow, and that of Hallow in one of the abandoned igloos. In the other igloo, they found Howmik and her two older daughters, plus the dead younger daughter. Howmik did not know the whereabouts of her husband and was told that he was dead. They all returned to Eskimo Point. Two days later, on 16 February, a search party of four Inuit was dispatched by the police on foot to follow the trail made by Yahah to Henik Lake in order to locate Kikkik and her children.

At the same time, a police plane piloted by Sgt. Ross and Cpl. Carter, and with Cpl. Gallagher, Cst. Laliberte, S/Cst. Gibbons, Henry Voisey, and NSO Kerr on board, conducted an aerial search between Padlei and Henik Lake. In the afternoon the plane spotted Kikkik and her family at an abandoned cabin approximately thirty kilometers from Padlei. When the police found Kikkik, she had only one deerskin blanket, one trade-type "Indian" blanket, a frying pan, and one or two tea mugs and spoons. She had no food (ibid.: 50). When asked where her other two children, Annacatha and Nesha, were, Kikkik told the officers that they had died that morning and that she had buried them. She and her other three children—Ailoyoak, Karlak, and Nokahhak—were airlifted to Eskimo Point. Cst. Laliberte and S/Cst. Gibbons used the HBC dog team from Padlei to re-trace Kikkik's trail and locate the missing children. The following day, on 17 February, at 5:20 P.M., Laliberte's party found Anna-catha and Nesha. The ground was covered with snow, and the temperatures were between −28° and −42°F (ibid.: 14). Kikkik was held in police custody at Eskimo Point for the next two months, awaiting trial.

Crisis Management of the Ahiarmiut Deaths

The Department responded to the emergency by dispatching two of its senior officers, Alex Stevenson, chief of the administration section, and Walter Rudnicki, chief of the welfare section, from Ottawa to Eskimo Point to undertake a full investigation into the deaths and the condition of the Ahiarmiut. Their report included recommendations for the survivors' immediate and long-term welfare. Phillips (1958b) instructed Stevenson and Rudnicki to reassure the three field officials who were closely involved in the relocation, NSO Bill Kerr, Cpl. Bill Gallagher, and HBC manager Henry Voisey, that the administration did not doubt the wisdom of the action they took in the circumstances. The investigation was in no way a reflection of lack of confidence in the field staff but only necessary so that the Department could respond to questions that were bound to be asked in public about the case.

Phillips was reacting to his Department's concern about the prime minister's view of the incident. On 21 February, R. A. Faibish, private secretary to the minister of northern affairs, sent a memo to Cunning-ham informing him:

The Prime Minister has received 18 telegrams regarding the outbreak of violence among the Eskimos which has occurred in the Keewatin District and the move of some 45 Eskimos to Eskimo Point from Henik Lake. Reports he has received from military personnel, the Church, two prominent university officials, and other interested parties are contradictory and somewhat disturbing. They generally seem to indicate that the outbreak of violence, discontent, and disease can be attributed to the initial dislocation and relocation and that departmental administrators are at fault insofar as they made decisions based upon inadequate social research. (Faibish, 1958)

Faibish requested that Phillips attend a briefing on the matter, since his name had been linked publicly with the relocation. In preparation, a summary of the events was drafted by Department officials. The original draft typifies the Department's immediate sensitivity about the way others would perceive Inuit compliance with the move. The notes state that before the move the Department conducted a study, and "the result pointed to Henik Lake as the best hunting and living area whence the Eskimos could trade at Padlei. The chief factors in the study were the social implications" (Canada, 1958d). The last sentence was crossed out and replaced with: "Particular care was taken to ensure that it was the true desire of the Eskimos concerned to move." The authors further wrote: "At the end it appeared that the Eskimos understood their deteriorated position at Ennadai and the need for moving to the good game country around Henik Lake." Upon revision, the words "the need for moving" were replaced with "desired to move."

Though Graham Rowley, who reported directly to Deputy Minister Robertson, had voiced his criticisms of the Department's management of the Ahiarmiut relocation to senior officials in December 1957 and January 1958, his concern about their welfare was marginalized at that time. Rowley expressed his frustrations in a personal letter to Geert van den Steenhoven:

I don't even know what I should do myself. In this case I had warned the Deputy Minister in writing that he could expect further trouble this winter when I got the report on the thefts, which was of course before the killings took place. The only result so far is that nothing later about this group has been referred to me. (Rowley, 1958a)

Initial reports indicated that Ootuk (see fig. 5.5) shot and killed Hallow, and that Hallow's wife Kikkik stabbed and killed Ootuk, either in self-defense or in revenge. On the previous day, Ootuk's daughter Igyaka had died of starvation (Canada, 1958b: 48). Following the death of her husband on 8 February, Kikkik and her five children abandoned their camp at Henik Lake and began walking towards Padlei. En route she left two of her children, Nesha and Annacatha, alive in a snow shelter.

Kikkik and her other three children were found by the RCMP. When Cst. Laliberte discovered the snow shelter on 17 February with the two girls inside, Annacatha was miraculously still alive, but Nesha had died. It was unknown why the killings had occurred, and officials could also not understand why Kikkik had left two of the children behind. Cpl. Gallagher (1958a) attributed the other deaths to the manner in which the Inuit made their exodus from Henik Lake:

In the course of this general movement towards Padlei three Eskimos died of exposure caused by nothing more nor less than idocy [sic], these people would leave their camps without even taking a tent or suitable sleeping equipment and then start to walk, some pushing small hand sleds towards Padlei, some forty miles distant and become tired, colapse [sic] and die.

At the trial, it later emerged that Cpl. Gallagher, who was the officer in charge of the Eskimo Point detachment, had never met Kikkik, Hallow, Ootuk, or Howmik before Kikkik's evacuation on 16 February (Canada, 1958b: 46). Despite the fact that he was the senior government agent in the area with direct responsibility for the Ahiarmiut, he had not visited Hallow's and Ootuk's camp during the eight months they had lived at Henik Lake (ibid.: 50). Rather than draw attention to this fact or to the causal factors associated with the relocation and the roles of external agencies, Gallagher placed the greater burden for the Ahiarmiut's misfortunes on the Inuit themselves:

The failure of the caribou again was largely responsible for this decline, however the major difficulty was in lack of initiative and of morale among this group, coupled with many of their pagan taboos. This group has long had the "something for nothing" attitude and had long been at the stage where they could not or would not live without continual handouts from the whites. (Gallagher, 1958a)

As I will discuss in this chapter and in chapter 7, the way officials attributed blame for the Ahiarmiut's demise became politically important during the postmortem on the relocation.

The Department's Investigation of the Truth

The Department investigators, Walter Rudnicki and Alex Stevenson (1958), described the fate of the Ahiarmiut survivors. According to their report, the "bout of starvation" left Owlijoot (a forty-six-year-old man) hard of hearing; Pallikal (a twenty-nine-year-old man), who was blind in one eye, was ill; Howmik (thirty-eight years old), who had lost her husband Ootuk and daughter Igyaka, survived although she had been crippled by polio and had no use of her legs or right arm; Howmik's daughter Karlak (thirteen years old), whose hearing and speech were impaired, also survived; Kikkik's daughter Annacatha was recovering in hospital; Agatiyoak (a twenty-three-year-old man) was hospitalized with frozen feet; Alikaswa (twenty-two years old), the wife of Kiyai (fig. 5.4) who died of exposure, had frozen feet and was hospitalized with her son Boonla. Oohootok was also hospitalized and was reported to be almost blind as a result of his accident while breaking rocks.

Rudnicki and Stevenson began their report with an epitaph for the band of Inuit: "The Ahearmiut [sic] as Rasmussen knew them, and more recently Steenhoven, are no more." This reality was what confronted both those who wished to see this culture preserved, remarked the authors, and those who were left with the problem of creating a new life for the survivors (Rudnicki and Stevenson, 1958: 1). Rudnicki also noted that the last of the Ahiarmiut were living in six igloos behind the policeman's house at Eskimo Point and no longer had dogs, sleds, or kayaks. He surmised that, with no more caribou to hunt, they no longer had any aim in life. Their present existence was based on only one awareness, claimed Rudnicki—"that they are now absolutely dependent on the white man."

Gallagher (1958a) reported that the survivors had become completely demoralized because of "the utter failure of this group to rehabilitate themselves at Henik Lake." He requested their evacuation to Eskimo Point, where they could be "kept under surveillance and given guidance." Gallagher's remark reflected the assumption behind the relocation project that it was the group's responsibility to reform themselves but that they had shown that they were not capable of doing so unsupervised (Forsythe, 1987: 1). While making their investigations, Stevenson and Rudnicki discovered a great deal about the background to the relocation and about Inuit reaction to being moved from Ennadai; however, this information was not made public.

Despite Gallagher's comments that the group's difficulties were largely self-inflicted, Rudnicki did not attempt to blame either the Ahiarmiut or the officials directly responsible for their welfare. Indeed, he deflected blame from the Department and seemed to suggest that it was a matter of fate:

The plight of this group cannot be attributed to defects of character or temperament among its members or to oversights among our field representatives. To seek such answers is to obscure the real issues. It is to obscure a basic human problem which stems from a combination of old and new conditions affecting the social and economic life of the Eskimos. (Gallagher, 1958a)

Rudnicki was a university-educated sociologist, and he applied professional research methods to the interview process. In March 1958 the two men conducted interviews with each member of the Inuit group at Eskimo Point and, in Churchill, with Lewis Voisey, who also served as their interpreter in discussions with the Inuit. In addition, all the officials at Eskimo Point were interviewed about the Ahiarmiut situation. In the report, Rudnicki quoted the interviewees' answers to his questions verbatim. It is one of the few sources of documentation from the 1950s in which Inuit points of view have been recorded at length. As such, the Rudnicki/Stevenson report provides a valuable, firsthand record of Inuit impressions. The only adult Inuk not interviewed was Kikkik. Rudnicki felt it would be improper to interview her while she was in police custody. He used two forms of interview: direct questioning and, later, recorded Inuit impressions of his series of drawings that depicted the sequence of events after the relocation from Ennadai. Rudnicki was responsible for the substance of the report (Rudnicki, personal communication) and is therefore referred to as the principal author in the following text.

Rudnicki concluded that Owlijoot was seen by the group "as the person who forms their opinions and decisions" (Rudnicki and Stevenson, 1958, appendix B: 3). This view was confirmed by Steenhoven's earlier description of Owlijoot as an *isumataq,* or "man of wisdom" (Steenhoven, 1962: 54–56; for descriptions of the role of an *isumataq,* see Riches, 1982: 134–46, or Brody, 1987: 113–23). Lewis Voisey described Owlijoot as the one whom the others looked to for advice and guidance (Rudnicki and Stevenson, 1958, appendix B: 15). When Owlijoot and Nootaraloo were asked about the hunting and fishing at Ennadai Lake before they left, they responded:

The fishing was good and there used to be caribou. We couldn't get at the caribou because we were always short of ammunition. The radio boys only issued us ten rounds at a time. We have lived near Padlei before but we never found good fishing spots such as at Ennadai. We used to be happy when the caribou came. We didn't know we were moving to Henik Lake till just before we went. Henry Voisey told us the day before. He didn't give any reasons. (Rudnicki and Stevenson, 1958, appendix B: 4)

Rudnicki found that the Inuit felt almost unanimously that a lack of ammunition had been a more serious problem at Ennadai Lake than a lack of caribou. The Inuit said there were no caribou to be found that first winter at Henik Lake, and Voisey agreed. Shikoak and Pallikal also confirmed: "There was lots of caribou at Ennadai, but we were always short of ammunition. There was lots of fish in the fall. We were moved to Henik Lake because we didn't have any ammunition. If we had ammunition, we would have been alright at Ennadai" (ibid.).

The Inuit agreed that after they had moved to Henik Lake they were given plenty of ammunition, but they could not find caribou. Owlijoot and Nootaraloo commented from past experience: "We never got any caribou this side of Ennadai. . . . We don't know why the caribou didn't come—but there never was much caribou around Henik Lake." Yahah and Howmik pointed out that, though there was a lake at Ennadai where they could get fish, at Henik Lake they did not have a boat for fishing. They were able to get a little fish through the ice during the winter, but Shikoak and Pallikal said that the only time they fished was when Voisey was with them (ibid.).

The question of whether the Ahiarmiut, who were Caribou Inuit, would eat fish to survive, whether they would indeed use fish nets, or whether they had certain taboos against eating fish, was the subject of much comment. Officials could not understand why the Inuit would not fish if there was no sign of caribou. Rudnicki tried to discover the basis for speculation about fish taboos but had little success. When Rudnicki asked whether there were certain kinds of fish they would not eat, all the Inuit replied that they would eat any kind of fish. Lewis Voisey, however, thought that the Ahiarmiut did have certain taboos about fish (later confirmed by Csonka, 1991: 339–40). Voisey's mother was an Inuk, and he grew up in the Padlei–Eskimo Point region. He said that several of the Inuit had told him they would die if they ate northern pike or certain kinds of trout, and when the Ahiarmiut used nets, they would select the fish they considered to be edible and leave the rest.

Owlijoot said that, because they were unable to obtain sufficient caribou or fish at Henik Lake, they had even eaten their kayak for food (Rudnicki and Stevenson, 1958, appendix B: 8). Pallikal said that Shikoak, who was an old man, never remembered starvation such as what happened that winter. Owlijoot accepted that if they had stayed at Henik, "there wouldn't have been many of us left in the spring." There was no food, he said. Yahah and Howmik agreed that many would have died during the winter at Henik Lake. Rudnicki felt that the game situation at Ennadai during the winter would probably have been as bad as at Henik Lake had the group remained there.

As far as Rudnicki could tell, the Ahiarmiut had little idea why they were moved from Ennadai, or from Padlei to Eskimo Point. They knew only that "they had been sent away" (*aulaktitaujuviniit nunamut ungasiktualukmut*) from Ennadai Lake. In fact, both Inuit and Whites appear to have regarded the relocation to Henik Lake as punishment for Inuit reliance on the Ennadai station personnel. The move was an act of social reform and commensurate with this view a first principle in establishing a reformatory setting is to isolate the "offender" from the external world and everything that motivated the offense (Foucault, 1977: 236). In this case, they were isolated from their lands, the Ennadai radio station, and ready access to provisions for the misdeed of relying too much on the Whites. According to Lewis Voisey, the Inuit were told they had to move to be near a place where they could trade, and Padlei was about three days' walking distance from Henik Lake. It was not clear whether they understood the roles of the White officials, regarding them all as "big bosses" who, according to Rudnicki, "seemed to be equally viewed with fear and suspicion" (Rudnicki and Stevenson, 1958, appendix C: 2). Apparently the group did not have "the vaguest concept of what government is or what its responsibilities are in the north" (ibid., appendix B: 1). The Ahiarmiut did not know the word for "school" or "teacher" and were unfamiliar with life at Eskimo Point and along the coast. Indeed, this was the first time that many of them had seen seals or whale meat.

Rudnicki also interviewed Lewis Voisey, who said that during the time he was with the Ahiarmiut at Henik Lake in August 1957, only four caribou were shot by the Inuit and eight by him. This was the only meat obtained before winter, and he thought that the Inuit were hungry even when he left in September. Voisey estimated that one caribou might last a family of five about three days. He did not think that there was much fish in the area and informed Rudnicki that the Ahiarmiut had told him they did not like Henik Lake. Indeed, they felt "that there could not possibly be caribou there because never in their living memory had the caribou gone to that region in significant numbers. They had not wanted to leave Ennadai and were very happy when the first plans for the move were delayed" (ibid.: 14).

When Bill Kerr (1955) had discussed the relocation to Henik Lake with the Ahiarmiut in 1955, they had told him that the Padlei area was a poor country for game and that they would be hungry there; thus they already had knowledge of the place and its resources. In fact, there is a range of hills between the Ennadai and Padlei regions that the Ahiarmiut called *Huinnakuluit* ("the bad ones"), where there were few caribou (Csonka, 1991: 307–8). These hills extend to Henik Lake and serve as a natural boundary between the Paallirmiut hunting area and *Ahiarmiut nunaat* (the country of the Ahiarmiut), also forming a relatively fixed territorial boundary (Riches, 1982: 128). Rudnicki thus acknowledged:

In the minds of this people Ennadai traditionally was home and a good hunting area. Henik Lake on the other hand was merely a place designated as "this side of Ennadai" and regarded as a poor hunting area. Understandably therefore, this group remain far more optimistic about the game possibilities at Ennadai than at Henik Lake. (Rudnicki and Stevenson, 1958, appendix B: 2)

Voisey noted that when the group was relocated to Henik Lake it split into four camps within a seven-mile radius. Each camp provided for its own needs, and during his time with them the Inuit rarely traveled fur-

TABLE 6.1: A record of the Ahiarmiut who visited the Hudson's Bay Company Padlei post, 19 September 1957 to 12 February 1958

Date	Individuals to visit the post
21 September 1957	Annowtalik [Anowtelik]
2 October	Annowtalik
3 October	Ootuk
6 October	Arloo
9 October	Alikaswa and Kalusigaot
21 October	Alikaswa, Owlijoot, Arloo, and Annowtalik
27 October	Kiyai
29 October	Ootuk
3 November	Alikaswa and Kalusigaot
8 November	Owlijoot
19 November	Hallow
22 November	Micki, Pallikal, Owlijoot, Arloo, and Anayoenak
3 December	Ootuk
11 December	Mounik, Annowtalik, and Kiyai
21 December	Ootuk, Owlijoot, and Arloo
29 December	Angnukoak, Nutarloak [Nootaraloo], and Angatayok
30 December	Alikaswa and Kalusigaot
4 January 1958	Annowtalik and Mounik
6 January	Ootuk, Oohootok, and Kiyai
8 January	Pallikal, Micki, and Ilungiayuk
13 January	Hallow
17 January	Annowtalik
18 January	Owlijoot, Arloo, and Micki
25 January	Pallikal and Shikoak
6 February	Mounik
10 February	Mounik

Source: Nichols, 1959: 13

ther than one day's walk from their camp to hunt. Voisey had the impression that the Inuit expected that the caribou would come to them. Only once during his month at Henik Lake did a family make the trip to Padlei to bring back ammunition and tea. He said that while he was there the Inuit were short of tea and store foods, and he accepted that (before his arrival) the Inuit had broken into the mine's stores because they needed food (ibid.: 15).

The records of the Hudson's Bay Company post at Padlei (see table 6.1) reveal a more complex story. Between 19 September 1957, when Lewis Voisey left the Ahiarmiut, and 12 February 1958, when Henry Voisey was informed of the first deaths, the Ahiarmiut visited the Padlei store numerous times and received regular amounts of food and supplies in exchange for furs, as relief, and in lieu of family allowances.

What do these visits to the Company post at Padlei, shown in table 6.1, reveal about the Ahiarmiut before the deaths that occurred between 8 and 15 February 1958? With the exception of Alikaswa, who made four visits, and Angnukoak and Nootaraloo, who made one visit each, only the men visited the post. Of the three men who died of malnutrition and exposure—Kiyai, Angatayok, and Ungmak—only Ungmak did not visit the post during this period. Angatayok visited it only once, on 29 December, six weeks before he died. Kiyai visited Padlei three times during the period, the last time on 6 January. These numbers contrast with, for example, Anowtelik's six visits and Owlijoot's and Arloo's five visits each; all three men were from the same camp. It is perhaps not surprising that no deaths occurred in Owlijoot's camp, which was comprised of a larger group of people and included more able-bodied men who could hunt, trap, and fish and make the journey to Padlei for supplies.

Hallow visited Padlei only twice, whereas Ootuk made five trips to the post. Ootuk's last visit was made on 6 January, almost five weeks before he killed Hallow. On that visit he traded one white fox, receiving a credit of sixteen dollars for the pelt, and purchased thirteen dollars-worth of supplies, which included small quantities of fish hooks and line, cloth, tobacco, matches, cigarette paper, coffee, tea, and some flour. When Hallow visited Padlei on his last trip on 13 January, he traded three white foxes, for which he was credited with $48. He obtained $56.75 in food and supplies in exchange for trade goods, and he received a further $51.95-worth of food and supplies in the form of a family allowance issue for his wife Kikkik. These items included flour, oats, sugar, cheese, powdered milk, syrup, molasses, biscuits, lard, coffee, tea, candles, tobacco, fish line, a blanket, needles, matches, and ammunition. Apparently, then, Hallow's family had comparatively more provisions in the weeks immediately before his murder. This factor explains Ootuk's remark that Hallow was not sharing enough food with them (Canada, 1958b).

Rudnicki used a psychological test on the Ahiarmiut in an attempt to understand their interpersonal relationships and the way they experienced their environments. The test was comprised of drawings of the series of events that the Ahiarmiut had experienced recently: being moved, the mine shed break-ins, the evacuation. Rudnicki found that Inuit responses to the pictures were limited, and in most cases their answers reflected their incomprehension about why they were being shown the drawings. In summary, Rudnicki stated that it did not appear that the hardships and violence of the past winter had created any mental pathology (Rudnicki and Stevenson, 1958, appendix C: 3). Instead, he believed that they felt "immobilized and helpless, mostly because they are in a new setting in which they do not know what is expected of them. There seems to be a large element of fear and distrust of the white men which suggests the need to win their confidence before any rehabilitation is attempted."

The Department was concerned that the Ahiarmiut were not the only Inuit in the Keewatin to be affected by the decline of caribou in the region. Rudnicki and Stevenson were therefore asked to make an assessment of the extent to which the factors affecting the Ahiarmiut might apply to other groups within the Keewatin District or elsewhere (Rudnicki and Stevenson, 1958: 1). Rudnicki commented:

Hardship and even starvation is not a new phenomenon in Keewatin. The Eskimos there have always lived close to the brink of disaster and most regard this precarious existence as a normal state of affairs. The failure of caribou this winter however has put most of these people over the brink. Because population is so thinly dispersed and because of communication problems, the inevitable result is that some people die.

Rudnicki duly reported that, although the Ahiarmiut were the first to be affected by adverse conditions, most of the other Inuit of the Keewatin were also under threat of starvation, deteriorating health, and the eruption of violence. He noted that the Paallirmiuts had lost most of their dogs during the winter and were existing "at a marginal level," and that the caribou had not arrived in any numbers at Baker Lake. Furthermore, the coastal Inuit were "no better off": the 225 Inuit at Eskimo Point were described as ill clothed, demoralized, and living chiefly on flour. After conversations with officials at Eskimo Point, Rudnicki surmised that the incidents at Henik Lake "were regarded as relatively minor symptoms of a general crisis" (ibid., appendix B: 16).

The Deaths Reconstructed

While conducting their investigation in March 1958, Rudnicki and Stevenson tried to find out more about the slayings of Hallow and Ootuk. Owlijoot and Nootaraloo explained that Ootuk and Hallow were not their relatives and that they had not seen them all winter. Mounik and Ookanak said that they, too, were some distance from Ootuk's and Hallow's camp, "maybe one or two sleeps" away; Yahah said he lived five kilometers from their camp and did not see them very often, and Shikoak and Pallikal said they lived about eleven kilometers from their camp. They mentioned that Ootuk was an *angatkuq* (shaman), and Mounik and Ookanak described Hallow as a better man than Ootuk. Ootuk's widow Howmik said that both Ootuk and Hallow were medicine men. She said that "we lived together because we were always helping each other" (Rudnicki and Stevenson, 1958, appendix B: 10). Howmik acknowledged her family's dependence on Hallow, saying that "we always went hungry if we lived away from Hallow." She said that she did not know of Ootuk killing anyone before and did not say why he killed Hallow. Howmik said that she was never angry with Hallow or Kikkik. Several of the Ahiarmiut said they were now afraid of Kikkik (ibid., appendix B).

According to Rudnicki, it was Ootuk and Hallow's custom to camp together, which is supported by the fact that close kin were regarded as providing the most reliable support (Riches, 1982: 119). Rudnicki found that "neither were happy with their new hunting grounds at Henik Lake" (Rudnicki and Stevenson, 1958, appendix D: 1). They talked often of the caribou that did not come. Rudnicki drew a portrait of Ootuk:

Although recognized as a medicine man among the Ahearmiuts, Ootuk also was known as a haphazard provider. When the Eskimos still lived at Ennadai, Ootuk sometimes showed up with a live rabbit. The Eskimos thought this most unusual and attributed Ootuk's ability to catch things alive to his special powers. However, the cooking pot on Ootuk's hearth was more often empty than full. This may have been because of his great confidence in his magic.

Though Gallagher had apparently never met Ootuk, he described him as "a witch doctor" (Canada, 1958b: 50). Ootuk's wife, Howmik, did not have use of her legs or right arm as a result of polio and needed help from her hearing- and speech-impaired daughter Karlak and her sister-in-law Kikkik. Rudnicki wrote that Kikkik was a good wife. "She kept her family well-clothed and her five children were always well looked after. She felt secure with Hallow for he had never failed to provide for his family" (Rudnicki and Stevenson, 1958, appendix D: 1). It was Rudnicki's impression that Hallow "did not mind sharing the spoils of the hunt with Ootuk and his family." Rudnicki found that "Hallow was a skilled hunter and he often obtained fish and game even when food was very scarce because he was patient and determined. The Ahearmiut regarded Hallow as a strong man and a good Eskimo." In their investigative report, Rudnicki and Stevenson reconstructed the deaths of Hallow, Ootuk, and Nesha:

As the winter progressed food became scarcer and scarcer. By February, hunger and despair filled the two igloos on the shores of Henik Lake. Hallow continued to jig for fish from early morning till late at night and managed usually to catch one or two to keep his family going. Ootuk and his family kept themselves alive by eating caribou clothing and fish bones which they got from Hallow's igloo.

According to the autopsy report, Ootuk's gastrointestinal tract contained the equivalent of one small fish and fragments of animal hair, greyish white in color, consistent with the consumption of caribou-skin

clothing. The pathologist estimated that Ootuk had eaten the fish within
half an hour or an hour of his death (Canada, 1958b: 82). Rudnicki and
Stevenson (1958, appendix D: 2) continued:

Soon, the children's clothing was gone and there was nothing more to eat. Not
long afterwards, Igyaka, Ootuk's son died of starvation [he was two years old].
Karlak and Kooyak, the two girls shivered naked in the igloo wrapped only in an
old skin.

   Hallow thought about how his family was now in danger of dying and how
Ootuk and his family must surely die now. When Ootuk came on one of his fre-
quent visits to Hallow's igloo looking for food, Hallow told him of his decision
to move away in search of a better fishing spot. Ootuk knew that he could not
move with Hallow. He was weak with hunger and his family did not have clothing to leave their igloo. Hallow's decision really meant that he was leaving Ootuk
and his family to die.

   On the eighth of February, a big storm came up with much driving snow and
bitter cold. That morning, Ootuk was very angry. He struck his daughter Kooyak
because she was crying for food. He then told his wife he would walk to Padlei
for help, a return journey that would take a week. Picking up his rifle, he stepped
out of his igloo and felt the fury of the storm. Instead of starting for Padlei,
Ootuk walked to Hallow's igloo.

   Hallow and Kikkik were eating strips of caribou skin and old tea leaves and
shared these with Ootuk when he entered. Ootuk also asked for and received fish
bones. Hallow talked of moving after the storm and Ootuk talked of his intention of walking to Padlei. After this conversation, Hallow announced he would
try to catch some fish and left for his jigging hole. Ootuk remained silent in the
igloo while Kikkik mended clothes. He then left the igloo without a word.

   Ootuk walked in the direction of the jigging hole. Driving snow obscured
vision and the wind deadened all other sounds. He came up behind Hallow who
was crouched over the fishing hole and had not heard him approach. Ootuk
stared at the huddled figure, then carefully aimed his rifle and fired. Hallow
slumped forward into the water, the back of his head shattered by the force of
the bullet.

   Rudnicki's account of Kikkik's struggle with Ootuk and her decision
to leave for Padlei followed her own version of events. Rudnicki and
Stevenson had therefore come to the conclusion that the families of
Ootuk and Hallow were starving and inadequately supplied to cope with
the severe winter conditions. They were isolated from officials. There was
insufficient game in the area to which they had been moved. Ootuk mur-
dered Hallow and tried to kill Kikkik, perhaps to save his starving family
by resorting to cannibalism. Ootuk may have been acting in an irrational manner on account of the dire circumstances, or perhaps he was
taking a socially justifiable action against a person whom he thought was
no longer prepared to share food (in order to increase his own family's
chance of survival) and was thereby abandoning him. Howmik later explained that the murder was the result of hunger and an unwillingness to

share (Csonka, 1993). This remark bears out Steenhoven's observation that in times of starvation food was shared, but priority could be given to feeding one's children (Steenhoven, 1962: 37). Kikkik killed Ootuk in self-defense, and seven days later, in desperation, she left her two daughters in an igloo because she no longer had the strength to pull them on the sled and thought she might still be able to save herself and her other three children if she carried on towards Padlei.

The Trial of Kikkik

News of the Ahiarmiut deaths was reported in the major Canadian newspapers (e.g., *The Globe and Mail*, 1958a). The immediate public response to the deaths did not concentrate on the effects of the relocation to Henik Lake (the general public was unaware of the connection), but on the pending murder trial of Kikkik.

The case of "Her Majesty the Queen and El-472 Kikkik" was a celebrated murder trial held in the Arctic before the Honourable John Sissons, the first justice of the Northwest Territories (1955–66). The testimony presented in the legal proceedings offers valuable insight into the Ahiarmiut culture, the difficulties the Ahiarmiut faced at Henik Lake, and the cultural interaction between the Inuit and the officials responsible for their welfare. The oral testimonies taken by officials from the Ahiarmiut in preparation for the trial and the cross-examination during the trial have produced a valuable and lengthy record of Inuit narratives.

The murder trial of Kikkik was held on 14–16 April 1958 at the coastal settlement of Rankin Inlet in the Territorial Court of the Northwest Territories. Rankin Inlet was selected because it was the largest settlement in the area, and the peripatetic Territorial Court was abiding by the principle that an accused person has a right to be tried in the area where the crime is alleged to have been committed. The list of dramatis personae and the preparations for the event were impressive. Kikkik and the Crown witnesses were flown up from Eskimo Point and Padlei. Kikkik's four surviving children were also brought to Rankin. The judicial party, including Justice J. H. Sissons and his staff from Yellowknife, Defense Counsel Sterling Lyon from Winnipeg, and Crown Prosecutor John Parker from Yellowknife, were flown in. NSO Bill Kerr flew in from Churchill, and NSO Doug Wilkinson came from Baker Lake. The pathologist who performed the autopsies, Professor James Stirratt, was flown up from Edmonton to present his findings. Six jurors were selected from Rankin Inlet, including two Inuit, Niatook and Chenitook. The trial was held in the recreation hall of the Rankin Inlet Nickel Mine. Following up its earlier feature on the Ahiarmiut, *Life* magazine sent a photographer to cover the trial. There was public interest in the trial not only because these Inuit were the subject of Mowat's book but because, in the 1950s, murder was punishable with death.

For the defense counsel, Sterling Lyon, this case was not only his first (and only) one in the Northwest Territories, it was also his first murder trial. A month after the trial, he was appointed attorney general of Manitoba and subsequently became premier of the province. The prosecutor, John Parker, was a distinguished attorney. The prosecutor informed the jury that he would produce evidence that Kikkik committed manslaughter under section 206 of the Criminal Code of Canada by killing Ootuk, and that she was guilty of criminal negligence and abandonment under section 192 of the Criminal Code in respect of the death of her daughter Nesha. The defense counsel entered a plea of "not guilty" on both charges.

At the trial, the prosecutor, defense attorney, and judge went to considerable lengths to satisfy themselves that the Inuit testifying understood the meaning of truth. The jurists decided that, for the Inuit witnesses, taking the oath should be linked to the nature of an Inuk's Christian beliefs. Dramatic tragedies can have comic interludes, and such an incident occurred during the murder trial when the Inuit actors had difficulties following the cultural script they were being presented with. When Howmik was asked to take the stand as a Crown witness, the prosecutor became embroiled in a philosophical and religious discussion with Justice Sissons (referred to in the transcripts as "the Court") and defense counsel Sterling Lyon about the legal status of her sworn oath. At the same time, they were trying to cope with an untrained court interpreter and had translation difficulties (Canada, 1958b: 53):

MR. PARKER: I note, My Lord, she was given a Christian oath. I wonder if Your Lordship might inquire about that.

THE COURT: (To interpreter): Ask her if she is a Christian.

MR. PARKER: My Lord, with great respect, can you start off with "Are you a Christian?" Isn't that the way these questions are going to have to come?

THE COURT: I do not quite follow.

MR. PARKER: As this interpreter is asked "Is she a Christian?" he must translate "Are you a Christian?" He must answer "I am . . ." or "I am not . . ."

THE COURT: We will ask this witness "Are you a Christian?"

A: She says "Yes."

Q (COURT):   What church?

A: Both of them.

MR. PARKER: A very wise precaution, My Lord.

Later that day, when Howmik was being cross-examined at the witness stand, Mr. Lyon, the defense counsel, tried to question the nature of her oath (ibid.: 59–61):

MR. LYON: Now Howmik, you are still under oath. Do you understand that?

A: Yes.

Q: You told us this afternoon that you go to two churches?

A: Yes.

Q: Did you go to them when you were out at Churchill with your polio cure?

A: Yes.

Q: Have you gone to church since you came back up north?

A: Yes.

Q: Where did you go to church?

A: In our land.

Q: And you know then what will happen to you if you tell a lie, do you?

MR. PARKER: My Lord, I am raising an objection. It is not open to the defense at this stage to question whether this witness is competent. Does she have to account for her religious beliefs and so on?

THE COURT: I don't think this is admissible for that purpose. I don't know what the purpose of the question is, whether to attack credibility, or whether to impress on the witness the compulsion to tell the truth.

MR. LYON: Perhaps I can qualify the situation, My Lord. She was sworn on the oath that she attends two churches.

THE COURT: She said she was a Christian.

MR. LYON: With the greatest of respect, I feel it is open on cross-examination to examine that situation and just see if, in fact, the witness is a Christian and if she is, she knows what will happen if she doesn't tell the truth.

MR. PARKER: I will let my objection go, My Lord. I don't think this line of questioning can be taken at this time. You can't have it both ways.

THE COURT: I am inclined to think you are right, and that there is authority for that, but I am letting it in. I believe there is authority for your statement . . .

(Mr. Lyon continues cross-examination of the witness)

Q: Well, as a question, Howmik, what will happen to you if you don't tell the truth here in court under oath?

A: She apparently does not understand that, what would happen to her if she . . . she doesn't understand.

Q: In your religion, Howmik, whom do you believe in?

A: She says she believes in Jesus.

MR. PARKER: (To interpreter) Can you say "I believe in Jesus"? Just say her words.

MR. LYON: What else did she say?

A: She believes, she said.

Q: And what will Jesus do to her if she tells a lie?

THE COURT: You are getting pretty deep there. I don't think she will be able to answer that.

MR. LYON: With respect, My Lord, a child—and in some senses this witness is in that category—a child is questioned along these lines "Is it right to tell the truth, and is it wrong to tell a lie," and if wrong "Why?" "Because God will punish you." I have seen that done on many occasions, and so has Your Lordship.

THE COURT: All right, go on.

MR. LYON: What was your answer?

A: She will be punished.

Q: That's fine, that's fine, that's all.

After this awkward process of examining the depth of Inuit religious convictions, swearing of subsequent oaths was a briefer process, although the witness's belief in a Christian god still appeared to be a precondition for being able to present acceptable testimony. Yahah (Anayoenak) was asked to take the witness stand for the Crown (ibid.: 62–63):

THE COURT: Are you a Christian?

A: Yes.

THE COURT: Do you believe in God?

A: Yes.

THE COURT: Well, I guess that's it. He says he believes in God, so he is entitled to take an oath.

MR. LYON: Will Your Lordship permit an examination?

THE COURT: Yes.

MR. LYON: Yahah, do you go to church?

A: He goes.

Q: What does he say?

A: I go to the other church, not the R.C., but the other one, what church you call it, the Bible . . .

THE COURT: Mr. Gallagher, what is it?

A: (By Corporal Gallagher) The Evangelistic Mission that travels over the country in a small aircraft.

Mr. Lyon continues:

Q: How many times have you been to church, Yahah?

A: Just when it comes I go.

THE COURT: If there was any question as to the competency to take an oath, we would come under 14(1) of the Canada Evidence Act. I think we are obliged to take this man's oath.

MR. PARKER: I don't think my friend will go so far as to say this man should be United Church to be questioned. This church comes, and he goes, which is a great deal better than a lot of people in the city.

THE COURT: I think it is an excellent church.

(The witness is sworn)

This passage provides an indication of the trial's cultural and ethical subtext. Lyon's statement that the adult witness Howmik, a mother of three children, could herself be regarded as a child was characteristic of the way many White officials perceived the Inuit. This perception is a prominent feature of both relocation case studies, particularly in the way it influenced the question of consensus. If, however, Lyon was making his comment with respect to her ability to comprehend the Western judicial proceedings, then it could be interpreted as a defense tactic. During the trial, officials deemed it necessary to instruct the Inuit at length on the virtues of Christian truth and examined in detail the deaths of Ootuk, Hallow, and Nesha, without addressing in a similar judicial forum the extenuating reasons for these deaths and those of the other Ahiarmiut. The premise that nature killed them conveniently obscured the truth.

In his summation, the prosecutor asked the jury for a verdict of manslaughter. He suggested that Kikkik's killing of Ootuk was not an act of self-defense. The defense counsel argued that there was no case for murder, or for manslaughter. He argued that the only conclusion Kikkik could draw was that Ootuk intended to kill her and the children, and she could not concern herself with niceties; she followed basic law. Mr. Lyon concluded that Kikkik acted in self-defense and thus "felt and feels she did no wrong" (Sissons, 1968: 104).

Sissons was sympathetic to Kikkik and instructed the jury: "If you find the accused acted in self-defense, or in defense of her children, as I have indicated to you, there is no crime, and you will find the accused not guilty." The judge had made allowances for Kikkik's actions by a liberal interpretation of Canadian criminal law. He came to the conclusion that Kikkik's actions were justifiable and that she should be found not guilty because of a "common sense basic law." Lyon later stated it was clear that Sissons's sympathies were with the accused "to the extent that, at times I felt I was the junior defense counsel" (Lyon, personal communication). Despite the prosecutor's objections to the judge that he had essentially instructed the jury to find the accused not guilty, the prosecutor's com-

ments were disregarded—and two hours later, the jury returned and
unanimously found Kikkik not guilty. Sissons then attempted to inform
Kikkik of the "truth" as reflected by the verdict:

THE COURT: Would you have the interpreter come forward. Would you
    tell the accused that the jury has found her not guilty.
(The interpreter complied)
THE COURT: Does she understand?
INTERPRETER: She hardly understands. I am trying to describe it to her.
    She has not killed anybody is what description I am giving her. She
    doesn't quite get that, you know.

In his desire to inform Kikkik properly of the verdict, Sissons temporarily forgot that she still had to be tried on another charge relating to
the death of Nesha.

THE COURT: Tell her now that she is free to go; she is free on this charge.
MR. PARKER: That is not quite the situation, My Lord.
THE COURT: She is acquitted on this charge.
MR. PARKER: Does it matter? She seems relaxed.
THE COURT: (To interpreter) Does she understand what the jury has
    said? That she is not to blame for the death of Ootuk?

The court reconvened on the evening of 14 April to hear the second charge against Kikkik: that by criminal negligence she caused the
death of her daughter Nesha and unlawfully endangered Annacatha and
Nesha by leaving them without adequate food, shelter, clothing, or protection. It was further alleged that she had failed to secure assistance for
the girls. According to Sissons (1968: 107): "This was the aspect of the
case that troubled and puzzled all who felt sympathy for Kikkik, including the crown." When the search plane found Kikkik a few hours after
she had left the two girls, she did not tell the police about their precise
whereabouts or that they had been alive that morning. Sissons thought:

It seemed out of character with the concerned, considerate mother who emerged
from the testimony—the one who sat up all night in the snow house because
there were blankets only for the children—and with the tiny figure in the print
dress whose moccasins didn't reach the floor of the courtroom. How could she
do such a thing?
    I believe the key to her action is purely and simply stated in three answers
she gave later to Corporal Gallagher. They were contained in the statement interpreted by Jimmy Gibbons which I ruled to be voluntary and admissible as
evidence:
Q: Were Nesha and Annacatha alive when buried?
A: Yes, both of them.
Q: Why did you bury them alive?
A: They could not walk. I had dragged them a long way. They were heavy.
Q: Why was it that when you were found that same afternoon that you did not

tell the police about Annacatha and Nesha, as there was still every possibility that they could have been saved?

A: I was afraid to say.

I considered that a reasonable explanation for Kikkik's action. She was afraid.

In their investigation, Rudnicki and Stevenson came to a similar conclusion. They noted that the police asked a great many questions, and Kikkik was very frightened. They wanted to know where Annacatha and Nesha were, and Kikkik told them that they were dead—for they surely would be by now (Rudnicki and Stevenson, 1958, appendix D: 4–5). *Ilira*, the fear that affected Inuit in their dealings with Whites, and particularly authority figures such as policemen, also prevented Kikkik from telling the police the truth, even though it might have saved her children. One can only speculate that she thought the children had already perished in the hours since she left them. But it was fear of the police that caused her to lie. In effect, the children were sacrificed out of fear. Her fear was understandable. These were the same policemen who had taken away the three men in the summer after they had broken into the White man's cache of food. Both case studies reveal that "fear of the police" was a key element in the relationship between the Inuit and the RCMP.

Sissons instructed the jury that in common law there is no abandonment if a person cannot supply, or cannot furnish, the support required. "If Kikkik could not, in this case, furnish adequate food, shelter, clothing and protection," remarked Sissons (1968: 109), "the jury could take it that she had no alternative to abandoning the children. Inability to do anything else does not constitute abandonment." The jury was out only a few minutes before delivering a verdict of not guilty. The jury had heard the truth, but not the whole truth. In his autobiography, Justice Sissons alluded to the larger picture not presented at the trial:

Those of us who were involved as spectators could never feel so easy about the matter. Many courtroom scenes are played against the backdrop of a larger drama. I was forced to conclude that Kikkik's tragedy was played against the backdrop of high official farce. Well-intentioned ignorance in high places had trapped her in deep below-zero winter, out on a trail as hard to follow as some of the reasoning of the Northern Affairs Department. . . . Unfortunately, certainty about what's going on in the north increases with one's proximity to Ottawa. (ibid.)

The trial transcripts demonstrate that officials succeeded in discovering, in minute detail, why events took place and what their chronology was. On the basis of this information, the jurists and jury hypothesized about the decisions that led to the deaths of a man and a child. Ultimately, they decided that Kikkik was justified in her actions. Yet they had uncovered only part of the truth. This part emerged in a context that ignored the very events—the relocations—that set the scene for the tragedy. It was thought necessary to hold Kikkik, separated from her children, for two months until the White participants could be assembled for an expensive Arctic show trial. Despite this public attempt to demonstrate to the Inuit the importance of truth and of right and wrong, the Whites were less attentive when reviewing their own actions. The Department made the decision to remove the Ahiarmiut from the traditional site of their camps at Ennadai Lake, where they were being assisted by the radio station personnel, and to relocate them to an isolated area. It was this act that precipitated the deaths of Ootuk, Nesha, and the other five Ahiarmiut. Henry Larsen came to a similar conclusion when he recorded a cogent observation in his unpublished memoirs: "In the Kikkik case the most annoying part for me and my men in the North was that the murder no doubt was the result of the many moves carried out amongst these Eskimos, especially to areas they did not like" (Larsen, n.d.: 31).

A few weeks before the Ahiarmiut deaths, Graham Rowley had cautioned Deputy Minister Robertson about the potential political ramifications if the Ahiarmiut ran into difficulties: "Another aspect that may cause trouble," said Rowley (1958b), "is that Oohootok, one of the three involved in the theft and vandalism this spring, is the 'hero' of Farley Mowat's book 'People of the Deer.' The fact that Mr. Mowat reports Oohootok's [fictional] death towards the end of his book may deter him from taking up his cause, but I doubt it." Indeed, despite the minor complication of this literary license, Farley Mowat did become interested in uncovering the truth about the events that took place after his first story ended in 1948. The sensational aspects of the trial also intrigued national newspapers, which reported the verdict to the public in such headlines as: "Woman Cleared in Arctic Killing of Witch Doctor" (*The Globe and Mail*, 1958b). Mowat proceeded to research the Ahiarmiut tragedy by visiting Eskimo Point and interviewing the survivors. He spoke to officials and was also given privileged access to government files. As a result, he produced a widely publicized article, "The Two Ordeals of Kikkik," and a book on the relocation, its aftermath, and the murder trial under the title *The Desperate People*. In chapter 7, I explore the truths Mowat presented to the public and how they compared with those forwarded by the Department.

· 7 ·

INFLUENCING PUBLIC PERCEPTIONS
OF THE RELOCATIONS

Farley Mowat, Crusader for Truth

I t was a striking coincidence that the group of Inuit who had been
adversely affected by government intervention was in fact the same
band that was the focus of Farley Mowat's best-selling book *People of the
Deer*, published six years earlier in 1952. Mowat had criticized officials
then for not assisting the Ahiarmiut, and in the intervening years he
had continued to write about conditions affecting the Inuit. One of his
articles, "The Case of the Disappearing Eskimos," was published in a
popular magazine in 1954. The minister of northern affairs requested a
briefing from Deputy Minister Gordon Robertson on the matter. Robertson (1954b) responded:

> It is to Mowat's interest, of course, to keep this controversy alive and we would be
> ill-advised, I think, to enter into it again, unless we are obliged to do so by ques-
> tions in the House. Instances of starvation have occurred in this and other areas
> from time to time and will continue to occur so long as the Eskimos continue
> to live in small isolated communities with which there is little or no communica-
> tion. It is one of the risks that Eskimos take as a matter of course, just as whites
> do in some of their more dangerous callings.

Although Department officials may have accepted Inuit deaths due
to starvation and disease as an inevitable reality of their "primitive" lifestyle in the unforgiving Arctic environment, Mowat was not so forgiv-
ing of what he called government negligence and indifference. In his
attempt to sway public opinion and influence government policy to improve the social and economic conditions of the Inuit, Mowat continued
to search for true stories to write about. The tragedies that befell the
Ahiarmiut and the murder trial that followed were certain to attract his

attention, particularly since one of the main characters in Mowat's book, Oohootok, had been incarcerated and then permanently blinded while in police custody. The crime for which Oohootok had been sentenced was the illegal theft of food for his group during a period of privation. Mowat decided to research the issue and to write a sequel to his first book. He started by interviewing the surviving Ahiarmiut and various officials at Eskimo Point.

In January 1959, Mowat published a series of articles about the Inuit. On 3 January, a story appeared in *The Globe Magazine* entitled "Integration and the Eskimo: A Success Story." He stated that the starvation deaths in the Keewatin the previous year "were the inevitable outcome of an antiquated policy . . . designed to keep the Eskimo as a separate racial entity" (Mowat, 1959b). Mowat argued: "All that this region now has to offer Eskimos who try to cling to the ancestral way of life is starvation, disease and spiritual and social disintegration." Instead, Mowat advocated that the Inuk be given an opportunity to prove himself an equal partner in the land of which he was a citizen. He saw the Inuk of the future as a fully integrated member of a wage-employment society, working (for example) as a miner at the Rankin Inlet Nickel Mine. Mowat explained that there "will be bums and misfits among them," but "given half a chance, the average Eskimo can fit himself into our scheme of things with an alacrity and a competence that is startling." Mowat's assimilationist argument concluded: "No matter how strongly the reactionary Europeans who claim to speak for the Eskimo demand that he stay in the igloo, the Eskimo himself would sooner not."

Mowat repeated his argument for assimilation of the Inuit in a series of articles in the major Canadian newspapers and journals. "It's Time We Treated Inuk as *a Man*" announced his article in *The Telegram* of 20 January 1959; "The Realities: Hunger, Disease, Death" was the headline of another of Mowat's articles in *The Telegram* two days later (Mowat, 1959c and 1959f). As if preparing the Canadian public for the big story to come, Mowat then published "The Two Ordeals of Kikkik" in *Maclean's Magazine* on 31 January 1959, describing the relocation of the Ahiarmiut to Henik Lake, the deaths that ensued, and the murder trial of Kikkik. The headline foretold the writer's dramatic treatment of the story: "She killed a man in cold blood—she had to—then she set off on foot, starved, across a frigid, merciless wasteland to try to save the lives of five children. When she achieved the impossible the white man's unbending law held her for murder" (Mowat, 1959g: 12).

The article, which was illustrated by pictures of Kikkik and the trial, was widely read and resulted in numerous letters being sent to the government. For example, a letter addressed to the prime minister by a member of the public, similar to many others he received, stated:

Dear Prime Minister,

I would like to know if the article by Farley Mowat entitled 'The Two Ordeals of Kikkik' is essentially true. If it is then for the first time in my life I'm ashamed to be a Canadian. (Hobbs, 1959)

Minister Alvin Hamilton (1959a) answered the letter, confirming that "Mr. Mowat's story is essentially true. . . . This tragedy did occur substantially as described by Mr. Mowat." Mowat had begun his article by stating that he became friends with the Ahiarmiut while living with them in 1947–48, and, when the trial of Kikkik was reported by the press, he could not understand why the deaths had occurred. Mowat (1959g: 13) explained that he had studied the verbatim account of the two trials and the related documents as well as the police investigation reports. This statement was a public confirmation that he had been given access to official documents, a fact that was to cause the Department some difficulties later. The RCMP had refused to give him access to its files, thus he could only have seen police files with the acquiescence of the Department. Mowat stated that there was a conflict in the facts but that there was even more conflict in the interpretation of those facts. Confidently, he assured the readers of the purpose of his article: "Now I have taken the facts which are the true ones, and I have told the story, and I believe it to be truth." Mowat had a reputation as a popular author who had a liberal approach to the facts. His own view was: "I never let the facts get in the way of the truth" (Mowat, personal communication). What truth did Mowat produce?

In the *Maclean's* article, Mowat's description of the 1950 Nueltin Lake relocation of the Inuit was highly critical of the police (Mowat, 1959g: 15). He said the Inuit were flown to the new place without having any understanding of the purpose behind the move and without any desire on their part to go. The police, he felt, were to blame, just as they were in the case of the move to Henik Lake. In May 1957, the police, accompanied by a representative of the Department of Northern Affairs, flew to the Ahiarmiut camps and carried out "a mass deportation of the people." When three of the Ahiarmiut broke into the mining shed to obtain food, Mowat recorded that a police aircraft took these men away from the families who depended upon them for all things. Mowat argued that in late autumn 1957 the police said they would make a patrol to Henik Lake to ensure that no critical emergency arose, but that patrol was never made. When word reached Henry Voisey that the Ahiarmiut were in danger of perishing, he radioed the RCMP for a plane, yet Mowat records that no plane arrived. The RCMP aircraft finally did fly to Padlei and then on to Henik Lake, where the police discovered Howmik and two of her children still alive. Mowat reported (ibid.: 44), however, that after flying them and the three corpses back to Padlei, the plane continued to Eskimo Point, "flying almost directly over the travel igloo where Kikik [sic] waited—and it did not pause." Mowat blamed the police for wasting two more days before searching for Kikkik and her family from the air. When she was rescued and taken to Eskimo Point, he said that she was not told that Annacatha, whom she had left with Nesha in the igloo, had survived "until it suited the needs of the police" (ibid.: 45).

Understandably, the RCMP were outraged by Mowat's interpretation, which publicly blamed them for the Ahiarmiut deaths. Robertson (1959c) informed his minister in February 1959 that Commissioner Nicholson was most upset by the criticisms of the Force in Farley Mowat's article in *Maclean's Magazine* and also in some of his later articles in the *Toronto Telegram*. Nicholson told Robertson that he was planning to make a statement about the matter at the Northwest Territories Council the following morning, because "the effects of the inaccuracies and unfair criticism have been quite damaging in the Force" (ibid.).

Supt. Henry Larsen (1959) prepared a written rebuttal of Mowat's version of events, detailing what he felt were distortions of fact. Larsen's submission was not made public but took the form of a memo to Commissioner Nicholson. He noted that the 1950 Nueltin Lake relocation was not a police project; rather, the Department's deputy commissioner of the NWT had considered it best to move them to Nueltin Lake. Likewise, Larsen explained, when the second Ahiarmiut relocation to Henik Lake was being planned, the move was made at the request of the Department. He pointed out that the RCMP had expressed considerable doubt about the Henik Lake relocation and in effect were against the move.

A week after receiving Larsen's report, Nicholson made his statement to the Northwest Territories Council and attempted to defend the reputation of the Force. Rather than explaining that the relocations had been authorized by the Department and had not been undertaken at the behest of the RCMP, as Larsen had made clear in his report, Nicholson—acting either on his own initiative or on orders from his minister —refrained from politically embarrassing the Department. Instead, Nicholson focused criticism on the *Maclean's* article and took issue with individual points it made. This tactic had almost the opposite effect to the one Nicholson intended and virtually confirmed Mowat's allegations of police negligence. For example, referring to the radio message the police in Eskimo Point received from HBC manager Voisey on 25 January 1958 requesting a plane to evacuate Kiyai, Nicholson (1959a) explained that it was not possible to send one until 11 February due to "other urgent demands." Nicholson did not mention what Larsen had noted in his briefing—that Kiyai had died on 10 February (Larsen, 1959).

Consequently, the Force's attempts to shield itself from the blame attributed to it by the *Maclean's* article were unsuccessful. Robertson (1959c) privately acknowledged that Mowat's "attacks on the RCMP, together with the relatively praiseful attitude toward Northern Affairs have led the RCMP to feel that we may have 'slanted' Mowat's criticisms." Robertson also told Hamilton that, in respect of "the 'blame' for the decision to undertake moves of certain Eskimos in 1950 and 1957, [they] were decided on by this department," and that Mowat had wrongly ascribed these relocations to the RCMP. When *The Desperate People* was published in October 1959, Phillips (1959a) also acknowledged that it was a "devastating denunciation" of the police. He argued that it was difficult to defend the police effectively by saying that they were merely carrying out the Department's orders, "true though it is." Indeed, Phillips told Robertson that Mowat was bending over backwards, "perhaps too far for our comfort," not only to exonerate the Department but also to identify the government as the hope of the Inuit. Despite officials' initial fears, Mowat's version of events served to deflect guilt from the Department. Unbeknownst to the public, the Department's role in the affair was masked, and the RCMP essentially became the scapegoat.

Mowat praised the humanitarian approach of Justice Sissons at the trial, saying that he was a judge who understood the nature of the abyss that separated Kikkik from the Whites. Sissons was aware "that justice can be terribly unjust," reported Mowat (1959g: 46), rightly observing that in his charges to the jury the judge virtually instructed them to bring in a verdict of acquittal. Mowat's cogent style was extremely effective in dramatizing the events that took place. Working from the official reports and from his interviews with officials, he accurately related most of the known facts.

He was wrong, however, on several major points concerning police involvement. The RCMP were not responsible for the 1950 relocation to Nueltin Lake, nor were they responsible for the 1957 relocation to Henik Lake or, primarily, for the deaths that occurred. The planning for the relocations had been undertaken by the Department, and it was the Department that had ignored the advice of the police in the months before the deaths. Larsen was against the 1957 relocation, and, before the deaths, his officers and Graham Rowley had advised the Department that the Ahiarmiut were in serious trouble and that action should be taken to move them to the coast so they could be under direct police supervision or the supervision of a Department official. Yet no action was taken by the Department. These factors Farley Mowat did not report. Although the details of his article were often correct, his conclusions were somewhat misdirected with reference to issues of responsibility. Why did Mowat commit key errors when he had so much information at his disposal and when he was prepared to state at the outset of his article that he was confident of having uncovered the truth?

The possibility that there was a collaborative arrangement between the Department and Mowat has not been discussed in the literature. Might Mowat's incorrect conclusions in reconstructing the Ahiarmiut affair be in any way connected with the special relationship he had formed with the Department in 1957–59 when researching and writing his articles and book? In the light of the Department's earlier attack on Mowat's character and on the veracity of his first book, it seems rather surprising that the government would publicly endorse Mowat's *Maclean's* article; but that is precisely what happened when, on 10 July 1959, the minister for northern affairs, Alvin Hamilton, made the following comments in the House of Commons:

A few months ago *Maclean's Magazine* published one of the most moving accounts of human thought and endurance that I have ever read. It was written by Farley Mowat. I recommend to every member of the House and every Canadian the reading of this story. Here, in clear and powerful prose, an attempt is made to look into the minds of people thousands of years removed from us in civilization. Read that story and you will understand why my department, and this government, is not going to overlook the tremendous assets and personal needs of these old and long-overlooked Canadian citizens. We cannot take unto ourselves the smugness that we will always be right in our dealings with these first Canadians. We know that they are human beings who have a great need and a great potential. This government, to the limit of its knowledge will not fail our Eskimo people. (Canada, 1959)

Mowat could not have received a more glowing recommendation, and from no less than the minister responsible for his old adversary, the Department. Ironically, it was Hamilton's predecessor who a few years earlier had reassured his colleagues that Mowat's criticisms were pure fiction. How could this transformation in attitude have come about? What did the Department have to gain by changing its posture towards Mowat?

Controlling Discourse for the Common Good

An indication of the nature of Mowat's new relationship with senior officials in the Department is revealed in a letter Mowat (1958b) wrote to Ben Sivertz in November 1958, curiously addressing him as "Dear Cap'n." Mowat informed him that he had finished an article on the

Ahiarmiut incidents for *Maclean's Magazine* and was completing the book version for his publishers, Atlantic–Little Brown. "They see the yarn as of very wide appeal in the States," remarked Mowat; "I hope so, since this will ensure its wide sale here." Mowat told Sivertz: "I doubt that even you have any conception of just how dreadful a commentary it is upon Canada, and Canadians. It is far, far worse than I had suspected. . . . It will be a pretty telling indictment of man's inhumanity to man." Mowat said that he would not refer to NSO Bill Kerr by name when discussing his part in the relocation, but "at this juncture I am not prepared to protect anyone who was involved in the whole frightful shambles. The RCMP are going to take the perfect devil of a beating though, and I may have to flee the country as a result." Mowat announced: "I conclude that this is the twelfth hour for the Eskimos, and that we cannot afford even one more major blunder" (ibid.).

Upon receiving Mowat's letter outlining his forthcoming publications, Sivertz (1958b) passed it to Deputy Minister Robertson with the following warning:

I am a little afraid however that he may yield to the temptation to be spectacular at the expense of accuracy and to use again the formula of shocking revelations which proved so successful in selling "People of the Deer.". . . The fact remains that any criticism of the Government's activity or lack of it among the Eskimos is going to reflect upon this Department, and we shall have to answer any questions that are raised.

Sivertz also informed Robertson that Mowat was in favor of the Department's new policies but was extremely critical of the RCMP; he apparently felt they should have no administrative responsibility for Inuit affairs. Sivertz noted that he had met Mowat several times over the previous year, that he had corresponded with him, and that Mowat had spent four days in the Department talking with his officers.

Robertson contacted the minister, Alvin Hamilton, to brief him on the situation. Robertson (1958b) told the minister: "I think we must expect some pretty extreme and intemperate criticism and judging from 'People of the Deer,' awkward facts will not be allowed to stand in the way of a good story—or of a sweeping condemnation. . . . Be braced!" He was particularly insistent that the Department take immediate measures to prevent more Inuit deaths during the present winter of 1958–59. Robertson's remarks to the minister reflect his Department's recognition of the influence Mowat's forthcoming publications were likely to have:

I have told the Northern Administration Branch that the knowledge that these articles are coming makes it particularly important that everything possible should be done during this winter to avoid cases of starvation and generally to take whatever measures are possible, within the staff limits that are imposed upon us, to look after the people of the area. . . . I think we should not underestimate the public impression that Mowat's articles may well make. He is a most persuasive writer.

By this time, Mowat's ability to harness public opinion was a reflection of the maxim that the real power to shape beliefs and the behavior of others often belongs to those who wield political influence outside the formal setting (Clark and Dear, 1984: 94). Robertson pragmatically recognized a potential advantage for the Department's future plans in Mowat's publications. Whether the Department was right in every detail of its policy or not, stated Robertson (1958b), it could not hope to take more effective action unless it increased the numbers of its staff. The realization that Mowat's publications on the "plight of the Eskimo" could be used as leverage for soliciting additional funding to respond to the crisis influenced Robertson's advice to his minister. He informed him that he could have Mowat's material available for the session they would be having with the Treasury Board regarding requests for higher staff numbers and departmental budget estimates.

Like his junior officials, Robertson—the mandarin of the Department —adopted a familiar tone in his correspondence with Mowat at this time. Robertson (1959a) addressed him as "Dear Farley," reaffirming that "we shall co-operate with your endeavour in every way." This intimacy stood in contrast to his usual reserved style of writing and illustrated the Department's attempt to turn Mowat into a friend of the Department, on easy terms with its senior personnel.

A fundamental component of state crisis management is reinterpreting the crisis in language that characterizes it as something inevitable (Clark and Dear, 1984: 99). An agency is thus seen as controlling a crisis that warrants an intervention. A week before the *Maclean's* article was to be published, Alvin Hamilton requested that his staff prepare a statement "praising the Mowat article as a powerful piece of writing which, in the minister's view, is a service to the purpose which the department is trying to achieve in bringing home to the people of Canada the utterly precarious conditions of life of these people, unless something is done to bring them into our civilization" (Robertson, 1959d). Mowat's assimilationist arguments in his articles published in 1959 and in the final chapter of *The Desperate People* were now compatible with the views of Sivertz and Phillips.

Official policy had thus shifted from "keeping the Eskimo an Eskimo" to one of assimilation. Sivertz (1959a) agreed that the Inuit could no longer remain "in a quaint backwater in the stream of human progress," arguing that there was no long-term future for the separate culture of a small group such as the Canadian Inuit. He thought the Inuit were "on the threshold of a great leap from the primitive culture of their fore-bears" and should be welcomed as full Canadian citizens. This nationalist view of Inuit assimilation prevailed throughout the 1960s, with advocates proposing "to lift them out of their present degradation, physical and mental, and make them useful, respected, and contented citizens of the richest nation in the world" (Jenness, 1966: 126). The worst of the obstacles in the path of Inuit assimilation was now past, Mowat (1960) explained to Minister Hamilton, hoping that the resistance of the old order was at an end. Mowat insisted that a long, intense program of assistance would ensure the Inuit's full and useful integration. He felt that only through assimilation into greater Canadian society would the Inuit have the opportunity to improve their standard of living and extricate themselves from their former subordinate relationships with the police, missionaries, and traders—all of which he abhorred.

Senior officials recognized that the media can have a powerful impact on the public's perception of the "symbolic goods" of the political process (Clark and Dear, 1984: 99). As a result of Mowat's articles, the Department was able to adopt the symbolic role of savior, while attempting to reassure the public that every precaution would be taken to prevent a repetition of the unfortunate incidents of starvation (Hamilton, 1959a). Phillips (1959a) told Robertson that he thought *The Desperate People* could be the most influential book ever published on any area of Departmental responsibilities. He pointed out that, in the book, Mowat allows the reader to infer that the present minister was sympathetic to the Inuit cause. Wishing to encourage this tone, Phillips drafted a statement for the minister that praised the book and the issues it addressed. For the Department to support the book, Phillips thought it best that Dr. Porsild, the government official who was the principal critic of Mowat's earlier book, *People of the Deer*, and who had attempted to discredit Mowat professionally, should remain quiet about *The Desperate People*. In a crisis situation, the state acts to control the flow and nature of information (Clark and Dear, 1984: 99). Mowat's version of events was the one the Department wanted to portray. Immediately before the book's publication, Phillips (1959a) strongly urged the deputy minister to ensure that Dr. Porsild decline any invitations to make a public comment on the new book, orally or in writing. If officials like Porsild did not wish to join the chorus, the Department wanted them at least to remain silent.

The Department was not able to restrain criticism from all the officials who disagreed with Mowat's version of the facts, however. At the Northwest Territories Council debate in February 1959, when Commissioner Nicholson condemned the *Maclean's* article for its misleading statements, as he saw them, another member of the Council, L. C. Audette, also attacked Mowat's work. Audette (1959) described Mowat's writings as highly descriptive and colorful but "a trifle lurid and over-ripe," and he characterized Mowat as "incautious in his use of factual material—an incaution amounting, at times, to what I could, in the most charitable vein, term negligence or downright carelessness." Audette reiterated Porsild's criticisms of *People of the Deer* and referred to the *Maclean's* article in similar terms.

Robertson completely disagreed with this assessment of Mowat's work. He felt that personal attacks upon the author, his intelligence, his sincerity, and even his personal honesty would help no one (Robertson, 1960). Criticism of the *People of the Deer* had had the opposite effect, and Robertson accepted that it may even have rallied support behind Mowat that he would not otherwise have received. Ironically, although the Department sought in the early 1950s to orchestrate a defensive, negative response to the *People of the Deer*, now its senior officials—Phillips, Sivertz, and Robertson—sought to orchestrate a positive government response to *The Desperate People*. It was important for the Department to try to control the discourse. In this way, they might use Mowat's writings to their advantage by bringing public opinion behind the Department's efforts to improve conditions in the North through increasing its northern staff and funding new programs. As Robertson acknowledged, in the past "the administration of Eskimo affairs fell far short of the standards which the Government and people of Canada today find acceptable. . . . It is our conviction that the real fault lay partly in the people of Canada as a whole and partly in history, in that we were too small and new a nation really to undertake the Arctic job which we had in theory inherited."

The Department demonstrated its commitment to "a new start" and its alignment with Mowat, in its response, for example, to a letter from the sociology class of the Barons Consolidated High School in Barons, Alberta, who had written to the prime minister commenting on the *Maclean's* article. The class stated in its letter that it was concerned by the story of the suffering of these Inuit and thought it was a great shame that, in a prosperous country like Canada, anyone should have to endure such hardship and privation. They urged the prime minister to take steps to give more attention to the Inuit so that such happenings could be prevented (Sociology class, 1959). Hamilton (1959b) responded by confirming that Mowat had done an excellent job in drawing public attention to the critical problems facing the Inuit. The minister agreed that the government had not done very well by the Inuit, but it was his conviction that today the Department was moving as rapidly as possible to correct the wrongs of the past. He added that, in Mowat's recently

syndicated articles, he himself had paid tribute to the work the government was doing in this regard.

Multiple Realities

Mowat's account in *The Desperate People* of what happened to the Ahiarmiut was so full of facts that one critic actually remarked that the account was far too detailed to be believable (Dunbar, 1959). The reviewer
questioned how the author was able to present the public with perfect
knowledge of events. This observation leads one to ask: Was Mowat given
access to confidential government files? and, Why did he focus blame on
the Force?

Answers to these questions may be found in the Department's files on
Mowat. In the autumn of 1957, Mowat wrote to the minister of northern
affairs, Alvin Hamilton, to request assistance for his next writing project.
In a letter to the deputy minister, Mowat (1957b) assured Robertson in
advance that, "if I accepted assistance from your Department in connection with gathering material, . . . I would be morally obligated to give full
consideration to your point of view." He promised that before publication he would submit his writings to the Department for their comments
"to ensure that your Department was satisfied." Mowat explained that
he wanted to be involved in the changes taking place in the North and
believed that he could do something to awaken the general public to a
new awareness of the North. This letter was written two months before
the Ahiarmiut deaths. When the deaths occurred and the news was made
public, Mowat contacted his publishers about writing both a sequel to
People of the Deer and some magazine articles.

Mowat would have been unable to write about the complex circumstances of the relocation, the deaths, and the trial without reading the
Department's internal reports and those of the RCMP. This requirement
placed the Department in a privileged position. They had the facts on
the relocation and knew why the deaths had occurred. They knew how
the relocation had been planned and implemented; they had information about the aftermath of the move and how the Inuit had interpreted
events—records of the investigations by Stevenson and Rudnicki, by the
police, and by the judiciary. A dialogue had already been opened with
Mowat about cooperating on research for his writing assignment. The
Department made a bold, calculated decision: given the controversial
circumstances of the Ahiarmiut deaths, senior officials felt it might prove
useful to turn Canada's foremost popular writer on the North into an

ally rather than a foe. Mowat (1957a) signed a memo, drafted by Sivertz, in which he agreed to obtain the permission of the chief of the division before copying any information from the files. Mowat was then given special access to files on the Ahiarmiut case in the Department's head-quarters, and he talked with Robertson, Phillips, Sivertz, and other officials about the events that took place. Sivertz wrote to Mowat in July 1958, informing him: "When you come to Ottawa we will give you every co-operation. . . . We here will look forward to your coming and we will give you all we can in the way of help in assembling the material for your book" (Sivertz, 1958a). Mowat (1958a) wrote to Minister Alvin Hamilton: "I assure you that I will be most grateful for your co-operation."

The RCMP, however, would not give Mowat permission to see their files. Sivertz contacted Nicholson on Mowat's behalf and suggested that the RCMP give him access, but the RCMP again refused (Sivertz, personal communication). In fact, the Department had copies of a great many of the RCMP's detachment reports on the Ahiarmiut, which were regularly sent to the Department as a matter of course. Mowat recalls that he was given a desk in the Department building at which to look at the files. One day, an official apparently asked him if he had checked a bottom drawer of the desk. Mowat opened it and inside found the RCMP's Ahiarmiut files (Mowat, personal communication). How, then, with all the facts and many of the files before him, did Mowat attribute to the wrong agency—namely, the RCMP—responsibility for the 1950 and 1957 moves? When I showed Farley Mowat the key reports in which Larsen argued against the 1957 move and Gallagher advised that the Ahiarmiut be evacuated from Henik Lake in the autumn, Mowat said he had not seen those documents. He apparently had also not seen Rowley's warnings to the deputy minister in advance of the deaths, or Phillips's memo that argued against the advice of Rowley and the RCMP to move the Ahiarmiut over to the coast for closer supervision. Those documents and others show clearly that the Department instigated the relocations and was ultimately responsible for the deaths because of its decision not to follow the advice of field staff and informed observers. The police, on the other hand, acted largely in a support capacity.

Mowat was given access to a pre-selected group of files, which would explain perhaps why he mistakenly erred in favor of the Department. The fact that the Department was cooperative and the RCMP was not might also have influenced his conclusions. The Department appeared to have nothing to hide. Amongst senior officials, it was known that Mowat experienced difficulties in his contact with Cpl. Gallagher at Eskimo Point (Mowat, 1959d). He could not have been pleased to learn that his hero

Oohootok from *People of the Deer* had been arrested by Gallagher and seriously injured while breaking rocks.

During his writing of the book and articles in 1958–59, Mowat discussed his publishing plans with senior officials. He wrote to Sivertz in January 1959 saying that he planned to finish the book with a chapter outlining the hopes and plans of the Department, confiding that at this early stage "the only thing we have to watch is too overt support for the Dept." (Mowat, 1959e). He asked Sivertz for additional facts and insisted there must be no confusion or careless errors in this book. Mowat informed Sivertz of his promotional strategy and its polemical intent: "The newspaper series should start the fire roaring. I have deliberately made it highly inflammatory and we will then go on to talk about the constructive possibilities open to the Govt, and to all of us." Mowat signed his letter, "Cheers chum."

The Department's calculated decision to accommodate Mowat proved highly successful. Mowat became a powerful advocate of the Department's efforts, and, to their delight, he refrained from blaming them in the *Maclean's* article as well as in *The Desperate People* for the errors that were made. The Department responded warmly, and Mowat (1960) wrote to Alvin Hamilton telling him how pleased he was about the minister's public statements on *The Desperate People*. Hamilton's attitude had disarmed Mowat's most dangerous critics, he said. Mowat described the ironic symbiotic position that placed him "in the same bed" with the Department. "I now feel that your Department will do a good job in this regard," Mowat assured the minister. "In fact I have apparently said so to such effect that certain reactionary groups are now bracketing my name with that of the Department. I don't know which one of us will be most uncomfortable in this propinquity." As a result of Mowat's writings and of the Department's support for his version of events, the Force was publicly made to bear the greatest burden of guilt for the Ahiarmiut tragedy. In retrospect, Mowat feels that he was used by the Department, despite his having solicited their cooperation (Mowat, personal communication).

· PART 4 ·

REASSESSMENT

· 8 ·

THE AFTERMATH: REFLECTIONS
ON RELOCATION

The End of the Experiment

The two case studies discussed here were roughly framed between two historical events: the first Conference on Eskimo Affairs in 1952, when the "Eskimo problem" was first identified publicly, and the tenth meeting of the Eskimo Affairs Committee, held on 25 May 1959, where for the first time Inuit representatives presented their views of the problems facing their people to the prime minister of Canada (see fig. 8.1). The significance of the latter event was widely recognized: "At Long Last, Eskimos Speak Out for Themselves at Historic Conference," announced a newspaper headline (Gray, 1959). One could argue that both events were prompted by public response to reports about a small group of fifty Inuit—the Ahiarmiut. Mowat's descriptions of their difficulties in *People of the Deer* provided a "trigger mechanism" resulting in a massive public outcry, which prompted the government to organize the first conference on Inuit affairs. After the reports of the Ahiarmiut deaths and those of other Keewatin Inuit in 1958, the Department responded once again by arranging the highly publicized 1959 meeting.

During the seven years between these two events, the Department was called upon to develop, virtually without guidelines, Inuit social welfare policies. In an effort to find solutions to the "Eskimo problem," it conducted a number of socioeconomic experiments. At the beginning of this transitional period, which Jenness (1964: 90) has characterized as "steering without a compass," the Department and the RCMP set in motion the ambitious 1953–55 High Arctic repopulation experiments. Given the difficulties the Inuit and their RCMP guardians faced, they were fortunate that the project did not collapse.

FIGURE 8.1 George Koneak speaking before the prime minister, John Diefenbaker (far right), at the tenth meeting of the Eskimo Affairs Conference in Ottawa (Ben Sivertz seated at table between Koneak and Diefenbaker), 25 May 1959. Credit: National Archives of Canada

The 1957 resettlement of the Ahiarmiut had much in common with the 1953 project. Both relocations demonstrated the Department's determination to sever the dependency relationship the Inuit had developed with the Whites. The public's negative response to the Keewatin deaths, however, caused the Department to reassess their solutions. The failure of this 1957 project signaled an end to the type of social experiment that placed Inuit lives at risk and placed the Department's reputation in jeopardy (Phillips, 1967: 174; Mackinnon, 1989: 165–66). Ironically, the Inuit had come to refer to the northern administrators as *inulirijik* (one who fixes up people). The act of asking the four Inuit to address the prime minister, John Diefenbaker, at the 1959 conference could be seen as a public relations exercise (in keeping with Diefenbaker's "northern vision" resource development policies); but it was also a symbolic gesture and an acknowledgment that the Whites could benefit from the assistance of the Inuit in developing effective policies that, first of all, were consensual and, secondly, would not result in the sort of disaster that led to murder and starvation (Diubaldo, 1989: 172). This chapter brings out the salient aspects of the relocation policy, relating them to the planners' ideological motivations and their social implications for the Inuit.

Positive Views

In spite of the Department's difficulties with the Ahiarmiut relocation and its aftermath, officials continued to view the Resolute Bay and Grise Fiord relocation projects in a positive light. Numerous press reports and internal documents attest to this view. The project proved that the Inuit could live on Ellesmere and Cornwallis Islands, as Inuit had done over five hundred years before (Cantley, 1953; *Arctic Circular*, 1955; *Polar Record*, 1957; Maxwell, 1985). The experiment also succeeded in demonstrating that families dependent on social benefits could be taken off relief and could survive off the land. The two Inuit colonies at Resolute Bay and Grise Fiord continued to be referred to in the late 1950s as "rehabilitation settlements" (Canada, 1958c). At Resolute Bay, Cpl. Moodie was able to report in 1958 that during the last year the twelve Inuit families had obtained some 50 whales, 790 seals, 50 walrus, 47 caribou, 1,025 white foxes, and 61 polar bears (Gould, 1958b: 3). Furthermore, because of the demand for Inuit labor at the base, the ten Inuit men had been divided into two groups of five and organized so that each group worked two-week shifts at the base, followed by two weeks hunting. At least one individual, Salluviniq (1977) was contented with life at Resolute Bay; however, the store continued to be short of supplies, and the community still did not have a school or other facilities. Cpl. Moodie had been asked several times by Markoosie Patsauq (then sixteen years old) if he could go to school in the south.

Perhaps equally important, the government had succeeded in creating permanent settlements of Canadian citizens in the High Arctic Islands, thus consolidating effective occupation and exercising sovereignty over the region. During the 1950s when the Department lacked the necessary field personnel, it was prepared to cede operational control of the settlements to the RCMP. Detachment reports from the two colonies usually reassured officials in Ottawa that "the natives generally are in good health, happy and prosperous" (Pilot, 1958). The Department in turn showed its untarnished confidence in a letter to the RCMP saying that they were pleased that conditions among the Grise Fiord Inuit were favorable and that they were in good health, happy, and prosperous (Bolger, 1959).

Admittedly, the rapport between the RCMP and the Department was not always so good. Conflicts arose, for example, between the RCMP and the Department over responsibility for Grise Fiord and Resolute Bay. In 1964, Chief Superintendent C. B. Macdonell, commanding "G" Division, informed a colleague in the RCMP: "We have striven to maintain control over the Eskimos at both Resolute and Grise Fiord and this has been no easy matter, as the Dept. of NANR have on a number of occasions expressed their desire to take over responsibility for welfare of the Eskimos at those points and handle it through their own staff" (Macdonell, 1964).

In a confidential internal memo of June 1964, Insp. E. R. Lysyk in the Criminal Investigation Branch of "G" Division stressed that the RCMP was particularly pleased with its administration of the two colonies:

It would not be boastful if we said that this relocation of Eskimos was a very successful venture and one which we are quite proud of. . . . We have received very favourable publicity over our management of Eskimo welfare at both Resolute Bay and Grise Fiord, and I do not want our members making any moves to lessen our responsibilities at those points. (Lysyk, 1964)

Officials were also gratified that one of the original aims of the relocation—to reduce the total of relief benefits paid to the Port Harrison area—had been achieved. Figure 8.2 shows that, by 1958, relief payments and family allowances had diminished as a percentage of average income. This reduction had been possible since 1951 as a result of increased income from trapping, handicrafts, and wage employment. In the late 1950s, the Department financed a detailed study of Port Harrison by anthropologist William Willmott (1961: 34), who observed that relief played only a small part in the economy of that Inuit settlement. His report noted that the list of those currently receiving relief included only "widows, cripples and old men," whereas in 1950 it had included many able-bodied young men who were classified as inefficient trappers.

In the years before Willmott's study, Port Harrison had been described by officials as overpopulated and hopelessly dependent on relief. The Department could now claim that, after the implementation of a prudent financial policy, Port Harrison was developing into a model northern community with a varied and balanced economy. Willmott observed that one of the reasons for such a dramatic improvement in the native economy was the phenomenal rise over the past decade of the soapstone industry, which provided most of the Inuit in Port Harrison with an income (ibid.: 35). Another contributing factor was the government's policy of reducing the population of Harrison through migration to the High Arctic, which had thus increased the land resources available to each household and allowed a greater dependency on country food (ibid.). The study therefore recognized the "success" of the Depart-

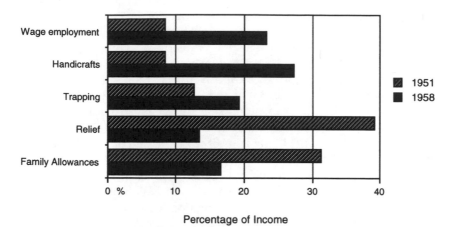

FIGURE 8.2 Comparative sources of Inuit income at Port Harrison, 1951 and 1958.
Sources: Canada, 1951b; Willmott, 1961

ment's policy, whose justification for the 1953 relocation was to reduce the pressure on available resources by depopulating the district. The Canadian government was able to confirm what European countries had already discovered—that emigration or relocation was a necessary safety valve for dealing with the social stresses generated by excess population (H. Johnston, 1972: 132).

By targeting the people dependent on relief, the Department was also able to realize a significant reduction in relief payments to the Port Harrison district—from $32,363 in 1952–53 to $12,265 in 1954–55 (see fig. 2.2). That 62 percent reduction to Port Harrison was in marked contrast to the 85 percent increase in relief payments for the other Inuit districts during the same period, from an annual average of $3,483 to $6,454; and an overall increase of 24 percent in total relief payments to Inuit for the same three-year period, from $128,887 to $160,671.

When Cst. Ross Gibson returned from Resolute Bay to Port Harrison in 1957, he did so without the relocatees. Upon arrival for his two-year reassignment there, Gibson (1957) was displeased to find a number of Inuit living in the settlement. He reintroduced the same strict measures he had implemented in 1952–53, moving out of Port Harrison all the Inuit who were not employed there and placing them on the land within a twenty-mile radius of the settlement. Geographical space is linked to social exclusion, and the control of space is a key element in the maintenance of social order (D. Smith, 1990: 9; P. Jackson, 1989: 101). Gibson's action exemplified the degree of operational autonomy and the power over the local population that constables enjoyed in the 1950s. He was not required to obtain the consent of his superior officers before carrying out this local resettlement operation. Moral order was thus restored by employing a spatial strategy, justified by Gibson: "This move has kept the settlement cleaner and ridded it of starving dogs and scrounging Eskimos" (P. Jackson, 1989: 100; Gibson, 1957).

In subsequent years, the Department continued to report that the 1953–55 relocations had been highly successful for all parties concerned. In his appraisal of the relocations, Alex Stevenson (1968), DIAND's administrator of the Arctic, wrote in 1968 that the outcome of these ventures had been more successful and satisfactory than had ever been anticipated. He recognized that the original "migration scheme" was an attempt to depopulate the Port Harrison region. Withdrawal of some of the hunters from the area not only benefited them, argued Stevenson, but also relieved Port Harrison of some of its large human population.

Dissenting Voices

As the officer in charge of the eastern Arctic patrol, Bob Phillips visited Port Harrison in 1955 and found that the original motivation for the relocation (namely, the poverty in that area) was somewhat suspect. In view of what he had heard previously about the difficulties of the Port Harrison economy, "especially in relation to the movement of its residents to the Queen Elizabeth Islands," Phillips (1955: 43) reported to the deputy minister, "I was a little surprised, though agreeably so, at the general level of prosperity." This observation was made by a senior official just two years after the Department had reported the district as being one of those in the Arctic with the most problems. Indeed, the settlement's new Company manager, Mr. Nichols, advised Phillips that the migrations from Port Harrison should cease (ibid.). Although 1955 was a poor year for fox trapping, economic conditions remained stable.

The senior RCMP officer at Port Harrison, Cpl. Decker, also felt that the Port Harrison people seemed to be reasonably well off and that inadequate sources of income were not putting pressure on the population (ibid.). Although the Inuit reportedly hunted less than in other districts, Phillips informed his superiors that it was pointless for them to do so when they could earn a large income from their soapstone carvings. Nevertheless, the plan went ahead as arranged, and the four Inukjuamiut families pre-selected for relocation were brought on board and transported to the High Arctic under Phillips's supervision. The observations in this report are highly significant because they raise questions about the credibility of the Department's statements two years before that the Port Harrison area should be depopulated to ease the dire circumstances there. Ironically, two years after Sargent (1954) referred to Grise Fiord as the Inukjuamiut's Garden of Eden, Phillips (1956: 26) suggested that, although Port Harrison was not exactly a Garden of Eden, this shortcoming was due to the disharmonious relations amongst the Whites in the community (a recurrent feature of settlement life; see Brody, 1975: 73; Riches, 1977).

When Phillips continued to Pond Inlet on the eastern Arctic patrol in 1955, he heard similar comments from officials there questioning the merits of any relocation. The Company manager particularly questioned its wisdom and pointed out that Pond Inlet was well endowed with all the natural resources necessary to support a community even larger than its present size (Phillips, 1955: 74). The manager told Phillips that game and trapping were good, and he regretted the decline in population, particularly when it involved his best hunters.

In the early 1960s, the Department was still considering whether to establish Inuit colonies in the vicinity of the High Arctic weather stations at Mould Bay, Isachsen, Eureka, and Alert. Radstock Bay, a site of oil and gas activity on Little Cornwallis Island, was also considered as a location that offered the opportunity for wage labor. When, in the 1960s, the Department embarked on a population centralization program for the Canadian Arctic, necessitating the resettlement of the entire Inuit population into communities, the coastal sites that were selected for supply access were those that had a recent history of human habitation. Resolute Bay and Grise Fiord therefore remained the only permanent settlements in the Queen Elizabeth Islands.

Walter Rudnicki, chief of the Department's Welfare Division, in 1960 highlighted the disadvantages of establishing wholly artificial colonies like Resolute Bay or Grise Fiord. The two communities were started with "a built-in conflict factor," warned Rudnicki (1960), that might result in their ultimate dissolution. He pointed out that Resolute was a community in which there was considerable animosity and bickering between the Port Harrison and Pond Inlet groups. There had been no intermarriage, and moreover, the two groups hunted separately, maintained separate caches, and generally preferred to stay out of each other's way.

Rudnicki also criticized the theory behind the original plan to establish the Inuit trading stores at Resolute Bay and Grise Fiord. On paper, the stores were part of an enlightened scheme to promote self-reliance by training the Inuit in financial and management practices so that they might handle their own trading affairs. Arguably, they could be seen as the forerunners of the 1960s Inuit cooperative movement. The philosophy was similar to Larsen's conception of a Crown trading corporation to replace the Hudson's Bay Company. Larsen was unsuccessful in persuading the Department to create the larger company, but his officers were given the opportunity to manage the government-operated stores at Resolute, Grise, and Herschel Island.

In practice, though, the stores at Resolute Bay and Grise Fiord did not function the way they were intended to. The Eskimo Loan Fund had been set up in 1952 by the Department and the Treasury Board in order to make returnable advances to Inuit groups or individuals and thereby help them purchase supplies and equipment (Eskimo Affairs, 1952a: 3). The Craig Harbour and Resolute Bay stores were each given a five thousand dollar loan. These loans were made out in the names of the two Inuit whom the RCMP had selected as the camp bosses: "Fatty" at Craig Harbour, and "Sudlavenich" at Resolute Bay. Though the loans were officially in their names, they were "trader in name only" (Larsen, n.d.: 46), and they were given no say in running the stores (Sivertz, 1954). The trader (*niuviqti*) at each of the stores was actually an RCMP officer. The officers ordered the supplies and allocated them, kept the accounts, valued the furs, and shipped the furs south to be sold. In fact, Rudnicki (1960) discovered that after seven years none of the Inuit at Grise Fiord or Resolute Bay knew anything about running the store.

During the 1950s, the Inuit at Grise Fiord and Resolute Bay, and elsewhere in the Arctic, were not paid in cash for furs traded or work done (money was *kiinaujaq* "something which looks like a face"—a reference to the head of the monarch on coinage). Instead, they received credit at the local store. The RCMP officers at the two colonies were responsible for keeping proper accounts for all the inhabitants, listing the amounts of standing credits or debts owed. The Inuit brought in the white fox furs, which the RCMP valued on the basis of a price set by the Department, after which the hunters' accounts were credited accordingly. The Inuit could then purchase merchandise up to that value or leave a credit on the books. It was the same system the Inuit had been accustomed to at the Company store in Port Harrison, but there were two differences. First, the officers carefully controlled Inuit spending, whereas the Company traders might have induced the Inuit to spend all their earnings. Secondly, in place of the Company, the Department assumed responsibility for the sale of the furs at auction.

James Cantley, with his background as a fur trader, was given the responsibility of organizing the trade supplies required for the new colonies, and he purchased them from funds made available from the Eskimo Loan Fund. He also handled the fur returns when they were sent to the auction house in Montreal (A. Stevenson, 1977). Proceeds from the Inuit fur catch paid off the two loans in the names of "Fatty" and "Sudlavenich," and profits accrued. Apparently, though, the detachment officers and the Inuit were not told about the profits in the loan fund. In fact, Bob Pilot, the constable at Craig Harbour and Grise Fiord from 1955 to 1958, said he was informed by the Department in the late 1950s that the loan was still in arrears, to his surprise (Pilot, personal communication). Yet records show that as early as November 1955 the loan account to the store at Craig Harbour had a credit balance of $3,153 (Canada, 1955b). Furthermore, although interest on the loan had been charged at the rate of 5 percent, there was no provision for paying interest on the profits that accumulated in the account after the loan had been paid off (Sivertz, 1959d).

Theoretically, the Department was to inform the Inuit of their financial affairs. Supt. Larsen (1952b) had felt it was important that each Inuk know what his credit standing was. When a state functionary who has the authority to decide what is good for an individual under his care is able to escape effective public scrutiny and control, destructive consequences can follow, as both case studies demonstrate repeatedly (Allen, 1981: 46). For example, on their visit to Resolute Bay in August 1956, Supt. Larsen and J. C. Jackson (the Department's officer in charge of the 1956 eastern Arctic patrol) were told by the Inuit that for three years Cst. Gibson had been withholding information from them about the amount of their credit at the store (Jackson, 1956). Inuit criticism of Gibson's actions was unusual, for in the event of disputes with him they would typically not have appealed beyond the local RCMP (Freeman, 1971: 36). When Cpl. Moodie replaced Gibson in May 1957, he discovered that no individual accounts had been kept since the store had started up (Gould, 1958b: 8), whereas Cpl. Sargent at Grise Fiord had maintained proper store records. Reports that Gibson did not keep accounts were consistent with a statement to the Royal Commission in June 1993 that he never looked after family allowances at Resolute Bay (Canada, 1993b: 200).

Cunningham (1954b) informed Supt. Larsen that Gibson's first-year store accounts were incomplete and that Inuit wages and proceeds from trapping and handicrafts were not being credited. Cunningham also noted that Gibson had taken from the store's stock goods to a value of $385 for his personal use, without yet having arranged for a remittance. In fact, because the stock was costed against the outstanding loan, the Inuit were being charged 5 percent interest for Gibson's provisions and for all other noncredited debts (ibid.). Government officials who purchased supplies and equipment for the relocatees before their embarkation in Port Harrison had also charged those provisions to the two loans (Stevenson, 1953).

Although the reformers' rehabilitative strategy was intended to en-

courage self-reliance, the inherent penal apparatus of the colonies favored the continuance of police hegemony over the Inuit. The officers
were natural agents for creating and policing a penitential environment,
exerting discipline within the enclosed space of what became a colony of
confinement (Foucault, 1977: 141). In the early years, the only way the
Inuit could leave the High Arctic, as in Markoosie Patsauq's case, was on
the hospital ship (see chapter 3). The police retained full supervision of
the local trading operations in Resolute Bay and Grise Fiord, thereby exerting exclusive economic control over the individuals living in the two
rehabilitation settlements. This situation created a micro-environment
for internal colonialism (Dryzek and Young, 1985: 125), which later became apparent to Walter Rudnicki. He criticized the RCMP's approach
to the management of the two stores, arguing that by transferring Inuit
to a new location, the Department merely transferred the former "Boss-
Eskimo" relationship that existed in the more established communities
(Rudnicki, 1960). Rudnicki reported in 1960 that the status quo was un-
changed, with the constable being the only person in the community who
knew the prices of goods on the shelves. The store items were not being
provided by the government at cost either. Officials decided to mark up
all supplies, adding 25–50 percent to the cost price of hardware and
50 percent to that of dry goods (Canada, 1958f). According to anthropologist Milton Freeman (1968: 116), in the mid-1960s the Grise Fiord
constable, who was secretary-treasurer of the store, controlled people's
spending habits according to their economic and moral standing. The
bookkeeping remained in the hands of the RCMP officers until 1967.

Though Supt. Larsen and the Department complained at various
times during the first four years that the Inuit at Resolute Bay and Grise
Fiord were not being credited properly, the RCMP later discovered a
critical flaw in the Department's management of the Inuit profits. In
1960, RCMP Assistant Superintendent W. G. Fraser learned that during
the previous trapping season the Inuit at Grise Fiord received $6,140
in credits for 379 white fox pelts. He further learned that the fox pelts
had been sold at auction by the Department for $17,953. The balance of
$11,800 in profit never reached the Inuit hunters (Fraser, 1960b). After
receiving a memo from the Department's officials Stevenson and Bolger,
Fraser tried to explain to his officers at Grise Fiord and Resolute Bay
why the Inuit could not receive the profits from their fur catches: "In
the past, concern has been expressed because the profit from the annual operation of the Eskimo Trading Stores has not been returned to
the Eskimos. We now understand that this cannot be done because of
the unusual circumstances whereby the Trading Stores were established"
(Fraser, 1960a).

It is clear from Fraser's explanation that this particular government policy would remain a mystery. When I asked Ben Sivertz (see fig. 8.1) about Fraser's memo, he confessed that, although he was the Department's director of northern administration at that time, he too never fully understood the intricacies of the Eskimo Loan Fund's administrative apparatus for financing the operation of the stores (Sivertz, personal communication). This form of paternalism, whereby the Inuit were not informed of the store prices nor credited properly for wages and profits made on fur catches, created a relationship inferior to the one they traditionally had had with the Hudson's Bay Company in Port Harrison. The Department was using the Inuit fur profits as a revolving fund from which to purchase supplies for the stores rather than covering the advances from its own funds. Considerable sums of money were involved: departmental accounts for the loan to Sudlavenich at Resolute Bay show that, after seven years, "repayments" on the original $5,000 loan totaled $103,000 (Canada, 1960). The $5,000 loan to "Thomasie's store" at Grise Fiord (Thomasie had been assigned the store, in name only, and the loan after the death of "Fatty" Aqiatusuk, the former "trader") had accrued repayments of $64,000 after five years, though Thomasie and the other Inuit in the community had no knowledge of this amount (ibid.; Inuit informants at Grise Fiord, personal communication).

Supt. Larsen (1952b) had suggested that Inuit employed at air force bases receive the same pay as Whites for comparable work. At the base at Resolute Bay, the Inuit were paid a percentage of the standard rate, according to their level of skill. At both Resolute Bay and Grise Fiord, the Inuit allege some of them were not paid at all for the work they did. Simeonie Amagoalik recalled that, whenever "the policeman and his friends wanted to go polar bear hunting, I had to act as their guide. I never got paid for those times" (*Makivik News*, 1989a). The Whites used to ask Simeonie and other Inuit to be guides for their hunting parties in return for some of the meat from the hunt. Cst. Gibson (1954) said he would invite members of the air force, United States Weather Bureau, and Department of Transport to accompany him on hunting trips. It was customary, he said, for the Inuit to consume some of the food while on the hunt, and any excess was distributed to them at the conclusion of the trip.

There were, however, other, more blatant examples of nonpayment for services rendered. John Amagoalik recalled how his father and other relatives spent months at a time taking government surveyors around the High Arctic, mapping the islands and collecting mineral samples, and they were never paid for their services (Canada, 1990b). Supt. Larsen (1954b) found evidence of this; he noted that, at Resolute Bay, Ama-

goalik and his wife earned five dollars per day for their employment with
the geological survey party but were not receiving their wages either in
cash or in goods from Gibson's store. Larsen brought this situation to
the attention of the Department, commenting that "the whole of their
wages goes to your Department to help pay off the Eskimo Traders'
Loan Account" (ibid.). Similarly, a Department of Transport receipt
dated 23 April 1954 shows that Alex, Simeonie, Salluviniq, and Amagoalik earned $13.75 each, and Jaybeddie earned $10, from wage employment at Resolute Bay (Canada, 1954b); however, the five payments
were grouped together to give a total of $65 and paid by check to the
Eskimo Loan Fund, not to the individuals themselves (Canada, 1954a).

The records and oral statements show that, between 1953 and 1957,
the Inuit at Resolute Bay were not individually credited with the proceeds of trapping, wages, or family allowance benefits (the distribution
of which were officially mandatory). Accounting appears to have been
better at Grise Fiord, although the Inuit did not individually receive
their full fur profits. This situation was corrected finally in 1961 when
the government stores became Inuit cooperatives. Rudnicki (1960) concluded that there was much to be said for striving toward something a
little more imaginative and significant in future resettlement projects.

A Sense of Place

The RCMP selected Lindstrom Peninsula as the site for the Inuit camp,
ostensibly because there were Thule ruins on the beach (see chapter 3);
moreover, on Supt. Larsen's sea chart of the area, Otto Sverdrup's winter
quarters for 1899–1900 are marked as being on Lindstrom Peninsula,
which Sverdrup named after the expedition's cook ("Henry Larsen's Sea
Navigation Chart of the Northwest Passage," 1927). Perhaps Larsen felt
that, since his fellow Norwegian had selected this site as the most prom-
ising spot for overwintering, it should be fine for the Inuit camp.

Resolute Bay was named after the ship HMS *Resolute*, which wintered
in the area in 1850–51 while searching for Sir John Franklin's lost expedition of 1845. How did Grise Fiord, of which Lindstrom Peninsula
is a promontory, get its name? "Gris" means pig in Norwegian, and on
some old maps the fiord is labeled "Pig Fiord." This name is curious because the large fiord does not resemble a pig, none of the surrounding
features is pig-shaped, nor are there any pigs within a distance of more
than two thousand kilometers. A possible explanation might be found
in the Norwegian word "grisevær," used to describe "piggish" or rotten
weather. Indeed, today the Inuit speak of the strong winds that come

howling down the fiord and that have been known to rip the roofs off the houses in the community. (The katabatic winds can also make landing there in a light plane an uncomfortable experience.)

No one had lived on the fiord in the fifty years since Sverdrup had named it. The Inuit thus found themselves in a place that had an interesting name but certain environmental shortcomings. Despite Cpl. Sargent's Edenic description of the area, soon after their arrival the dark period began, and the Inuit found themselves on a narrow beach at the base of a steep, forbidding mountain in "grisevær," with high winds whistling down the fiord. Such were the differences in climate and environment from their old homeland that they used to ask each other: *silarjuarmiinginaaqitaa*, "are we still in the same world"? (Patsauq, personal communication).

In a report to Sivertz in 1960, Rudnicki described the social difficulties the Inuit were experiencing in adjusting to the prospect of permanent residence at Grise Fiord and Resolute Bay. "It is known that many of these resettled Eskimos still speak of returning to their original settlements though they have been gone for seven years," Rudnicki (1960) reminded Sivertz, but added that without more evidence he did not know how much of this attitude stemmed from genuine discontent (ibid.). Graham Rowley, the secretary of the ACND who had lived with the Inuit and spoke Inuktitut, also belatedly acknowledged Inuit homesickness (*anarrasiktuq*) and the importance to the Inuit of a sense of place. "To us, one part of the barrens may appear very much like another," Rowley (1958c) observed, "but this is not the case with the Eskimos." As discussed in chapter 4, the identification of places is vital to human development, and whereas an unknown space is in a sense empty, it requires bounding and identification by an individual in order to become a meaningful place (Lee, 1982: 161).

Place is a condition of human experience. The two elements place and culture are fundamental to the construction of one's individual and collective identity (Entrikin, 1991: 1). These universal needs had particular implications for Inuit identity and survival, as Rowley appears to have acknowledged with reference to the relocations. He informed Deputy Minister Robertson that, for the Inuit, the region wherein they have lived for many years has associations that mean a great deal to them, and detailed knowledge of any area is essential for hunters wishing to exploit its potentialities fully (Rowley, 1958c). With reference to the Ahiarmiut, Rowley commented on the question of consensual relocation in relation to a sense of place and suggested that, in view of the remarks in Steenhoven's report, the Ahiarmiut liked the Ennadai region and did not want to leave it. Thus, he ventured, "it appeared unlikely that the move was really accepted by them" (ibid.). Although Rowley was in the influential position of reporting directly to Robertson, his post at the ACND placed him outside the Department's command structure. He could comment on policy but had limited control over its implementation, and in the Ahiarmiut case, his warnings before tragedy occurred were ignored.

When planning the northward move to Henik Lake, it is surprising that officials did not take into account the consequences of the earlier southward move to Nueltin Lake in 1950. Had they done so, they would have noted that the project's failure was due in part to the distress caused by leaving Ennadai. On their return to Ennadai, the Ahiarmiut report-edly claimed that there were too many trees in the Nueltin Lake area and they could not stalk caribou (Larsen, 1959: 8). From this and other observations, the police acknowledged that the relocatees were unhappy in unfamiliar surroundings and simply returned to their accustomed haunts (ibid.). The Nueltin Lake experiment should have provided the officials organizing the 1953 and 1957 relocation experiments with evi-dence of the problems caused by a lack of consensual planning.

When Larsen analyzed the 1957 relocation, he accepted that the fail-ure to obtain informed consent had been a flaw in the planning. He quoted from an earlier report on the Nueltin move, which concluded that "the natives apparently never had understood the move or what they were expected to do"; in fact, they apparently thought the Whites were going to fish for them at Nueltin Lake (ibid.). When the Port Har-rison relocation was being planned, however, the only cautionary remark about the consequences of moving the Inuit to a quite different environ-ment was made by Alex Stevenson (1952), who informed his superiors that the Port Harrison Inuit could have difficulties adjusting to the dark period. Stevenson (1968) confirmed this view fifteen years later when commenting on the relocation: "It was thought at the time of the move that the Harrison group would not only find the environment strange," Stevenson recalled, "but as they had never experienced the dark period the assumption was that travelling and trapping would be most difficult." The sole notation on his memo of 1952 would suggest that either there was little interest among officials in introducing perspectives that con-flicted with relocation policy or that there was a lack of understanding of Inuit culture within the planning group.

The Final Drawing Back

Because the RCMP and the Department considered the colonization of the High Arctic Islands a success, it is perhaps not surprising that plans were made to extend the operation. In the spring of 1956, the idea of establishing additional Inuit communities in the High Arctic was discussed. Pleased with the Grise Fiord operation in particular, Supt. Larsen (1956a) recommended to Commissioner Nicholson that a similar Inuit colony and RCMP detachment be re-established at Dundas Harbour on Devon Island, where officers could supervise the operation of a trading store funded by the Eskimo Loan Fund.

Nicholson and Robertson discussed creating a colony at Dundas Harbour in the light of what was learned from the 1934 Devon Island relocation experiment (see chapter 2). Robertson (1956) recognized that in the previous relocation to Devon the wildlife population quickly decreased even with a minimum of killing and was not capable of regenerating at a rate anywhere near sufficient for the needs of the small group of Inuit that were moved in there. The Wildlife Service felt that two years' habitation at Grise Fiord and Resolute Bay was not a long enough time to assess the potential impact on available resources (ibid.). Indeed, it was later found that, in comparison with the southern Arctic, only a much greater land and sea area per hunter could provide sufficient food in the High Arctic because of the "sterility of the landscape" (Riewe, 1991: 297). For example, each Grise Fiord hunter needed more than eight times the area required for each hunter in the Eskimo Point area, which is at the same latitude as Port Harrison (ibid.). Without proper resource studies to help him make an informed decision about further repopulation of the High Arctic, Robertson decided in 1956 that it was better to postpone the establishment of a colony on Devon Island until at least the following year. Graham Rowley (1956b), secretary of the ACND, was relieved about the postponement, reminding Robertson that this location was the one selected by the United States Air Force for a photoflash bombing exercise by the Strategic Air Command. Significantly, Robertson (1956) also sounded a note of caution about the attitude of the Inuit toward the location:

The sociological problems have not yet been entirely worked out. We do not know what proportion, if any, of the Craig Harbour Eskimos and those at Resolute Bay may wish to return to their former homes after a stay of, say, three or four years in the High Arctic. We have been hoping that the majority of them would regard their new locations as permanent. If, on the other hand, they are not content to stay and demand to be sent back, this would be a factor to be considered in connection with establishing other groups.

Officials also recognized the growing need for schools, nursing stations, and other facilities in northern settlements, but the cost of establishing these services in multiple northerly locations was seen as a problem. Cantley (1956) advised Sivertz that, with all the changes that were taking place in the Arctic now, they should be cautious in their approach to setting up new communities in the far North. He queried the merit of further relocations to the High Arctic:

Before we decide on any large scale moves I think it would be desirable to carefully consider what the general pattern for Eskimo development is to be. Are we to encourage and assist Eskimos to remain scattered in small groups, or to congregate into larger settlements where they will have access to educational facilities for their children at least, and where they themselves may be better taken care of and trained in skills other than those of the hunter and trapper. I think we should attempt to look at the whole picture before making any temporary piece meal arrangements. (ibid.)

Cantley's questioning of the basic direction of the government's Inuit administration policies marked a pivotal change — a change toward using resettlement as a means of centralizing Inuit populations rather than further scattering them. In one meeting to discuss further resettlement to the High Arctic, Supt. Larsen also expressed the opinion that large settlements be established rather than a lot of small settlements and that full facilities be provided, such as schools, hospitals, small industries, and so on, for, ultimately, such would be required (Bennett, 1956).

By the mid-1950s, there was a growing feeling in the Department that the Inuit were no longer able to subsist exclusively on the proceeds of an unstable, fur-based economy. The price of white fox fur was tied to the whims of fashion, and in Robertson's view, that base was not suitable for securing long-term economic stability in the North. Wariness about Inuit subsistence led to a shift in the resettlement policy towards sites of wage labor and away from unoccupied wilderness sites, as illustrated by the decision in 1955 to increase the population of Resolute, which provided wage employment, and not to increase the population of Grise Fiord, which had a subsistence and trapping-oriented economy.

The Department's concern about the future of the fur economy was a key factor in its development strategy and relocation policy in the mid- to late-1950s. There was little sense in pursuing a policy of relocation to wilderness sites as a form of work relief (in order to reduce welfare dependency and encourage self-reliance) if there was no long-term stability in the fur market. A working group that included Walter Rudnicki was set up to examine resettlement possibilities in the south, such as "a cottage colony" on an island in Great Slave Lake or on Anticosti Island (Eskimo Affairs, 1956). As with the moves to the High Arctic a few years earlier, it was felt that "Eskimos would not co-operate singly in a resettlement project," and therefore the family unit was regarded as the nucleus around which the experiment would be built (ibid.). The relocation in

1953 from Fort Chimo to Churchill (see chapters 3 and 4) had demonstrated the difficulty of transplanting men without their families.

While considering plans to move Inuit to isolated islands in the south, the Department encountered another idea. According to Phillips, the RCMP constables posted to Port Harrison in 1956 had their own island-relocation scheme—"the Nottingham Island Plan." Phillips noted that their solution to the Eskimo problem had a certain simplistic quality: "put all the Eskimos on Nottingham Island and drop a hydrogen bomb on it" (Phillips, 1956: 28). After his discussions with the Port Harrison RCMP, Phillips informed Robertson in confidence that "their publicly expressed contempt for the Eskimos gave some of us pause" (ibid.).

A report on "Proposed Eskimo Resettlement in Southern Canada" was prepared by an internal working group organized by the Department, and it was discussed by the Eskimo Affairs Committee in 1957. The report began auspiciously, stating that the traditional relationship between the Inuit and their physical environment had ceased to exist (Eskimo Affairs, 1957). If a "surplus population" were to develop that was dependent on relief rations, it was argued that they could be resettled in the south and trained for wage employment. The option of a mass southern resettlement scheme was not pursued, however, perhaps because of how it might have been perceived by other countries (Paine, 1977: 12).

The quandary over whether to resettle Inuit in the south or north became apparent when government officials met in October 1956 in response to Robertson's request that two places be selected as possible locations for relocating more Inuit to the High Arctic (Richards, 1956b). Officials considered a number of possible sites for the new relocation, including Resolute Bay, Alexandra Fiord, Prince Patrick Island, Somerset Island, Igloolik, and Coats and Mansell Islands. Port Burwell was also discussed as a resettlement site, but Alex Stevenson was of the opinion that Eskimos would not want to go to Port Burwell unless trading facilities were provided (Bennett, 1956). It was decided that Dundas Harbour and Banks Island were the most appropriate, and the Department asked the Wildlife Service and Fisheries Department to make resource surveys of those areas to assess the feasibility of introducing future Inuit populations.

In the spring of 1958, the Department considered moving more families from Port Harrison to Grise Fiord. Cst. Gibson, now stationed back in Port Harrison, advised against the proposal, citing the local Company manager's concern that the area was being depleted of its good hunters (Larsen, 1958). Larsen informed the Department of this concern and (aware, as in 1954, of the problem of obtaining spouses in Resolute Bay and Grise Fiord) stated that, if more people were sent, they should be "marriageable young people." He also advised that no more large families be relocated since there was no long-range plan for these people to stay at Grise Fiord, and their opportunities at this location were considerably less than those afforded the Inuit farther south (ibid.). Larsen recognized, five years after the 1953 relocation, that Grise Fiord had obvious drawbacks as a community, thereby distancing himself from the original assumption by officials that the relocation would improve the Inuit standard of living.

At this stage, the colonization of Ellesmere Island was still considered an experiment whose future was in question. Some of the Grise Fiord Inuit were trying to move to Resolute, where living conditions were materially better. In 1959 Cst. Moodie at Resolute advised against any further relocation to that colony, noting, for example, that essential commodities were now becoming scarce. These commodities included lumber for building and heating homes (Moodie, 1959). Sivertz (1959f) informed Larsen in 1959 that the Department would no longer relocate families from Pond Inlet or elsewhere to Resolute Bay, and to discourage potential applicants, it would refuse to provide them with transportation, housing, and electricity (Sivertz, 1959g).

The Inuit at Pond Inlet and Port Harrison saw a change in Department attitude in the space of just a few years—from being actively recruited to relocate to the High Arctic to being discouraged from doing so. In 1960, for example, the Department asked the RCMP to instruct its officer in Port Harrison to convince one Inuk related to a resident of Resolute Bay that the move would not be in his best interests (Bolger, 1960c). This complete revision of the Department's policies was demonstrated when Sivertz (1958d) reported to Deputy Minister Robertson that the interdepartmental committee set up in 1958 to study further relocation to the High Arctic had recommended that:

1. no Eskimos be relocated in areas of poor transportation and communication;
2. Eskimo relocation would generally be within rather than across natural Arctic areas such as Northwest Quebec, Keewatin, and Western Arctic.

The adoption of these two principles would rule out any consideration of additional resettlement from Port Harrison to the High Arctic. Phillips admitted that it had been "a risky procedure" to relocate Inuit to Resolute and Grise without prior resource studies, and he pointed out that, owing to past disasters, settlements in areas of no or poor communication and transportation must be avoided; this view virtually eliminated consideration of the islands in the central Arctic as well as the Queen

Elizabeth Islands (Canada, 1958e). The adaptation problems of the Inuit who moved from one Arctic region to another were finally being recognized, as is illustrated by an internal Department memo in 1960 about the relocation from Port Harrison to the High Arctic: "It was thought at the time of the move that the Harrison group would not only find the environment strange, but, as they had never experienced the dark period, the assumption was that travelling and trapping would be most difficult" (Bolger, 1960b).

Colonization of the High Arctic Islands was, nevertheless, still being considered by the Department in the 1960s. Ben Sivertz was interested in establishing new colonies at Mould Bay, Isachsen, Eureka, and Alert. The plan was to use Resolute Bay as a hub community that would service a number of satellite Inuit colonies throughout the archipelago. Ultimately, the project was not implemented. Perhaps the government realized that the old problem of welfare dependency might recur but in even more distant locations. Resolute Bay and Grise Fiord were at the farthest end of the supply chain, and it would be both difficult and increasingly expensive to maintain them, especially if the Inuit became less able to support themselves by hunting and trapping. In the 1960s, the cost of providing schools and other facilities, teachers, mechanics, and other necessary personnel for the colonies outweighed the possible advantages of redistributing the Inuit in the High Arctic Islands.

Senior officials came to recognize the difficulties the Inuit were experiencing at Grise Fiord, but they continued to stress the colony's political value. In a confidential memo to Alex Stevenson in 1960, C. M. Bolger, administrator of the Arctic, commented on a conversation he had had with Ben Sivertz (Bolger, 1960a). They had discussed "some of the problems we have had with Grise Fiord in respect of supply and of medical services and his own feeling is that while Grise Fiord should be continued for sovereignty purposes, it should not be duplicated at other isolated locations." Although the government was determined to keep the community functioning for political reasons, despite the hardships and health risks to which the Inuit were exposed, officials now recognized that it would not be cost-effective to repeat this experiment in other isolated locations within the Queen Elizabeth Islands. Bolger also noted that the Inuit at Resolute Bay were becoming a useful source of labor for the oil exploration work taking place on Cornwallis Island and the adjacent islands (ibid.). In order to satisfy the government's political and economic needs, Grise Fiord and Resolute Bay were thus destined to remain the two most northerly Inuit settlements in Canada.

Utopia on Trial

When he made *Nanook of the North*, Robert Flaherty tried to capture the essence of a "traditional" Inuit lifestyle. The camera is an extension of our perception, and in effect, he was attempting to re-create an Arctic Eden on celluloid (Beloff, 1985: 9). As shown in chapter 1, Nanook was the iconographic representative of a happy, innocent people who enjoyed life in a land that was apparently abundant in game, if one had the specialized knowledge necessary to obtain it. What Flaherty accomplished on film, Henry Larsen later attempted in reality. In both cases, myth and nostalgia played important roles. Flaherty's prophetic remarks that the Inuit were in danger of moral corruption were confirmed thirty years later by Larsen's vision of a people in need of salvation. Like Flaherty, Larsen was appalled by what he saw as the detrimental influence of the Whites. He viewed traders and missionaries as external agents who exploited the Inuit. Fearful that the introduction of relief and government benefits would foster a "mentality of dependence" (Dryzek and Young, 1985: 132), Larsen felt that the unfortunate consequence would be a debasement of the Inuit by reducing them to the status of "loitering bums." Although the views of these two men may now seem naïve and romantic, they were deeply felt and had developed over years of traveling and living among the Inuit.

The conflicting perceptions of the Inuit, who were regarded both as proud hunters and as being too dependent on benefits, persuaded the planners that they could reform the Inuit socially by relocating them. This belief arose from an apparent contradiction in which "civilized man is painfully divided between the desire to 'correct' the 'errors' of the savages and the desire to identify himself with them in his search for some lost paradise" (Mannoni, 1964: 21). Larsen's utopian vision of an ideal Inuit society was founded on the belief that one could return a group of people to an Arctic Eden.

Larsen was not alone. The documents are replete with statements by Whites that link Inuit relocation with visions of paradise, such as Sargent's (1954) remark on a Grise Fiord "Garden of Eden." A Company official proposing the total relocation of the Belcher Island Inuit in the 1940s spoke of picking out a "promised land" in the High Arctic Islands (Cruickshank, 1944). When the Ahiarmiut were to be relocated to Nueltin Lake in 1950, the radio station personnel recorded in their diary: "[we were] advised they will be moved to paradise for Eskimos" (Steenhoven, 1955). Ironically, when Larsen visited the Ahiarmiut camp at Ennadai Lake in 1955, he noted that if other Inuit "found themselves in these Ihalmiut's camps with lakes abundant in fish [they] would think they had been transferred to Paradise" (Larsen, n.d: 26). The Arctic wilderness became a symbol of an earthly paradise (Short, 1991: 10). White perspectives of an ideal, "traditional" Inuit society were conditioned by images of self-reliant Eskimos living in an Arctic paradise, in keeping with the scenes of Inuit life presented in the films *Nanook of the North, Land of the Long Day,* and *Savage Innocents* (see chapter 1).

Peopling the High Arctic also served a prevailing Canadian nationalist sentiment of the 1950s to expand northward. In Canada, as in the United States, the theme of conquering the wilderness had become a symbol of progress and a prominent feature of national identity (Short, 1991: 19). This aspect of nation building was consistent with the drive to fulfill geopolitical objectives of effective occupation, as discussed in chapter 2, and with establishing permanent settlements in the North. When Larsen was given the responsibility for re-opening his High Arctic detachments, it thus seemed fitting that Canadian Inuit should be given the heroic opportunity of repopulating the northern islands. The Inuit had abandoned this land several hundred years ago, but Larsen believed it to be habitable because Greenlanders were hunting seasonally on Ellesmere Island.

The archaeological work undertaken by the National Museum of Canada in the High Arctic, published in 1951–52 and referred to in chapter 3, provided the timely scientific evidence that a large population of Inuit had indeed lived there and that game had been plentiful. Did Larsen or Gibson see themselves in the mold of Qitdlarssuaq, leading Inuit to the High Arctic on a "vision quest"? Larsen was proud that "these Eskimos then were the first to return to the old haunts and places inhabited by their early ancestors" (Larsen, n.d.: 50). Larsen and his officers hoped that placing the Inuit campsites beside those of their "forebears" might bond the relocatees to their new homeland (see fig. 8.3). With satisfaction, he remembered how "seeing the ruins of the many old houses reassured our Eskimos that the country must be good" (Larsen, n.d.: 50). The utopian scheme was given substance by a romantic archaeological interpretation of the prospects for Inuit rehabitation of the High Arctic Islands.

In the 1950s, officials viewed the problems of Inuit poverty and "overpopulation" and the relocation solution fundamentally in geographical terms (Jackson, 1989: 91). Though the Department perhaps saw the 1953 move from Port Harrison primarily as a depopulation or geopolitical experiment (see chapter 2), the Department's public rationale and the private beliefs of reformers like Larsen were that the project provided the Inuit with an opportunity to better themselves. All the right components were in place. The Inuit would be released from their eco-

FIGURE 8.3 Pauloosie on Ellesmere Island, 1955. Credit: Bob Pilot

nomic and spiritual bondage to the traders and missionaries and be transported to a land rich in game where they could prosper under the benevolent guidance of the RCMP. It also offered the prospect of Inuit "returning to ancestral territory." In effect, the reformers were drafting a new "map of morality" (Vitebsky, 1992: 223), identifying the southern areas as places where Inuit had become dependent on "handouts" and viewing the High Arctic as a place free of contamination, offering the prospect of moral redemption. This idealism had much in common with the earlier views of General William Booth and of the proponents of a British emigration policy of "shovelling out paupers" during the nineteenth century. The aim was to encourage emigration to the "un-populated and virgin lands" of Canada and Australia, both as a means of socially reforming unwanted indigents and reducing "surplus popula-tions" in Britain (see Booth, 1970 [1890]; H. Johnston, 1972; and Con-stantine, 1991.)

The ideological rehabilitative component of the Inuit relocations, however, camouflaged the latent penitential environment they engen-dered (Allen, 1981: 54). Cst. Gibson was aware of this dichotomy by interpreting the rehabilitation project as both an altruistic act and a punitive measure—recalling the religious notion of self-improvement through flagellation. He saw fit to choose those individuals whom he thought were both dependent on relief and in need of reform and, with almost evangelistic zeal, approached the task of ridding the settlement of "scrounging Eskimos." For the Department, the project was a para-digm of social action—an inexpensive, quick-fix, trial solution to the complex "Eskimo problem," quite apart from its geopolitical merits. The plan also had the advantage of being cost-effective, because the Eskimo Loan Fund allowed the operation to be self-financing (the Inuit would pay for it themselves) and the RCMP had volunteered to supervise it in the field. Only later did the government realize that it would be too expensive to reproduce the prototype in other isolated locations of the High Arctic because "progress" would require more facilities in keeping with the higher standard of living in the south.

The relocations of the Inukjuamiut and the Ahiarmiut were linked by more than just their media prominence and a press release that pre-sented the projects as philanthropic attempts to assist the Inuit in mov-ing to areas abundant in game (Canada, 1957b). Both groups were seen by officials as an unnecessary nuisance to the local White populations and as people addicted to living on "handouts." When the Inukjuamiut were moved out to the Sleeper and King George Islands by the RCMP in 1951–52, they returned after several months, and the operation was later repeated. After the radio station personnel occupied the Ahiar-miut's lands around Ennadai Lake, the Inuit were relocated away from it. When the Ahiarmiut drifted back after being moved to Nueltin Lake in 1950, they were relocated again in 1957. This recurrent pattern of push-ing the Inuit away from the White settlements was justified by the notion that there was better game further north. Human experience has shown that geographical space must be shared and divided. The inevitable outcome of this territorial paradox, though, is conflict (Smith, 1990: 1). In both the 1953 and the 1957 moves, the Inuit were transported northwards to wilderness sites more distant than in the earlier sideways moves, and taken away from their homelands, because the latter areas had become centers of White occupation.

The Department assured the public that the Inukjuamiut and the Ahiarmiut were voluntary migrants. The basis of this claim was that the Inuit were attracted by the prospect of moving to a land rich in game. How important was this feature of the projects? When Capt. Ejnar Mikkelsen (1951) described his 1924 Scoresby Sund colonization project in east Greenland (see chapter 2), he found that the Inuit "are very conservative and do not take kindly to the idea of leaving their place of birth." Mikkelsen thus had to come up with an effective way of encouraging Inuit to embark on a government-sponsored relocation: "They have, consequently, to be cajoled to go, tempted by accounts of better hunting and living conditions" (ibid.). Mikkelsen's candid advice was published in the *Canadian Geographical Journal*'s issue for August 1951, a year before the Canadian Department's decision to use similar tactics in their relocation discussions with the Inukjuamiut.

The availability of game was the principal public justification for the relocations; yet no scientific resource studies of the destination sites were undertaken before either relocation, and planners did not have firm evidence that the relocatees would be able to sustain themselves there. These experiments were purely speculative. Was food a sufficient lure in itself to persuade the Inuit to leave their homelands permanently? If the Department had closely examined the results of its two earlier relocation experiments, in 1934 on Devon Island and in 1950 at Nueltin Lake, they would have discovered that, although the availability of food had been the primary inducement (and the publicly stated objective), both projects had ended in failure. This result was due in part to a lack of informed consent as well as a scarcity of game. To obtain informed consent, subjects should agree to intervention based on an understanding of relevant information, and the act of consent should not be controlled by influences that manipulate the outcome (Faden and Beauchamp, 1986: 54). After reviewing the Henik Lake tragedy, officials agreed that consensual acceptance of the scheme had been compromised, for the Ahiarmiut were reluctant to move to the Padlei district because of their strong associational ties with the Ennadai Lake area.

On one occasion, Cunningham (1955) had referred to the Ahiarmiut as "Padleimiut" (see chapter 5) and had used that designation in saying that they belonged in the Padlei area. As a result, some people were under the illusion that the group were being returned to their "ancestral lands". This idea was also a convenient concept for the 1953 High Arctic relocation; however, the Inukjuamiut had no prior knowledge of the High Arctic, whereas the Ahiarmiut knew of the Padlei and Henik Lake areas. Two years before the move, the Ahiarmiut had described it to NSO Bill Kerr (1955) as a region with few caribou (see chapter 6). In fact, Larsen recorded privately that he had received a letter from the Department about the proposed Ahiarmiut relocation to Henik Lake informing him "that these people would be moved whether they liked it or not" (Larsen, n.d.: 27). After the collapse of the Department's relocation policy in the wake of the Ahiarmiut deaths, Graham Rowley (1958c) commented in a letter to Deputy Minister Robertson that relocations "have rarely been successful unless they are done with the full consent of the people concerned."

The Department's description of the relocation experiments as "migrations" or "assisted moves" leads one to question the use of the word "migration." The term implies that the reformers were not imposing their will on Inuit society; rather, they were assisting the Inuit to migrate naturally to a land rich in game. Because the reformers stated repeatedly that the project was voluntary, one might have imagined that it was honestly their intention to help the Inuit "to help themselves." The project can then be envisaged as a self-contained scheme of self-reform. This strategy for self-improvement signified the projects' "rehabilitative ideal" (Allen, 1981: 19). Thus migration metaphorically becomes a means of social reform. Larsen (n.d.: 44) stressed that the 1953 move would give "these natives . . . a chance *to prove themselves under new conditions in a completely strange country*" (italics mine). This notion of self-improvement also appears in statements made by the officers directly responsible for supervising the two schemes. Two weeks after the RCMP had moved the relocatees to Lindstrom Peninsula on Grise Fiord, Cst. Fryer (1954a) stated: "This concluded the assistance intended to be given by the detachment, so that *it was now up to the natives to make a success of their undertaking*"; similarly, Cpl. Gallagher (1957b) reported that, six months after their relocation to Henik Lake, the Ahiarmiut "have made little, if any progress towards *rehabilitating themselves* in their new environment" (my italics). In fact, the project's reformist intention was emphasized by the nature of the selection process.

Yet Gibson's chosen people were bound for an Arctic Eden of which they knew nothing. Inuit expectations of temporary displacement from Port Harrison (or an extended hunting expedition) and the planners' expectations for permanent High Arctic colonies conflicted with any preconceived notion that this move was a voluntary experiment. Fear of the police and other officials, and intimidation by them, combined with an inability to surmount cross-cultural barriers, undermined any thoughts the Inuit might have had of extricating themselves from the "migration" schemes.

Was the Department's use of the phrase "voluntary migration" applied euphemistically to a rehabilitation and social reform experiment (or, indeed, as a subterfuge for geopolitical motivations)? In her comprehensive study of Inuit mobility patterns (referred to in chapter 3), Susan Rowley (1985a: 3) observed that, traditionally, migration could play an important role in Inuit society as a "risk buffering strategy in times of environmental and social stress." From this perspective, officials were helping the Inuit do what they might have done if the White man had not been there—namely, to migrate "as a means of escape from a region when resources became scarce" (ibid.: 17). For the Inukjuamiut, it would have meant leaving what officials described as the "overpopulated" and "resource-poor" area of northern Quebec to move to a land thought to be "more suitable"; and the Ahiarmiut would have been abandoning an area with increasingly limited prospects for caribou in order to adopt a "more balanced" diet of fish and other game at Henik Lake.

Not only was Arctic Eden to be re-created for the Inukjuamiut, Larsen's comments and those of Cst. Fryer give the impression that they thought the High Arctic wilderness would transform the Inuit morally with its redemptive qualities (Short, 1991: 10, 96). The act of social reform would take place naturally, because the land and sea would yield its animals in abundance and the Inuit would no longer be in need of "White man's handouts"—an Eden without apples. A work ethic would prevail, old subsistence hunting instincts would resurface, and only minimal guidance would be required from the RCMP. Fryer confirmed the self-sufficient features of this endeavor by noting that the Pond Inlet Inuit were successfully assisting their charges from the southern Arctic to adjust to the new conditions. The role of the RCMP would thus be reduced to that of bookkeepers and guardians, warding off outside interference (from people like nurses, teachers, missionaries, and military personnel).

Although the officials may have seen the Inuit relocatees as migrants and volunteers, those relocated to the High Arctic in 1953–55 have consistently described themselves over the last ten years as "exiles" (the term also employed by the Royal Commission; Canada, 1993a). These contrasting labels indicate the key distinction between Inuit and official views of the issue and show how they wish to see these events represented. I believe this conceptual difference originates in the way "migration" is interpreted. Susan Rowley (1985a: 17) found that Inuit migration was sometimes "a method of ridding the community of an undesirable individual or group of individuals"; historically, that act was not dissimilar to the role of banishment in other societies (Helms, 1988: 54). The Inukjuamiut and the Ahiarmiut thus interpreted the act of relocation as an expulsion from their homeland. As a form of internal social control in Inuit society, individuals could be ostracized if they exhibited deviant behavior, such as theft and non-sharing. In a severe case, they could even be banished, for example, if they were seen to be a danger to the rest of the group (Inukjuamiut informants, personal communication; Williamson, 1974: 47–48). In the Arctic environment, as the Ahiarmiut realized, exile and banishment from a land you know could pose a threat to survival (ibid.). In fact, two years before the 1953 Inukjuamiut relocation to the High Arctic, Stevenson (1951a) recorded his impression that "the average Eskimo does not care to go too far afield, especially if he is told he will never be allowed to return to his home." In view of this situation, Stevenson suggested that rather than incarcerate Inuit who had been found guilty of a crime, "it is sufficient punishment if a native is moved from his home region and banished permanently to another area of the Arctic." His prophetic observation was realized when the Inukjuamiut and the Ahiarmiut were moved away from their homelands.

In the show trial of Kikkik—a consequence of the Ahiarmiut deaths— the government tried again to control the public perception of the circumstances of the relocations. The trial demonstrates what enormous cultural barriers prevented the Inuit from understanding the mechanisms of the government's bureaucratic apparatus. This incomprehension included their selection process for relocation "volunteers," the workings of the Eskimo Loan Fund, the review procedures for requests to return home, and the Western judicial ritual surrounding Kikkik's trial. Whites set the rules and guided the events. Only when circumstances got out of control and members of the Ahiarmiut band and other Caribou Inuit died in the winter of 1957–58 did the Department accept the need to re-evaluate and alter its relocation policies. Even then, the Department was able to influence the way the public perceived the events.

When reviewing the factors that led to the Ahiarmiut deaths and the verdict of the Kikkik trial, the Crown prosecutor, John Parker, provided an apt epigram for the entire scenario—"The Crown never wins and the Crown never loses" (Parker, personal communication). Whenever it was faced with external criticism of the relocations, the government tried to show the events in the most positive light. Two reports the Department commissioned on the relocation issue (Hickling Corporation, 1990; Gunther, 1992) are an example of this approach. I review the first of these reports in a 1991 article, and the second has been analyzed and rebutted at length (Royal Commission, 1994; Tester and Kulchyski,

1994). Now that the Inukjuamiut relocatees have succeeded in having the circumstances of their relocation "tried" over the last three years in investigative hearings conducted by the Royal Commission on Aboriginal Peoples, the Parliamentary Committee on Aboriginal Affairs, and the Canadian Human Rights Commission, and debated in the House of Commons in Ottawa, the Department has responded defensively. It has questioned the veracity of Inuit descriptions of the hardships imposed by relocation and their suggestions that the project may not have had the full, informed consent of the "volunteers."

Shortly before he died, Henry Larsen warned: "I shudder to think of the criticism which will be levelled at us in another fifty years time" (Larsen, n.d.: 1004). While Stevenson, for example, did foresee the possibility that the dark period might hinder the acclimatization process by the Inuit, little value appears to have been attached to this concern. One may posit, therefore, that the planners in general were not unduly worried about the psychological aspects of adjusting to a new environment. I believe this nonchalance was largely due to a popular misconception about the Arctic—as a barren, white land without regional differences. Geopolitical insecurity over effective occupation of the High Arctic highlighted the national vertigo about the extensive, empty space of unoccupied Canadian territory (Ley, 1989: 44). Many officials saw the High Arctic as a void to be filled. In the Western world, space is a common symbol of freedom and opportunity (Tuan, 1977: 54); however, this frontier spirit was incompatible with the goal of permanent relocation.

When the imaginative solution to relocate the Inuit was proposed, planners underestimated or were unaware of the strong bond that Inuit maintained with a particular area, or of the localized web of landscape knowledge necessary for successful resource harvesting. The intellectual security that came with a knowledgable sense of place and the desire to be with one's relatives and friends were ultimately key factors in Inuit dissatisfaction with the High Arctic relocation project. Historically, of course, these considerations have been a common experience of many migrants or relocatees, regardless of their ethnicity or the geographical setting (Sutton, 1975), and separation from homeland was the intrinsic flaw in both these case studies. As early as 1888 Boas had recorded that the desire to die in one's birthplace was a compelling reason for Inuit wanting to return to their homeland (Boas, 1888a: 466).

Upon learning of recent attempts by the Inuit to record their grievances on the relocation, Ross Gibson commented: "I guess they were not as nomadic as we thought they were" (Gibson, personal communication). Given the period when these relocations took place—in the 1950s —perhaps Gibson's remark was not surprising; still, even in the 1940s a Hudson's Bay Company manager, Ralph Cruickshank, had readily appreciated that the Inuit were bound to a particular place and regional environment. When in 1944 Cruickshank proposed the relocation of the Belcher Islanders to a High Arctic "paradise," he advised his superiors:

Total evacuation must however be our objective; none must remain; all ties with the homeland must be severed. There is sound sense in this for the Eskimo at heart is a family man, and does not like to be away for long from his people. We must recognize this basic fact in all our dealings with him, and act accordingly. (Cruickshank, 1944)

Cruickshank's all-or-nothing recipe for relocation highlights a fundamental difference between the 1953 and 1957 operations. Not long after relocating the small group of Inukjuamiut to the High Arctic, officials received requests from them to visit or return to northern Quebec. In the relocation to Henik Lake, the entire group of Ahiarmiut were moved, and (in keeping with Cruickshank's advice) all human ties to the homeland were thought to have been severed. But, as officials soon discovered, this mass relocation was not enough to prevent the project's failure. Homeland meant something more. Inuit concepts of homeland had been presented numerous times in the literature before the relocations; for example, Rink observed in his *Tales and Traditions of the Eskimo*, published in 1875: "The Eskimo may more properly be classed among the people having fixed dwellings than among the wandering nations, because they generally winter in the same place through even more than one generation, so that love of their birthplace is a rather predominating feature in their character" (Rink, 1875: 9).

This insight became common knowledge with the publication in 1904–05 of Mauss's classic work on seasonal migration. Inuit testimonies, such as those presented to the Royal Commission on Aboriginal Peoples, confirm the importance of Inuit attachments to a specific locale or homeland. For the government, migration could be regarded as a means for attaining social reform and geopolitical goals. For the Inuit, however, the Resolute Bay, Grise Fiord, and Henik Lake migration projects were more like deportations. Inuit were reluctant to be separated permanently from the land they knew and to be treated as nomads who could be relocated to foreign places, however Edenic according to White perceptions.

· EPILOGUE ·

Those Inukjuamiut presently living in Resolute Bay and Grise Fiord who are more or less content to remain there are those who were young children at the time of the move or who were born in the High Arctic. Most of the elders have returned to Inukjuak (Port Harrison) in recent years. In 1988, the Department finally accepted that it had made a two-year promise of return thirty-five years earlier, and it paid the transportation costs for those people who wanted to move back to Inukjuak. The three elders who have remained in the High Arctic have stayed primarily because their children live there. At Resolute Bay, everyone was relocated again in 1975, when the Inuit village was transplanted eight kilometers away in another utopian government plan, this time to build a modern, racially integrated community, complete with domed tropical park. After the Inuit were moved, however, the scheme was abandoned, and today few Whites live in the Inuit village.

At the airport at Resolute Bay there is a sign that reads "Resolute, pronounced Desolate." Indeed, the community has a reputation in the North as being an environmentally unpleasant place to live, with a paucity of fauna and particularly poor weather conditions. A number of airplane crash sites eerily litter the area around the airstrip. Resolute underwent a dramatic conversion in the mid-1960s, from model community to a dystopian "no place," when RCMP paternalism was moderated and Inuit relations with the military base at Resolute changed. Alcoholism and prostitution became commonplace, and Resolute developed a reputation as a town with serious social problems.

In stark contrast, Grise Fiord has few visible socioeconomic problems. Indeed, the RCMP officer stationed at Grise Fiord recently called it a "Garden of Eden," echoing Cpl. Sargent's remark forty years ago. In 1988, nineteen of the original relocatees moved back to Inukjuak when the government paid for them to do so. Grise Fiord was in danger of being closed as a result, but some large North Baffin families moved in, and the government built a new school and nursing station as an inducement for people to stay. Most of the town's 120 residents have chosen to remain there.

In many ways, Grise Fiord is an Eden today. Unlike any other northern community, with the exception of Sachs Harbour on Banks Island, which also has a population of only 120 people (Whittles, personal communication), Grise Fiord has no unemployment and no welfare cases, except for two Inuit who receive disability pensions. It has the ideal jobs-to-workers ratio. Grise Fiord is physically a beautiful location and, as elsewhere in the Canadian Arctic, its inhabitants live in modern, centrally heated homes with triple-glazing. It is still very isolated, but with the new airstrip, there are two weekly flights by Twin Otter light aircraft from Resolute, weather permitting. Transportation, however, is extremely expensive.

In the 1960s and 1970s, with the arrival of commercial aviation in the Canadian Arctic, it became feasible for some relocatees to visit or move back to Port Harrison, if they had the money to do so. The visit had to be for an extended period, though, even up to a year, due to the difficulties of arranging transport. Meanwhile, they would be separated from their family back at Grise Fiord or Resolute Bay, so for many of the relocatees, it was not a viable option. For those Inuit who have returned to Inukjuak in the last five years, reintegration has been a complicated process. Inukjuak is a modern Arctic community with a population of around eleven hundred people. Housing and jobs tend to go to long-term residents, and many of the relocatees found themselves at the bottom of the social scale. Many of the younger members of the group have had a particularly difficult time adjusting to life in Inukjuak, and some have been ostracized as "foreigners." The ridicule exchanged between the two Inuit groups at Resolute and Grise is mirrored in the way local schoolchildren in Inukjuak treat the "exile children" from the High Arctic.

Salluviniq and Aqiatusuk, the two original "camp bosses" at Resolute Bay and Grise Fiord, have died. Paddy Aqiatusuk's son, Larry Audlaluk, who still lives at Grise Fiord with his family, took me by boat to visit their old camp on Lindstrom Peninsula. Nellie, who was over eighty years old at the time of the move, died five years later, but most of the relocatees are still alive, including the three Pond Inlet elders—Amagoalik, Akpaliapik, and Anukudluk—all of whom have returned to Pond Inlet. Joseph Idlout, the film star of *Land of the Long Day*, died tragically. In the 1960s, the personification of the proud, self-reliant hunter became a regular visitor to the Arctic Circle Bar at the Resolute military air base. Leaving the bar inebriated one night in 1968, Idlout drove his snowmobile off a cliff and was killed. A recent film documentary, *Between Two Worlds*, in which filmmaker Doug Wilkinson had an advisory role, speculated that

Idlout committed suicide. Some Inuit in Resolute feel it was simply an accident. The controversy surrounding his death is evocative of the fate of Nanook. Although it is the accepted view that Nanook (Alakarial-lak) died of starvation while hunting caribou two years after the film was made, Inuit told me that, before he died, he was seen spitting up blood. That condition would indicate hemoptysis, a common symptom of tuberculosis (*puvalluk*, "bad lungs"), the deadly illness that has killed a large number of Inuit this century (Fortuine, 1989). Aqiatusuk was also accorded a heroic death by the media, for though his relatives and the police reports state that he died from a heart attack, according to *Time* magazine (1954) he slipped off an ice floe.

After the moves to Nueltin Lake in 1950, Henik Lake in 1957, and Eskimo Point in 1958, the Ahiarmiut "migration" continued with a relocation the following year to the Keewatin Rehabilitation Center at Rankin Inlet. Around 1960, they were moved again, this time to Tavani on the coast, where a small settlement was established. During the 1960s, most of the Ahiarmiut drifted back to Eskimo Point (Arviat), where they remain today. Arviat is similar in size to Inukjuak. Kikkik remarried after the trial and stayed in Eskimo Point until she died in 1971 of cancer. Her daughter Ailoyoak, who had to testify as a Crown witness, committed suicide in 1981. Kikkik's other children—Annacatha, Karlak, and Nokah-hak—still live in Arviat.

Howmik, who was rescued by the police after the death of her husband Ootuk, died in Arviat in 1990. Oohootok, who was blinded while breaking rocks for Cpl. Gallagher, died tragically in the winter of 1984 when he got lost in Arviat during a snowstorm and was found frozen near the airstrip. The two men with whom he was arrested, Mounik and Iootna, live in Arviat across the street from one another. Aulatjut (Owli-joot), the *isumataq*, and his wife Nutaraaluk (Nootaraloo) live in Arviat, and I stayed with them in December 1991 while I was doing fieldwork.

Henry Larsen, Hugh Young, James Cantley, Alex Stevenson, Glenn Sargent, Frank Cunningham, and John Sissons have all died. At the time of this writing, many of the other officials are still living in Ontario or have retired to British Columbia, including Ben Sivertz, Gordon Robertson, Graham Rowley, Bob Phillips, Bob Pilot, Clay Fryer, Walter Rudnicki, Doug Wilkinson, and Farley Mowat. Among the other participants in the Kikkik trial, Henry Voisey and Sterling Lyon live in Manitoba, and John Parker lives in British Columbia. Former Cst. Ross Gibson, who testified at the Royal Commission hearings in June 1993 by telephone from his hospital bed, died of cancer two months later.

List of Inuit Relocated to Grise Fiord and Resolute Bay, 1953–55

Families relocated from Port Harrison to Craig Harbour (Grise Fiord) in 1953

Paddy Aqiatusuk	husband	55 years old
Mary	wife	44
Anna	stepdaughter	26
Elijah	stepson	21
Samwillie	stepson	17
Minnie	stepdaughter	13
Larry	son	3
Joadamie Aqiatusuk	husband	22
Ekoomak	wife	17
Lizzie	daughter	3 mos
Phillipoosie Novalinga	husband	51
Annie	wife	51
Pauloosie	son	26
Elisapee	daughter	10
Thomasie Amagoalik	husband	39
Mary	wife	31
Allie	son	7
Salluviniq	son	4
Charlie	son	7 mos

Families relocated from Port Harrison to Resolute Bay in 1953

Simeonie Amagoalik	husband	20
Sarah	wife	18
Jaybeddie	Simeonie's brother	18
Nellie	grandmother	80
Daniel Salluviniq	husband	36
Sarah	wife	21
Allie	son	4
Louisa	daughter	1
Jeannie	single female	26
Alex Patsauq	husband	36
Edith	wife	35

Families relocated from Port Harrison to Resolute Bay in 1953 (cont.)

Lizzie	daughter	15
Markoosie	son	13
Johnny	son	5

Families relocated from Pond Inlet to Craig Harbour (Grise Fiord) in 1953

Simon Akpaliapik	husband	33
Tatigak	wife	44
Ruthie	daughter	7
Tookahsee	daughter	3
Inutsiak	son	1 mo

Samuel Anukudluk	husband	
Qaumayuk	wife	
Mukpanuk	grandmother	
Tamarisee	daughter	
Rhoda	daughter	
Jonathan	son	
Phoebe	daughter	

Family relocated from Pond Inlet to Resolute Bay in 1953

Jaybeddie Amagoalik	husband	37
Kanoinoo	wife	36
Ekaksak	son	10
Merrari	daughter	2

Family relocated from Port Harrison to Craig Harbour (Grise Fiord) in 1955

Josephie Flaherty	head	35
Rynee	wife	28
Martha	daughter	5
Mary	daughter	2
Peter	son	6 mos

Families relocated from Port Harrison to Resolute Bay in 1955

Levi Nungak	husband	31
Alici	wife	25
Annie	daughter	8
Minnie	daughter	5
Philipusie	son	4
Anna	daughter	1

Johnnie Echalook	husband	46
Minnie	wife	45
Lizzie	daughter	17
Rynee	daughter	15
Dora	daughter	12
George	son	9
Mary	daughter	5
Leah	daughter	2

Families relocated from Port Harrison to Resolute Bay in 1955 (cont.)

Mawa Iqaluk	mother	53
Andrew	son	26
Martha	daughter	20
Emily	daughter	14
Jackoosie	son	22
Mary	Jackoosie's wife	22

Families relocated from Pond Inlet to Resolute Bay in 1955

Joseph Idlout	head	40
Kidlah	wife	39
Leah	daughter	16
Mosesee	son	11
Pauloosee	son	9
Noah	son	6
Ruth	daughter	3
Susan	daughter	1
Anknowya	Idlout's mother	69
Ilksoo	adopted son	18
Daniel	adopted son	15
Oodlaleetah	husband	20
Isigaitok	wife	19
Philiposie	son	2

Inuit Relocated to Henik Lake, 1957

Micki	husband	39 years old
Kahootsuak	wife	37
Kukigiak	daughter	17
Ilungiayuk	son	13
Hickwa	son	5
Owlijoot	husband	45
Nootaraloo	wife	43
Arloo	son	16
Agnasadeak	son	12
Paneguak	son	10
Neebainak	son	5
Kukigiak	adopted daughter	17
Mounik	husband	23
Ookanak	wife	19
Tabloo	son	1
Ungmak	husband	39
Nutarloak	wife	39
Shikoak	father	57
Pallikal	son	29
Pongalak	husband	57
Ootnooyuk	wife	39
Angatayok	son	7
Akkagalak	daughter	7
Angnukoak	daughter	1
Kiyai	husband	19
Alikaswa	wife	21
Pongalak	son	4
Boonla	son	2
Oohootok	husband	37
Nanook	wife	47
Igloopalik	daughter	12
Kerkoot	daughter	1

Ootuk	husband	41
Howmik	wife	37
Karlak	daughter	13
Ooyah	daughter	4
Igyeka	daughter	3
Hallow	husband	43
Kikkik	wife	37
Ailoyoak	daughter	12
Karlak	son	8
Annacatha	daughter	5
Nesha	daughter	3
Nokahhak	daughter	1
Yahah [Anayoenak]	husband	50
Atatloak	wife	38
Atkla	son	7
Agatiyooak	single male	22
Aleykoosuak	husband	39
Kudluk	wife	34
Kalusigaot	son	17
Kowtak	son	15
Akalak	daughter	12
Olipa	son	7
Ahlayan	daughter	2
Anowtelik	husband	25
Akjar	wife	19
Owlijoot	son	2
Igyekah	son	1

· APPENDIX C ·

Presentation Given by the Author to the Royal Commission on Aboriginal Peoples at a Public Hearing in Ottawa on 30 June 1993

I have listened with great interest over the last three days to the presentations made before the commission, and after this time, I have to agree with Commissioner Dussault's comment made on Monday that this most certainly is a difficult issue to assess. The Royal Commission has played an important role in this issue by providing a forum for the relocatees, government officials, and researchers to present their views. This has been greatly valuable, but people will want to know, What are the facts, what is the truth? Has the issue become so politicized and divided that the truth will elude us? Why are so many well-meaning individuals looking at the same thing from radically different perspectives?

First, let us look at the reasons for the relocation. Was it sovereignty, was it humanitarian, or was it something else? History is not so tidy. I believe there were several factors for the move. One was related to "effective occupation." Researchers have been looking for a political motive—a document which categorically states that the Inuit were moved to safeguard sovereignty. Yet, Ben Sivertz and others have told us of the government's desire to Canadianize the High Arctic Islands above Lancaster Sound in the 1950s. The Canadianization of this territory in the face of growing American military activity has already been recorded in history books about the period. It is no secret and no surprise that Canada should wish to show in the 1950s as a matter of national pride that it was demonstrating a presence in this vast unoccupied space on the map which was, in fact, a part of Canada.

It might be useful at this point to quote from an ACND document marked "confidential," entitled "Memorandum for the Advisory Committee on Northern Development: Policy Guidance Paper for Release of Information on the North." It is dated May 28, 1954. On the object of public information on the North the memo states: "The first object of public information on the north is to emphasize that the northern regions are as much a part of Canada as any other area in the country. It is most important that all Canadians should be aware of this fact in order that the measures to stimulate and encourage the development of our northern frontier will be supported and sustained" (Rowley, 1954).

Notice the use of the word "frontier," and, What do you do with a frontier? You often colonize it. Under the heading "Canadian–United States Relations and Sovereignty," the memo states: "No emphasis should be placed on Canadian claims in the north lest we seem to be on the defensive." This statement indicates a weakness, an unease regarding external perceptions—hence the drive towards Canadianization of the northern Arctic Islands. This process of Canadianization, for example, involved the re-establishment of the RCMP posts at Craig Harbour in 1951 and at Alexandra Fiord in 1953.

Had the posts at those locations not been remanned as "flag detachments," the Inuit would never have been moved to Ellesmere Island. Throughout the 1950s, officials at the Department of Northern Affairs discussed the repopulation and colonization of the High Arctic Islands. This relocation experiment was referred to in government documents as a colonization project, a potential forerunner of more Inuit moves to come. A prototype.

The government's actions to re-establish a native population in the High Arctic Islands and their actions to re-establish RCMP posts in the area were twin instruments of Canadianization, of demonstrating "effective occupation"—which refers to *de facto* sovereignty. We are not doubting the issue of *de jure* sovereignty over Canadian title, but we are acknowledging that the actions were taken as part of the government's broader desire to Canadianize this vast territory, which in the early 1950s looked particularly empty due to the noticeable lack of a Canadian presence.

In the early 1950s, the Department of Northern Affairs successfully sought to encourage Inuit from the Mackenzie Delta region to relocate on Banks Island by offering financial assistance from the newly created Eskimo Loan Fund. Repopulating Banks was part of the same thinking behind repopulating Devon Island, Ellesmere, Cornwallis, and others. Devon Island was considered several times by the Department for native repopulation during the 1950s, as it had been in 1934–36 during a failed colonization project. For the Department of Northern Affairs, it was perfectly simple—it would be useful to have the northern Arctic Islands repopulated, and the Inuit were the only people able to do so. The rationale of good hunting would be used, and Inuit could be moved from areas designated as "overpopulated" to a region which was unpopulated. It would give these Inuit an opportunity to hunt and trap in virgin territory, potentially rich in game. They could leave their dependence on relief and become self-reliant once again. It would kill two birds with one stone, and everyone would benefit. That was the idea.

The specific decision to target Inuit from Quebec for relocation was, I believe, largely political. As Doug Wilkinson has recalled, Farley Mowat's book *People of the Deer* and its controversial indictment of the government's Inuit administration policy, or lack thereof, was indicative of rising public concern in the early 1950s about the plight of the Inuit. There were a number of documented cases of starvation and epidemics amongst the Inuit that the public was made aware of by the media in the early 1950s. The Department was responding to a crisis of confidence when it undertook the relocation experiment amidst great publicity as a high-profile opportunity to be seen to be finding a solution to what was then known as "the Eskimo problem."

The move was motivated by a political response to reduce dependency on relief. Was it also a humanitarian gesture? Gordon Robertson told us that 95 percent of the motivation of the move was to reduce the overpopulation of Quebec. However, Ottawa's process of labeling northern Quebec as overpopulated is an interesting one. Reuben Ploughman, the Hudson's Bay Company store manager at Inukjuak in 1953, informed us that starvation didn't enter into the relocation at all. Nobody was starving, he said, and the RCMP records reported no cases of starvation either. It wasn't for lack of food that the move was made, Mr. Ploughman said. In fact, he reported that 1952–53 was a bumper year for fox at Inuk-juak, with five thousand fox pelts traded, far exceeding expectations. He should know, that was his job. There was no starvation or serious lack of food in the Inukjuak area in 1953. That is a fact.

Was this therefore an attempt to depopulate Quebec of a portion of its native population? I believe it was. But it wasn't done because of scarcity of game. It was done because of a concentration in the E-9 Port Harrison district of high relief and family allowance benefits which were collectively viewed by officials as "white man's handouts."

This takes us to the next point. There are a number of references in the documents that officials regarded the experiment, as Gordon Robertson told us, as a means to establish Inuit in the manner of the traditional way of Inuit life — in self-reliant communities, so they wouldn't be dependent on handouts. That is what he said. The Department of that day, we are told, thought the Inuit way of life should be preserved and insulated from the seductive, easier way of life the Whites had. Rehabilitation was the term used at the time. The RCMP called the relocation at Grise Fiord a rehabilitation project, and the constables wrote articles explaining how they were managing to rehabilitate the relocatees. In other words, this was an experiment in social reform. It is ironic that the Inuit themselves had no knowledge that they were being relocated for a rehabilitation experiment in social reform.

How was the word experiment used? What were its implications?

It was an experiment to repopulate the Queen Elizabeth Islands with a native population. It was an experiment to see if Inuit from southern regions of the Arctic could adapt to life in the High Arctic environment. The government had never tried such a move before — to take Inuit from the southern Arctic and move them to the northernmost Arctic regions. As James Cantley, chief of the Arctic services section, said in the meeting held on August 10, 1953, to discuss the relocation: "The main purpose of the experiment is to see if it is possible for the people to adapt themselves to the conditions of the high North and secure a living from the land" (Canada, 1953b).

It was an experiment to see if there were sufficient resources in the vicinity of Grise Fiord and Resolute Bay to support a native population; and, it was an experiment to effectively depopulate northern Quebec, which was repeatedly referred to at the time as overpopulated. This move was therefore not a humanitarian gesture but a pseudo-scientific experiment being undertaken not by scientists, but by bureaucrats.

We have been told that the Inuit who took part in the government's experiment were "volunteers." It has been suggested in various presentations that because the government considered the people to be volunteers this was somehow sufficient justification for any hardships they might experience while participating in the experiment. It was cold — well, they volunteered. They didn't have the same amenities in the High Arctic as in Inukjuak — well, they volunteered. They wanted to return home — well, it was difficult to take them back, maybe they will change their minds once they are out of the dark season — and besides, they volunteered.

I would suggest to you that the word "volunteer" has been used by the government as an overriding justification for whatever difficulties the Inuit may have experienced. There has been considerable discussion during these proceedings about what it meant to be a volunteer for the relocation. How can we define the depth of meaning for being a volunteer in this case?

The Inuit told us in their April testimonies that they did not volunteer. In this context, "volunteerism" is related to fear. Hugh Brody's excellent paper, which he has submitted to the commission, describes the Inuit concept of fear, *ilira*, particularly as it pertained to White people and authority figures like RCM policemen. Inuit descriptions of *ilira* in the April hearings, together with Brody's paper, provide us with a basis for understanding the fear the Inuit experienced from their encounters with the police at that time.

But, let us say for the sake of argument that they were keen volunteers— Where does that take us? First, we must ask: How well were they really informed? As Commissioner Sillett has pointed out, they did not participate in the planning of the relocation. Did they volunteer to go to a place of better hunting, a place they were told would be rich in game? Perhaps.

But, did they volunteer to go to a distant northern land that essentially had a foreign environment—where they would have to learn new hunting and trapping skills suited to living in the High Arctic?

Did they volunteer to endure the three-and-a-half-month dark period, during which they would have to hunt—having never experienced anything like the dark period before?

Did they volunteer to be separated on board the boat as they reached Craig Harbour, when they thought they were going to all stay together—as the oral testimonies and records clearly show us, and as Prof. Daniel Soberman reaffirmed from his report yesterday?

Did they volunteer to go to a place where they would have difficulty finding spouses because of the small groups of related family members?

Did they volunteer to go to a place where there was no Hudson's Bay Company store to which they were accustomed, no Anglican church, no school, and no nursing station—all of which they had access to in Inukjuak?

Did they volunteer to be permanently separated from their extended families and homeland?

The list goes on and on. I would suggest to you that the Inuit did not volunteer for these eventualities. It was not part of the bargain, regardless of the fact that a two-year promise of return was made. That is a fact. However much officials thought that they had actual "volunteers" for their quota of ten families in 1953, the Inuit from Inukjuak had virtually no idea what was going to happen to them—it was a voyage into the unknown—which challenges any notion that the government had the people's "informed consent."

Gordon Robertson suggested that "it was quite possible there was a major misunderstanding"—there certainly was. We have all agreed now that the government through its representatives made a promise of return that after two years if the Inuit wanted to move back, they would be assisted to do so. When J. C. Jackson, the Department's officer in charge of the annual eastern Arctic patrol, held a meeting with all the Inuit men in Resolute Bay on 21 August 1956, together with Supt. Larsen, Cst. Ross Gibson, and an interpreter, he reported that the Inuit asked about going back to Inukjuak and seemed to think a promise had been made. He reported to his superiors in Ottawa that he told them he had no knowledge of a promise (Jackson, 1956). But on 22 October 1956 Ben Sivertz, chief of the Arctic Division, reminded Cunningham, director of Northern Administration and Lands Branch, that "they only agreed to go in the first place on condition that we promise to return them to their former homes after two or three years" (Sivertz, 1956a). But the promise was not honored until thirty-five years later.

Ben Sivertz told the commission that the plan was to take some of the population of Quebec away for a better life. Commissioner Erasmus responded with the question—"What do you mean by a better life?" This question goes to the heart of the controversy. Mr. Sivertz replied, "so that they would be independent and wouldn't live on relief." That was his perception—and the perception of a government department as a rationale for carrying out an interventionist act. It was not an Inuit perception—it was a White man's perception. And the government turned to the instrument of relocation as a result.

We have been told that, after a few years or so, the Inuit at Resolute and Grise enjoyed a rich harvest of game—walrus, seal, polar bear. Did this constitute a better life? No, not from what was said at the April hearings. However good the hunting for marine mammals may have become, it did not in itself constitute a better life.

What did they miss from being relocated to the High Arctic? Did their relatives in Inukjuak starve? No. In fact, the Inuit back in Inukjuak enjoyed the economic benefits derived from a rise in the price of fur and in income received from soapstone carvings—after a temporary period in the late 1940s and early 1950s when the Inuit economy was depressed due to the unstable fur market. But fur prices rose again, and the Inuit in Inukjuak received one of the highest levels of income from handicrafts in the eastern Arctic in the 1950s. Within a matter of a few years, the Port Harrison district was no longer labeled "overpopulated," and in fact became relatively prosperous. That was a better life. But the relocatees, who included among them, as Mr. Ploughman and the records have informed us, a number of excellent carvers, did not experience that better life, because they were separated from their homeland.

For five years I have been in search of the facts and the truth, however difficult it may be to find forty years after the event. I have listened to the relocatees in their homes for many hours telling me of their experiences as a result of being moved to the High Arctic. And I reached the conclusion, as the commissioners may have done after hearing the Inuit testimonies in April, that the people did suffer as a result of the relocation. That, I believe, is a fact.

Perhaps the controversy surrounding the claim for $10 million in compensation has clouded and served to further politicize the issue. But when a person suffers as a result of an external act of intervention, compensation is a natural process. Some critics have suggested that clever lawyers and a $10 million pot of gold have induced the relocatees to act out tales of hardship. We have heard critics suggest that those Inuit testifying today were only children at the time of the move and have been influenced by events. This is part of the myth surrounding the controversy.

Yet, the commissioners have had to repeatedly point out to witnesses at different times during the last few days that that was not the case at the April hearings, and that in fact there were ten or twelve elders who appeared who were adults at the time of the relocation. And, what about those relocatees who have testified who were children or teenagers at the time of the move—have forty years clouded their memories—or is it not the case that children can suffer too? And, that children or teenagers who experienced difficult circumstances, such as permanent separation from their families and friends, or hardship and cold, can carry those experiences for the rest of their lives? Of course they can, that is a fact.

But, we are told, these are Eskimos, they are used to cold, they are used to migrating long distances. Hardship and uncertain survival were their lot in life. We were only trying to do the best thing for them. This is where I believe there are, in effect, two truths.

In my discussions with the planners of the relocation, and the RCMP constables responsible for supervision of the relocatees, I have been struck by the integrity of the individuals and the sincerity of their motivation to implement the relocation for "the common good of the people."

We have heard presentations from various people over the last few days: men from the Department of Northern Affairs who were based in Ottawa, like Ben Sivertz, Gordon Robertson, and Graham Rowley, or RCMP Supt. Henry Larsen —as we heard his thoughts told by his son Gordon—or the constables in the field—Bob Pilot and Ross Gibson. There is no doubting their sincerity, I believe, when they said they were acting in what they thought were the best interests of the people. But, what they believed to be in the best interests of the people, and what was actually in their best interests as the Inuit saw it, are two different things.

I do not believe that officials set out overtly to deceive, to coerce, or to cause the hardship that we have heard the Inuit experienced. They wanted to help them. And yet, where does that leave us? On the one hand we have people of authority who wanted to do good, who planned and carried out the relocation, and on the other hand we have people who have suffered for forty years as a result of those actions. It is no wonder that this issue is confusing. But I would argue that you can have people acting for what they believe to be the best intentions, and yet, people suffer as a result. This is the argument for two truths.

Ross Gibson told us that he thought "he was working for the Inuit." Bob Pilot told us on Monday of when he was a senior official with the Territorial government in the early 1970s and became aware that people wanted to move back to Inukjuak, he tried to do the right thing, to facilitate their relocation back to Inukjuak. But it wasn't so easy. What happened? Reality got in the way. Bureaucracy blocked good intentions. As Pilot said, "the federal government and I nickeled and dimed each other to death."

But still, despite the fact that some were moved back in the 1970s, most of the people were not assisted by the government to move back until 1988. That was fifteen years after Bob Pilot learned of their wish to do so. If it could happen in the 1970s that moving back to Inukjuak was made so difficult, we can imagine how much more difficult it was in the 1950s to obtain permission and assistance to move back to Inukjuak.

The Inuit have told us that they wanted to move back from the start—from that first dark winter when they were hungry and cold and missing their friends and extended families, and their homeland in Quebec. Yes, they were Inuit who could survive one of the severest environments on earth, as their ancestors had done, but they were human beings too. And it was then, as it is now, a natural human response to miss the place you know and the people you know.

They wanted to go home, but they couldn't. They had been placed, for whatever good intentions, in a location from which they physically could not return to their homeland without the benevolent assistance of the government. They were beholden completely to the government and its officials. This is a fact.

It may not be useful to point fingers at who was right and who was wrong, but let us face reality. The Inuit were separated from the officials in Ottawa who now controlled their destiny. They were separated by geographical distance, separated by language, separated by cultural differences. This had two results. It insulated those small Inuit communities at Resolute Bay and Grise Fiord from contact with the outside world, and it insulated the well-meaning officials in Ottawa, who were of the assumption that everything was working out just fine with their High Arctic relocation experiment. In other words, it insulated those Ottawa officials from the reality of the hardships those Inuit were experiencing. I believe that to be a fact.

The reality was, as the Inuit have told us, and as Ross Gibson informed me— "the cold was something the Quebec Eskimos had never endured the like. I am sure they would have all gone home right then if they could" (Gibson, 1983; Gibson, personal communication). In effect, the government created a grand experiment to relocate Inuit to the High Arctic where they could be self-reliant happy hunters once again, free from the temptation of White man's handouts, and yet—the people could not go home on their own. That was the basic flaw with the entire project.

Somehow, not one of the planners recorded his concern that the relocatees would not be able to go home on their own. Commissioner Wilson was incredulous, it appeared to me, when she interviewed Ross Gibson on Monday, when told by him that not one of the Inuit chosen for relocation had apparently asked him, "What if?" "What if I want to go home?"

What happened? The relocation plan, in effect, offered the Inuit a one-way ticket on the *C.D. Howe* to a foreign land from which there was no return.

Co-chairman Dussault said yesterday that the commission hoped by holding these hearings to help the Canadian public to understand what had happened in the relocation, in light of the conflicting views. It would be a bonus if these hearings would allow both sides to come closer to a conciliation.

In closing, I would like to say that I have presented what I believe to be some of the salient facts in this issue, which serve to explain, I hope, why there are, in effect, two truths. But differences in opinion have not kept the two parties from finally coming together, and those differences need not prevent the Canadian government and the Inuit from reaching a solution.

Thank you.

· APPENDIX D ·

List of Individuals Interviewed for This Study

In Arviat (Eskimo Point), Northwest Territories:

Anautalik, Luke*
Aulatjut, Andy*
Aulatjut, Nutaraaluk*
Aulatjut, John*
Iootna, Edward*
Irkok, Martha
Kalluak, Mark
Kalluak, Mary
Karetak, Elizabeth*
Karetak, James

Manik, Joe
Micki, Mary*
Muckpah, Jimmy
Muckpah, Elizabeth
Mukjungnik, Eva*
Mukjungnik, Job*
Sewoee, Annie*
Suluk, Joy
Suluk, Luke
Williamson, Jean

In Grise Fiord, Northwest Territories:

Akeeagok, Japatee
Akeeagok, Seeglook
Aqiatusuk, Tommy
Audlaluk, Annie
Audlaluk, Larry*
Flaherty, Rynie*

Iqaluk, Oolateetah
Nungaq, Lydia
Pijamini, Abraham
Pijamini, Geelah
Scott, Cora
Wentzell, Brian

In Inukjuak (Port Harrison), northern Quebec:

Amagoalik, Lizzie*
Amagoalik, Jaybeddie*
Battisti, Andre
Echalook, Mary
Eliasialuk, Samwillie*
Epoo, Daniel
Epoo, Jobie
Gunn, Barrie
Iqaluk, Andrew*
Inukpuk, Johnny
Inukpuk, Martha

Livingstone, George
Lowi, Manny
Nungaq, Anna
Nutaraq, Elijah*
Nutaraq, Elisapee*
Ohaituk, Anna
Palliser, Lizzie
Patsauq, Charlie
Patsauq, Edith*
Patsauq, Markoosie*
Weetaluktuk, Mary

*Inuit relocatees

In Resolute Bay, Northwest Territories:

Alexander, Ralph	Kalluk, Zipporah
Allakariallak, Elizabeth	Manik, Saroomie
Allakariallak, Minnie*	Manik, Tony
Amagoalik, Paul	Nungaq, Anna*
Amagoalik, Sarah*	Nungaq, Philip*
Amagoalik, Simeonie*	Nungaq, Sarah*
Idlout, Martha	Salluviniq, Allie*
Jesudason, Bezal	Salluviniq, Susan*
Kalluk, Herodie	Sliney, Florence
Kalluk, Lydia	Vera, Betty

In Ottawa, Ontario:

Amagoalik, John*	Phillips, Robert
Baker, Carol	Riedel, Doreen
Bolger, Clare	Robertson, Gordon
Fedor, Loanna	Rowley, Diana
Flaherty, Martha*	Rowley, Graham
Gunn, Lynda	Rudnicki, Walter
Inuksuk, Rhoda	Smith, Gordon
Neville, Bud	

Individuals interviewed elsewhere:

Bielawski, Ellen (Sidney, British Columbia)
Brody, Hugh (London, England, and Montreal, Quebec)
Chambers, Brian (Yellowknife, Northwest Territories)
Clancy, Peter (Cambridge, England)
Csonka, Yvon (Basel, Switzerland)
Diubaldo, Richard (Montreal, Quebec)
Erskine, Ralph (Drottningholm, Sweden)
Freeman, Milton (Edmonton, Alberta)
Freeman, Minnie (Edmonton, Alberta)
Fryer, Clay (Vancouver, British Columbia)
Gerber, Betsy (Washago, Ontario)
Gerber, Earl (Washago, Ontario)
Gibson, Grace (Victoria, British Columbia)
Gibson, Ross (Victoria, British Columbia)
Graburn, Nelson (Quebec City, Quebec)
Grant, Shelagh (Quebec City, Quebec)
Hiller, James (Cambridge, England)
Houston, James (Stonington, Connecticut)
Knight, Ralph (Winnipeg, Manitoba)
Larsen, Gordon (Quebec City, Quebec)
Larsen, Mary (Vancouver, British Columbia)
Lyck, Lise (Copenhagen, Denmark)
Lyon, Sterling (Winnipeg, Manitoba)
MacDonald, John (Igloolik, Northwest Territories)
Mackinnon, Stuart (Edmonton, Alberta)

MacRury, Ken (Cambridge, England)
Mascotto, Lino (London, Ontario)
McAllister, Leon (Yellowknife, Northwest Territories)
Mowat, Farley (Port Hope, Ontario)
Parker, John (Delta, British Columbia)
Pilot, Bob (Pembroke, Ontario)
Ploughman, Reuben (North Bay, Ontario)
Riewe, Rick (Quebec City, Quebec)
Rowley, Susan (Quebec City, Quebec)
Russell, Chesley (Sidney, British Columbia)
Schollar, Lauren (Yellowknife, Northwest Territories)
Silverstone, Sam (Montreal, Quebec)
Steenhoven, Geert van den (Hernen, The Netherlands)
Sivertz, Ben (Victoria, British Columbia)
Tidmarsh, Geoff (Winnipeg, Manitoba)
Tolboom, Wilf (Winnipeg, Manitoba)
Voisey, Henry (Sandy Hook, Manitoba)
Welch, Buster (Winnipeg, Manitoba)
Whittles, Martin (Cambridge, England)
Wilkinson, Doug (Kingston, Ontario)
Williamson, Robert (Saskatoon, Saskatchewan)
Wissink, Renee (Cambridge, England)

Biographical Details of Officials and Other Whites

CANTLEY, JAMES   trader, civil servant; b. Aberdeen, Scotland, 1896; emigrated to Canada in 1913 in the service of the Hudson's Bay Company (HBC); trader, HBC, 1913–21, appointed district accountant, then assistant district manager, HBC, 1921–30; assistant fur-trade commissioner, HBC, 1930–38; organized and managed the Baffin Trading Company, 1939–49; head, Arctic Services Section, Dept. of Resources and Development, 1950–53; appointed chief, Administration Section of Arctic Division, Dept. of Northern Affairs and National Resources in 1954.

CUNNINGHAM, FRANK   lawyer, civil servant; b. Regina, Saskatchewan, 1903; ed. Univ. of British Columbia, B.A. 1924; law school in Toronto, admitted to the Law Society of Upper Canada in 1927; lawyer in Regina, 1927–40; served in Canadian Army overseas, 1940–46, retired as lieutenant-colonel; stipendiary magistrate and administrator with the Dept. of Mines and Resources in Yellowknife, 1946–48; officer with the Dept. in Ottawa, 1948–52; director, Northern Administration and Lands Branch of the Dept. of Resources and Development and Dept. of Northern Affairs and National Resources, 1952–60.

DIEFENBAKER, JOHN   politician; b. Neustadt, Ontario, 1895; ed. Saskatoon Collegiate Institute and Univ. of Saskatchewan, B.A., M.A., LL.B.; elected to the House of Commons for Lake Centre, 1940; prime minister of Canada, June 1957–April 1963; died in 1979.

FLAHERTY, ROBERT   filmmaker, explorer; b. Iron Mountain, Michigan, 1884; ed. Upper Canada College and Michigan College of Mines; worked for Sir William Mackenzie as an explorer and mining engineer in the eastern Arctic, 1910–17; made his first film on the Inuit on Baffin Island and the Belcher Islands, 1914–16, but it was destroyed by fire; directed *Nanook of the North*, 1920–21; *Moana*, 1925; *Man of Aran*, 1934; *Elephant Boy*, 1937; *The Land*, 1942; *Louisiana Story*, 1948; died in 1951.

GIBSON, ROSS   policeman; b. Gibson's Landing, British Columbia, 1922; served in the Royal Canadian Navy, chief petty officer, North Atlantic convoy duty during WWII; officer with the provincial police in British Columbia, 1947–50; became an RCMP officer in 1951; constable at Port Harrison detachment, 1952–53; Resolute Bay detachment, 1953–57; Port Harrison detachment, 1957–58; other postings; retired from RCMP in 1968; died in 1993.

HAMILTON, ALVIN   politician, businessman; b. Kenora, Ontario, 1912; ed. Univ. of Saskatchewan, B.A. 1937; served in RCAF overseas, 1941–45; elected to the

House of Commons for Qu'Appelle, 1957; minister of Dept. of Northern Affairs and National Resources, August 1957–October 1960.

HINDS, MARGERY   teacher, writer; b. Kent, England; ed. Univ. College London and l'Université de Grenoble, France; schoolteacher in England, Australia, and New Zealand; lecturer for the Ministry of Information in England during WWII; emigrated to Canada in 1948; government welfare teacher in Fort McPherson, 1949; welfare teacher in Port Harrison, 1950–54, transferred to Cape Dorset in 1954; died in 1991.

HOUSTON, JAMES   art dealer, designer, writer, civil servant; b. Toronto, Ontario, 1921; ed. Ontario College of Art, 1939; served with the Canadian Army in Canada and overseas, 1940–45; Canadian Handicrafts Guild, 1948–52; Northern Service Officer, Dept. of Northern Affairs and National Resources, 1953–62. Author of a number of books and screenplays.

JACKSON, JOHN   civil servant; b. Birnie, Manitoba, 1908; ed. Univ. of Saskatchewan, B.A. 1933; administrative officer, Arctic Services Section, Dept. of Resources and Development, 1948; appointed assistant to the chief, Forests and Game Section, Dept. of Northern Affairs and National Resources in 1951.

KERR, WILLIAM   policeman, trader, civil servant; b. Ottawa, Ontario, 1900; Royal Northwest Mounted Police, 1919–45; trader for Baffin Trading Company, Port Harrison, 1946–49; joined Dept. of Northern Affairs and National Resources as a Northern Service Officer and appointed to Churchill in 1954.

LARSEN, HENRY   seaman, police officer; b. Fredrikstad, Norway, 1899; at age fifteen joined merchant navy; ed. navigation school, Norway; emigrated to Canada, 1927; joined the RCMP as a constable in 1928, and later took command of the *St. Roch*; completed a west-to-east trip through the Northwest Passage, 1940–42, and east-to-west trip in 1944; subinspector, 1944; inspector, 1946; superintendent, 1953; stationed in Ottawa as the commanding officer of "G" Division, RCMP, 1949–61; died in 1964.

LESAGE, JEAN   politician; b. Montreal, Quebec, 1912; ed. Univ. of Laval, B.A. and LL.L; Crown attorney, 1939–44; elected to the House of Commons for Montmagny-L'Islet, 1945; Parliamentary assistant to the secretary of state for external affairs, 1951–52; served in various Cabinet positions, including minister of Dept. of Resources and Development, Sept. 1953–Dec. 1953, and minister of Dept. of Northern Affairs and National Resources, Dec. 1953–June 1957; died in 1980.

LYON, STERLING   attorney, judge, politician; b. Windsor, Ontario, 1927; ed. Univ. of Manitoba, B.A. 1948; Manitoba Law School, LL.B. 1953; Crown attorney, Dept. of attorney-general of Manitoba, 1953–57; elected to Manitoba legislature in 1958; attorney-general of Manitoba, 1958–63 and 1966–69; minister of the provincial government of Manitoba in various departments, 1960–68; premier of Manitoba, 1977–81; justice, Court of Appeal, Manitoba, 1986–.

MOWAT, FARLEY   author; b. Belleville, Ontario, 1921; ed. Univ. of Toronto, B.A. 1949; served in Canadian Army overseas, 1940–45, retired as captain; made two trips to the Arctic in 1947–48; first book, *People of the Deer*, published in 1952; has subsequently written over twenty-five books, numerous articles, and television scripts; has received a number of awards and honors for his writings.

PARKER, JOHN   solicitor, crown prosecutor, judge; b. Brentwood, England, 1911; ed. Queen's University, Kingston, Ontario, B.A. 1934; Osgoode Hall Law School, Toronto, 1934–37; entered into private practice in the firm of Parker and Parker, Yellowknife, 1944; Crown attorney for the Northwest Territories, elected member of the Territorial Council of the Northwest Territories; appointed as the sole resident judge of the Supreme Court of the Yukon Territory at Whitehorse, 1958; died in 1992.

PEARSON, LESTER   diplomat, politician, author; b. Toronto, Ontario, 1897; ed. Victoria College, B.A. 1919, Oxford Univ., England, B.A., 1923; first secretary, Dept. of External Affairs, 1928–35; Office of Canadian High Commissioner in London, 1938–41; assistant under-secretary of state for external affairs, 1941; minister plenipotentiary, 1944; minister-counsellor to the Canadian legation in Washington, 1942; minister plenipotentiary, 1944; ambassador to the United States, 1945; under-secretary of state for external affairs, 1946; elected to the House of Commons for Algoma East, 1948; secretary of state for external affairs, 1948–58; president of the United Nations General Assembly 1952–53; prime minister of Canada, 1963–68; awarded the Nobel Peace Prize, 1957; died in 1972.

PHILLIPS, ROBERT   civil servant, writer; b. Toronto, Ontario, 1922; ed. Univ. of Toronto, B.A. 1942; served in Canadian Army overseas, 1943–44; joined Department of External Affairs in 1945, Canadian embassy in Moscow, 1947–49; National Defence College, 1949–50; Canadian secretary, Permanent Joint Board on Defence, 1950–52; Privy Council Office, 1952–54; executive officer, Dept. of Northern Affairs and National Resources (DNANR), 1954–56; chief, Arctic Division, 1957–63; director, Northern Administration Branch, DNANR, 1964–65; assistant secretary of the Cabinet, Privy Council Office, 1965–69; deputy director, General Information Canada, 1970–72.

PLOUGHMAN, REUBEN   trader; b. 1920; joined Hudson's Bay Company in 1939, trader in Hebron 1940–41, Eskimo Point 1942–43, Tavani 1944–47, Igloolik 1947–50, Port Harrison 1951–54, and further postings.

RICHARDS, JAMES   civil servant; b. England; emigrated to Canada in 1912; Northwest Mounted Police, 1914–15; served in the Royal Canadian Engineers in France, 1916–19; joined the Dept. of the Interior, 1919; chief, Wildlife Conservation Division; secretary to the officer in charge of the eastern Arctic expedition to Bache Peninsula, Ellesmere Island, in 1930; major, Royal Canadian Engineers, overseas and in Canada, 1940–45, retired as colonel; assistant to the chief, Canadian Wildlife Service in 1947.

ROBERTSON, GORDON   civil servant; b. Davidson, Saskatchewan, 1917; ed. Univ. of Saskatchewan, B.A. 1938, LL.D. 1959; Oxford Univ., B.A. (Juris.) 1940, D.C.L. 1983; Univ. of Toronto, M.A. 1941, LL.D. 1973; secretary, Dept. of External Affairs, 1941; assistant to under-secretary of state for external affairs, 1943–45; secretary to the Office of the Prime Minister, 1945–49; member of Cabinet Secretariat (Privy Council Office), 1949–51; assistant secretary to the Cabinet, 1951–53; deputy minister, Dept. of Northern Affairs and National Resources, and commissioner of the Northwest Territories, 1953–63; clerk of the Privy Council and secretary to Cabinet, 1963–75; secretary to Cabinet for Provincial-Federal Relations, 1975–79; chancellor, Carleton Univ., 1980–90.

ROWLEY, GRAHAM   educator, civil servant; b. England, 1912; ed. Univ. of Cambridge, B.A. 1934, M.A. 1936; Staff College Camberley, 1941; archaeological excavation Hudson Bay, Foxe Basin, and Baffin Island, 1936–39; served in Canadian Army overseas, 1939–46, retired as lieut.-col.; Arctic research for Defence Research Board, 1946–51; secretary, Advisory Committee on Northern Development, 1951–67; scientific advisor, Dept. of Indian Affairs and Northern Development, 1969–74.

RUDNICKI, WALTER   social worker, civil servant; b. Winnipeg, Manitoba, 1925; ed. Univ. of Manitoba, B.A. 1949; Univ. of British Columbia, M.A. in social work 1951; served in Canadian Army overseas, 1944–46; social worker with the Dept. of Social Welfare and Rehabilitation in Saskatchewan in 1950; psychiatric social worker with provincial government of British Columbia and casework supervisor at the Vancouver General Hospital, 1951–55; appointed chief, Welfare Section, Arctic Division, Dept. of Northern Affairs and National Resources in 1955.

ST. LAURENT, LOUIS   politician, lawyer, educator; b. Compton, Quebec, 1882; ed. Laval Univ., B.A. 1902, LL.L. 1905; became a Professor of Law, Laval Univ., 1914; minister of justice, attorney-general of Canada, 1941; elected to the House of Commons for Quebec East in 1942; secretary of state for external affairs, 1946; prime minister of Canada, 1948–57; died in 1973.

SISSONS, JOHN   judge, lawyer, politician; b. Orillia, Ontario, 1892; ed. Queen's Univ., B.A. 1917; law student, Edmonton, 1918; lawyer in Alberta, 1921–46; elected to the House of Commons for Peace River, 1940–45, district court judge, 1946; chief judge, district, southern Alberta, 1950–55; first judge of the Territorial Court of the Northwest Territories, 1955–66; died in 1969.

SIVERTZ, BEN   seaman, civil servant; b. Victoria, British Columbia, 1905; became a seaman on a square-rigger in 1922, sailed to Australia, South America, New Zealand, the Pacific Islands, and the Bering Sea; returned to school and then university in British Columbia in 1932; instructor in navigation, commanding officer of HMCS *Kings* and the R.C.N. Officers' Training School, Halifax, 1940–46; foreign service officer, Dept. of External Affairs, 1946–49; executive assistant to deputy minister, Dept. of Resources and Development, 1950–54; chief, Arctic Division, Dept. of Northern Affairs and National Resources (DNANR), 1954–60; director, Northern Administration, DNANR, 1960–63; commissioner of the Northwest Territories, 1963–66.

STEVENSON, ALEX   trader, civil servant; b. Verdun, Quebec, 1915; worked in the eastern Arctic for the Hudson's Bay Company (HBC), 1935–40; enlisted in the RCAF in 1940, POW in Germany 1942–45; rejoined the HBC in 1945; joined the Dept. of Mines and Resources in 1946 as assistant to the superintendent of the eastern Arctic; frequently served as officer in charge of the eastern Arctic patrol; assistant administrator of the Arctic, Dept. of Northern Affairs and National Resources (DNANR), 1959; administrator of the Arctic, DNANR, 1960–70; died in 1982.

WILKINSON, DOUG   filmmaker, author, civil servant; b. Toronto, Ontario, 1919; served with the Canadian Army, 1941–45, retired as captain; made films for the National Film Board, 1945–52, including *Angotee (Story of an Eskimo Boy)* and *Land of the Long Day*; Northern Service Officer at Frobisher Bay and Baker Lake, Arctic Division, Dept. of Northern Affairs and National Resources, 1955–58.

YOUNG, HUGH   civil servant, soldier; b. Winnipeg, Manitoba, 1898; ed. Univ. of Manitoba, B.Sc.E.E. 1924, Staff College Camberley, England, 1933–34; served in Canadian Army overseas in WWI; Royal Canadian Corps of Signals, served in the sub-Arctic and Arctic, 1924–30; served in the Canadian Army overseas in WWII, commanded Infantry Brigade in Normandy landing operations, promoted to major-general, 1944, quartermaster-general of the Canadian Army; deputy minister of Dept. of Resources and Development, October 1950–November 1953; deputy minister of public works, 1953–63.

· REFERENCES ·

The classification numbers of documents from the National Archives of Canada (NAC) in Ottawa are abbreviated, listing: Record Group (RG), Volume, File, Part. The classification numbers of documents from the Alex Stevenson Collection held in the Northwest Territories Archives (NWTA) of the Prince of Wales Northern Heritage Centre in Yellowknife are abbreviated, listing: Stevenson Collection (SC), Accession number and Box. The Hudson's Bay Company Archives (HBCA) are held in the Provincial Archives of Manitoba in Winnipeg. Documents held in private collections are noted as such. Authors with more than one reference for a given year are distinguished by "a, b, c. . . ."

Agnew, J., and S. Duncan. 1989. *The power of place*. Boston: Unwin Hyman.
Allen, F. 1981. *The decline of the rehabilitative ideal*. New Haven: Yale University Press.
Arctic Circular, The. 1953a. Eskimo identification discs. Vol. 6, no. 5:42.
———. 1953b. The 1951 census in the Northwest Territories. Vol. 6, no. 4:42.
———. 1955. Eastern Arctic patrol, 1955. Vol. 8, no. 4:61.
Arima, E. 1984. Caribou Eskimo. In *Handbook of North American Indians*. Edited by D. Damas. Vol. 5, *Arctic*. Washington, D.C.: Smithsonian Institution, pp. 447–62.
Asch, T. 1992. The ethics of ethnographic film-making. In *Film as ethnography*, edited by P. Crawford and D. Turton. Manchester: Manchester University Press, pp. 196–204.
Audette, L. 1959. Notes for Northwest Territories Council debate. 3 February. NAC/RG85/1514/1012-1/7.
Avataq. Cultural Institute. 1981. *Inuit place name inventory of the Inukjuak region*. Inukjuak: Avataq.
Bain, G. 1952. Eskimo hunting less since pensions granted. *Toronto Globe and Mail*, 22 May.
Baldwin, J. 1954. Memorandum to the deputy minister, DNANR. 20 October. NAC/RG22/298/40-8-1/5.
Banfield, A., and J. Tener. 1958. A preliminary study of the Ungava caribou. *Journal of Mammalogy* 39:560–73.
Barnouw, E. 1974. *Documentary: A history of non-fiction film*. New York: Oxford University Press.
Barr, W. 1977. Eskimo relocation: The Soviet experience on Ostrov Vrangelya. *Musk-Ox* 20:9–20.

————. 1984. Otto Sverdrup (1854–1930). *Arctic* 37, no. 1:72–73.

Barthes, R. 1972. *Mythologies*. London: Jonathan Cape.

Bassett, J. 1980. *Henry Larsen*. Don Mills: Fitzhenry and Whiteside.

Basso, K. 1984. Stalking with stories: Names, places, and moral narratives among the western Apache. In *Text, play and story: The construction and reconstruction of self and society*, edited by E. Bruner. Washington, D.C.: Proceedings of the American Ethnological Society.

Beloff, H. 1985. *Camera culture*. Oxford: Basil Blackwell.

Ben-Dor, S. 1966. Makkovik: Eskimos and settlers in a Labrador community. *Newfoundland Social and Economic Studies 4*. St. John's: Memorial University of Newfoundland, Institute of Social and Economic Research.

Bennett, E. 1956. Memorandum for Mr. Reeve. Establishment of Eskimo settlements in High Arctic. 5 October. NAC/RG85/1070/251-4/3.

Berry, J. 1951. Royal Canadian Army Service Corps in northern trials and operations. *The Arctic Circular* 4, no. 1:3–9.

Birket-Smith, K. 1929a. *The Caribou Eskimos. Material and social life and their cultural position. Descriptive part*. Report of the Fifth Thule Expedition 1921–24. Vol. 5, pt. 1. Copenhagen: Gyldendalske Boghandel Nordisk Forlag.

————. 1929b. *The Caribou Eskimos. Material and social life and their cultural position. Analytical part*. Report of the Fifth Thule Expedition 1921–24. Vol. 5, pt. 2. Copenhagen: Gyldendalske Boghandel Nordisk Forlag.

Boas, F. 1888a. The central Eskimo. *Sixth annual report of the Bureau of American Ethnology for the years 1884–1885*. Washington, D.C.: Smithsonian Institution, pp. 399–699.

————. 1888b. The Eskimo. *Proceedings and Transactions of the Royal Society of Canada for the Year 1887* 5, sec. 2:35–39.

Bolger, C. M. 1959. Letter to RCMP Inspector W. J. Fitzsimmons, "G" Division C.I.B. "Annual report—Grise Fiord detachment," 2 April. NAC/RG85/1446/1000-133/1.

————. 1960a. Memorandum to A. Stevenson. 4 October. NAC/RG85/1962/A-1012-13/1.

————. 1960b. Memorandum to the director. 15 November. NAC/RG85/1962/A-1012-13/1.

————. 1960c. Memorandum to Supt. W. G. Fraser. Relocation of Eskimos— Resolute Bay. 27 June. NAC/RG85/1962/A-1012-13/1.

Booth, W. [1890] 1970. *In darkest England and the way out*. Reprint, London: Charles Knight and Company.

Bravo, M. 1992. Science and discovery in the admiralty voyages to the Arctic regions in search of a North-West Passage (1815–25). Ph.D. diss., University of Cambridge.

Briggs, J. 1968. *Utkuhikhalingmiut Eskimo emotional expressions*. Ottawa: Department of Indian Affairs and Northern Development.

————. 1970. *Never in anger*. Cambridge: Harvard University Press.

Brody, H. 1975. *The people's land*. Harmondsworth: Penguin.

————. 1976. Land occupancy: Inuit perceptions. In *Inuit land use and occupancy project*, edited by M. Freeman. Ottawa: Department of Indian and Northern Affairs.

————. 1981. *Maps and dreams*. London: Jill Norman & Hobhouse.

————. 1987. *The living Arctic*. London: Faber and Faber.

————. 1993. Some historical aspects of the High Arctic exiles' experience. Submission to the Royal Commission on Aboriginal Peoples.

Brown, A. H. 1955. Weather from the white North. *National Geographic Magazine*, April, pp. 543–72.

Burch, E. 1978. Caribou Eskimo origins: An old problem reconsidered. *Arctic Anthropology* 15, no. 1:1–35.

————. 1986. The Caribou Inuit. In *Native peoples, the Canadian experience*, edited by R. Morrison and C. Wilson. Toronto: McClelland and Stewart, pp. 106–33.

Calder-Marshall, A. 1963. *The innocent eye: The life of Robert J. Flaherty*. London: W. H. Allen.

Canada. House of Commons. 1925. *Debates*, vol. 4, 1 June, pp. 3772–73.

Canada. Department of the Interior. 1935–36. *Annual report*, p. 36.

Canada. Department of Resources and Development. 1951a. Recent changes in Eskimo economy. NWTA/SC/acc. no. N92-023/box 17.

Canada. Department of Resources and Development. 1951b. Report on eastern Arctic patrol 1951, Montreal to Churchill. NAC/RG85/1127/201-1-8/2A.

Canada. 1953a. Minutes of a meeting of the cabinet in the Privy Council Chamber. 19 January. NAC/RG2/2652/Cabinet Conclusions—Meeting-7-1953.

Canada. Department of Resources and Development. 1953b. Minutes of a meeting held at 10:00 A.M. August 10, 1953, in room 304, Langevin Block, to discuss the transfer of certain Eskimo families from northern Quebec to Cornwallis and Ellesmere Islands. NAC/RG22/254/40-8-1/4.

Canada. House of Commons. 1953c. *Debates*, vol. 1, 8 December, pp. 696–700.

Canada. House of Commons. 1953d. *Debates*, vol. 1, 10 December, p. 773.

Canada. Department of Resources and Development. 1954a. Treasury Office receipt. 5 May. NAC/RG85/1474/251-2/4.

Canada. Department of Transport. 1954b. Accounts payable voucher. 23 April. NAC/RG85/1474/251-2/4.

Canada. House of Commons. 1954c. *Debates*, vol. 2, 19 January, pp. 1243-44.

Canada. House of Commons. 1954d. *Debates*, vol. 5, 13 May, p. 4680.

Canada. Department of Northern Affairs and National Resources. 1955a. Editorial and Information Division. Press release. 23 June. NAC/RG22/319/40-2-20/4.

Canada. Department of Northern Affairs and National Resources. 1955b. Eskimo Loan Fund. 17 November. NAC/RG85/1474/251-2/7.

Canada. Department of Northern Affairs and National Resources. [1956a]. Relief to Eskimos. NWTA/SC/acc. no. N92-023/box 5.

Canada. House of Commons. 1956b. *Debates*, vol. 7, 2 August, p. 6888.

Canada. Department of Northern Affairs and National Resources. 1957a. Movement of Eskimos. 27 November. NWTA/SC/acc. no. N92-023/box 14.

Canada. Department of Northern Affairs and National Resources. 1957b. Press release: Eskimos fly to new hunting grounds. 24 May. NAC/RG22/335/40-8-14/1.

Canada. Department of Justice. 1958a. Copy of statements and evidence given at the inquest into the death of E.1-471 Hallow, held at Eskimo Point, NWT on February 20th, 1958, before Coroner W.G. Kerr. Territorial Justice Department Library in Yellowknife.

Canada. Department of Justice. 1958b. Transcript of the proceedings of a trial before the Honourable Mr. Justice J. H. Sissons and jury, at the settlement of

Rankin Inlet, in the Northwest Territories, on the 14th, 15th, and 16th days of April A.D. 1958, in the matter of: Her Majesty the Queen—and—E1-472 Kikkik. Territorial Justice Department Library in Yellowknife.

Canada. Department of Northern Affairs and National Resources. 1958c. Caribou conservation and Eskimo population. NWTA/SC/acc. no. N92-023/box 1.

Canada. Department of Northern Affairs and National Resources. [1958d] Ennadai Lake—Henik Lake Eskimos murder. NAC/RG22/335/40-8-14/1.

Canada. Department of Northern Affairs and National Resources. 1958e. Minutes of the meeting held November 18, at 10:30 a.m., in the conference room to discuss resource studies for the proposed relocation of Eskimos. 24 November. NAC/RG85/1382/1012-13/5.

Canada. Department of Northern Affairs and National Resources. 1958f. Selling price of supplies shipped to Resolute Bay—season 1957–58. NWTA/SC/acc. no. N92-023/Box 5.

Canada. House of Commons. 1958g. *Debates*, vol. 2, 7 July, p. 1989.

Canada. House of Commons. 1958h. *Debates*, vol. 4, 14 August, p. 3540.

Canada. House of Commons. 1959. *Debates*, vol. 5, 10 July, p. 5799.

Canada. Department of Northern Affairs and National Resources. 1960. Financial status of active Eskimo loans as of June 8, 1960. NWTA/SC/acc. no. N92-023/box 5.

Canada. Department of Transport. 1970. *Climate of the Canadian Arctic*. Ottawa: Department of Energy, Mines and Resources.

Canada. 1977. *Document on Canadian External Relations, 1946*. Vol. 12. Ottawa: Minister of Supplies and Services Canada.

Canada. 1990a. *Document on Canadian External Relations, 1952*. Vol. 18. Ottawa: Minister of Supplies and Services Canada.

Canada. 1990b. Evidence given at a hearing before the House of Commons committee on aboriginal affairs. 19 March. Available from the House of Commons, Ottawa.

Canada. 1993a. Transcripts of a public hearing held in Ottawa by the Royal Commission on Aboriginal Peoples on the "High Arctic Exiles." 5–8 April. Available from the Royal Commission, Ottawa.

Canada. 1993b. Transcripts of a public hearing held in Ottawa by the Royal Commission on Aboriginal Peoples on the "High Arctic Exiles." 28 June. Available from the Royal Commission, Ottawa.

Cantley, J. 1950a. Memorandum for Mr. Wright. 17 November. NWTA/SC/acc. no. N92-023/box 6.

———. 1950b. Survey of economic conditions among the Eskimos of the Canadian Arctic. Department of Resources and Development, Ottawa.

———. 1951. Memorandum for Mr. Wright. 20 November. NWTA/SC/acc. no. N92-023/box 5.

———. 1952a. Eastern Arctic patrol report, Northern Section. NAC/RG85/1207/201-1-8/3.

———. 1952b. Memorandum to Meikle. 18 December. NAC/RG85/1234/251-1/2.

———. 1953. Memorandum to the director, Northern Administration and Lands Branch. 12 November. NAC/RG85/316/201-1/29.

———. 1956. Memorandum for Mr. Sivertz. Additional Eskimo resettlement in High Arctic. 28 March. NAC/RG85/1070/251-4/2.

Cantor, G. 1989. The rhetoric of experiment. In *The uses of experiment,* edited by D. Gooding and others. Cambridge: Cambridge University Press, pp. 159–80.

Clancy, P. 1987a. The making of Eskimo policy in Canada, 1952–62. *Arctic* 40, no. 3:191–97.

———. 1987b. *Native hunters and the state: The "caribou crisis" in the Northwest Territories.* SNID Occasional Paper No. 87–101. Kingston: Queen's University Programme of Studies in National and International Development.

———. 1991. State policy and the native trapper: Post-war policy toward fur in the Northwest Territories. In *Aboriginal resource use in Canada: Historical and legal aspects,* edited by K. Abel and J. Friesen. Manitoba Studies in Native History VI. Winnipeg: University of Manitoba Press, pp. 191–218.

Clark, G., and M. Dear. 1984. *State apparatus.* Boston: Allen and Unwin.

Clifford, J. 1992. Travelling cultures. In *Cultural studies,* edited by L. Grossberg and others. New York: Routledge, pp. 96–112.

Collins, H. 1951. Excavations at Thule culture sites near Resolute Bay, Cornwallis Island, NWT. *Annual report of the National Museum of Canada for the fiscal year 1949–50.* Bulletin No. 123. Ottawa: Department of Resources and Development, Canada.

———. 1952. Archaeological excavations at Resolute Bay, Cornwallis Island, NWT. *Annual report of the National Museum of Canada for the fiscal year 1950–51.* Bulletin No. 126. Ottawa: Department of Resources and Development, Canada.

———. 1955. Excavations of Thule and Dorset culture sites at Resolute Bay, Cornwallis Island, NWT. *Annual report of the National Museum of Canada for the fiscal year 1953–54.* Bulletin No. 136. Ottawa: Department of Resources and Development, Canada.

Condon, R. 1982. Seasonal variation and interpersonal conflict in the central Canadian Arctic. *Ethnology* 21, no. 2:151–64.

———. 1983. *Inuit behavior and seasonal change in the Canadian Arctic.* Ann Arbor: UMI Research Press.

Constantine, S. 1991. Empire migration and social reform, 1880–1950. In *Migrants, emigrants and immigrants,* edited by C. Pooley and I. Whyte. London: Routledge, pp. 62–86.

Cross, M., and others. 1970. *The frontier thesis and the Canadas.* Toronto: The Copp Clark Publishing Company.

Crozier, A. 1952. Statistical and financial report of Eskimo family allowances as at 31 March 1952. NAC/RG22/254/40-8-1/2.

Cruickshank, R. 1944. Hudson's Bay Company departmental memorandum to the manager, Ungava District. 29 May 1944. HBCA/RG7/1/1753.

Csonka, Y. 1991. Les Ahiarmiut (1920–1950) dans la perspective de l'histoire des Inuit Caribous. Ph.D. diss., Université Laval.

———. 1993. Letter to author. 30 June.

Cunningham, F. 1953. Memorandum for the deputy minister. Assisted Eskimo projects. 16 March. NAC/RG22/254/40-8-1/3.

———. 1954a. Memorandum for the deputy minister. 2 November. RG22/298/40-8-1/5.

———. 1954b. Memorandum to Supt. Larsen. 23 November. NWTA/SC/acc no. N92-023/box 5.

———. 1955. Memorandum to Supt. Larsen. 8 June. NAC/RG18/acc. no. 8586-048 box 14/G-577-14/3.

Damas, D. 1963. Igluligmiut kinship and local groupings. *National Museum of Canada, Bulletin No. 196.* Anthropological Series No. 64. Ottawa: Department of Northern Affairs and National Resources.

———. 1968. The Eskimo. In *Science, history and Hudson Bay,* vol. 2, edited by C. Beals. Ottawa: Department of Energy Mines and Resources, Canada.

———. ed. 1984. *Handbook of North American Indians.* Vol. 5, *Arctic.* Washington, D.C.: Smithsonian Institution.

Diubaldo, R. 1985. The government of Canada and the Inuit, 1900–1967. Research Branch, Corporate Policy, Indian and Northern Affairs, Canada.

———. 1989. You can't keep the native native. In *For purposes of dominion. Essays in honour of Morris Zaslow,* edited by K. Coates and W. Morrison. North York: Captus Press, pp. 171–88.

Dorais, L.-J. 1990. *One thousand Inuit words.* Inuit Studies Occasional Papers 3. Québec: Université Laval.

Downes, P. 1943. *Sleeping island.* New York: Coward-McCann.

Dryzek, J., and O. Young. 1985. Internal colonialism in the circumpolar North: The case of Alaska. *Development and Change* 16:123–45.

Dunbar, M. 1959. Book review of *The desperate people. Critically Speaking.* CBC radio broadcast. 18 October.

Edelman, M. 1977. *Political language.* New York: Academic Press.

Entrikin, J. 1991. *The betweenness of place.* London: Macmillan.

Eskimo Affairs. 1952a. Minutes of the first meeting of Special Committee on Eskimo Affairs held Thursday, 16 October 1952, in Room 304, Langevin Block, Ottawa. NAC/RG18/acc. 8586-048 box 42/D1512-2-4-Q-27 (1952).

———. 1952b. Summary of the proceedings at a meeting on Eskimo Affairs held 19 and 20 May 1952, in the board room of the Confederation Building, Ottawa. RCMP Information Access Directorate, D1512-2-4-Q-27 (1952).

———. 1954. Agenda for the fourth meeting of the Committee on Eskimo Affairs to be held in room 304, Langevin Block, Ottawa, on Monday, May 10, 1954 at 10:00 A.M. NAC/RG22/298/40-8-1/5.

———. 1956. Meeting of subcommittee of the Committee on Eskimo Affairs to discuss Eskimo resettlement in southern Canada. 1 June. NAC/RG85/1514/1012-1/5.

———. [1957]. To the Committee on Eskimo Affairs—report on proposed Eskimo resettlement in southern Canada. Discussed at meeting on 13 May 1957. NAC/RG85/1514/1012-1/5.

Faden, R., and T. Beauchamp. 1986. *A history and theory of informed consent.* Oxford: Oxford University Press.

Faibish, R. A. 1958. Memorandum to Mr. Cunningham. 21 February. NAC/RG22/335/40-8-14/1.

Fienup-Riordan, A. 1990. *Eskimo essays.* New Brunswick: Rutgers University Press.

Fitzsimmons, W. 1957. Memorandum to the commissioner, R.C.M. Police. Movement of Eskimos from Ennadai Lake, NWT to Henik Lake, NWT.— assistance to Department of Northern Affairs and National Resources. 13 December 1957. NAC/RG18/acc. no. 8586-048 box 14/G-577-14/3.

Flaherty, M. 1986. *Nunavut* 5, no. 6:4–6.

Flaherty, R. 1924. *My Eskimo friends: "Nanook of the North."* New York: Doubleday.

Forsythe, W. 1987. *The reform of prisoners 1830–1900.* New York: St. Martin's Press.

Fortuine, R. 1989. *Chills and fever.* Anchorage: University of Alaska Press.

Foucault, M. 1977. *Discipline and punish.* London: Allen Lane.

Fraser, W. G. 1960a. Memorandum to the constable in charge, RCMP, Grise Fiord, NWT, "Eskimo trading stores, Resolute Bay and Grise Fiord, NWT." 15 July 1960. NAC/RG18/acc. no. 8586-048 box 55/TA-500-8-1-5.

———. 1960b. Memorandum to the director, Northern Administration Branch, Department of Northern Affairs and National Resources, "Eskimo trading store, Grise Fiord, NWT." 5 May 1960. NAC/RG18/acc. no. 8586-048 box 55/TA-500-8-1-5.

Freeman, M. 1968. Patrons, leaders and values in an Eskimo settlement. *Symposium on the contemporary cultural situation of the northern forest Indians of North America and the Eskimo of North America and Greenland.* 12–18 August. Stuttgart-München: Verhandlungen des XXXVIII. Internationalen Amerikanistenkongresses, pp. 113–24.

———. 1969. Adaptive innovation among recent Eskimo immigrants in the eastern Canadian Arctic. *Polar Record* 14, no. 93:769–81.

———. 1971. Tolerance and rejection of patron roles in an Eskimo settlement. In *Patrons and brokers in the East Arctic,* edited by E. Paine. Newfoundland Social and Economic Papers No. 2. St. Johns: Memorial University of Newfoundland, pp. 34–54.

———. 1984. The Grise Fiord project. In *Handbook of North American Indians.* Edited by D. Damas. Vol. 5, *Arctic.* Washington, D.C.: Smithsonian Institution, pp. 676–82.

Freeman, M., and others. 1976. *Inuit land use and occupancy project.* Ottawa: Department of Indian and Northern Affairs.

Fryer, A.C. 1954a. Eskimo rehabilitation program at Craig Harbour. *RCMP Quarterly* 20, no. 2:139–42.

———. 1954b. Rehabilitation program of Eskimo at Craig Harbour. RCMP Craig Harbour detachment. 1 February. NAC/RG18/acc. no. 8586-048 box 55/TA-500-8-1-5.

Gallagher, W. 1957a. Memorandum to the officer commanding, "G" Division, R.C.M. Police. Conditions amongst Eskimos—generally—year ending—December 31, 1956. 3 January 1957. NAC/RG18/acc. no. 8586-048 box 14/G-577-14/3.

———. 1957b. Memorandum to the office commanding, RCMP "G" Division. Movement of Eskimos from Ennadai Lake, NWT to Henik Lake, NWT.—assistance to Department of Northern Affairs and National Resources. 3 December 1957. NAC/RG18/acc. no. 8586-048 box 14/G-577-14/3.

———. 1958a. Memorandum to the officer commanding, "G" Division, R.C.M. Police. Conditions amongst Eskimos—generally—year ending—December 31, 1957. 18 March 1958. NAC/RG18/acc. no. 8586-048 box 14/G-577-14/3.

———. 1958b. RCMP statement of E.1-472 Kikkik. 21 February. Territorial Justice Department Library in Yellowknife.

Garland, D. 1985. *Punishment and welfare.* Aldershot: Gower.

Gennep, A. van 1960. *The rites of passage.* London: Routledge and Kegan Paul.

Gibson, F. R. 1953. Eskimo project—Resolute Bay, North-west Territories. RCMP Resolute Bay detachment report. 14 October. NAC/RG18/acc. no. 8586-048 box 55/TA-500-8-1-14.

———. 1954. Conditions amongst Eskimos—Resolute Bay, NWT. RCMP

Resolute Bay detachment report. 26 March. NAC/RG18/acc. no. 8586-048 box 55/TA-500-8-1-14.

———. 1955. Conditions amongst Eskimos—Resolute Bay, NWT. RCMP Resolute Bay detachment report. 22 March. NAC/RG18/acc. no. 8586-048 box 55/TA-500-8-1-14.

———. 1956. Conditions amongst Eskimos—Resolute Bay, NWT. RCMP Resolute Bay detachment report. 14 November. NAC/RG18/acc. no. 8586-048 box 55/TA-500-8-1-14.

———. 1957. Conditions amongst Eskimos—Port Harrison Area. (Annual Report). RCMP Port Harrison detachment report. 30 December. NAC/RG18/acc. no. 8586-048 box 55/TA-500-8-1-13 (1960).

———. 1958. DOT message to the director. 2 July. NAC/RG85/1070/251-4/4.

———. 1983. Letter to Bob Pilot. 24 September.

———. 1990. Letter to author. 7 May.

Gibson, R. A. 1950. Note to the acting deputy minister. 6 September. NAC/RG22/254/40-8-1/2.

Globe and Mail, The. 1958a. Violence brings move for band of Eskimos. 21 February.

———. 1958b. Woman cleared in Arctic killing of witch doctor. 1 May.

Gooding, D. and others. 1989. *The uses of experiment.* Cambridge: Cambridge University Press.

Gould, R. 1958a. Eastern Arctic patrol report for 1958. Grise Fiord— August 27, 1958. NWTA/SC/acc. no. N92-023/box 16.

———. 1958b. Eastern Arctic patrol report for 1958. Resolute Bay—August 7, 1958. NWTA/SC/acc. no. N92-023/box 16.

Graburn, N. 1969. *Eskimos without igloos.* Boston: Little, Brown and Company.

———. 1976. Eskimo art: The eastern Canadian Arctic. In *Ethnic and tourist arts,* edited by N. Graburn. Berkeley: University of California Press, pp. 303–19.

Grant, S. 1991. A case of compounded error. *Northern Perspectives* 19, no. 1:3–29.

———. 1993. Inuit relocations to the High Arctic 1953–60: "Errors exposed." A submission to the Royal Commission on Aboriginal Peoples, 30 August. Available from the Royal Commission, Ottawa.

Gray, W. 1959. At long last, Eskimos speak out for themselves at historic conference. *The Globe and Mail,* 26 May.

Great Britain, Colonial Office. 1879. Colonial Papers, Canada, original correspondence (CO42), vol. 759, p. 19. Public Record Office, London.

Greig, D. W. 1976. *International law.* 2d ed. London: Butterworths.

Gunther, M. 1992. The 1953 relocations of the Inukjuak Inuit to the High Arctic—a documentary analysis and evaluation. A report for the Department of Indian Affairs and Northern Development. Held in the Department library, Hull.

Hamilton, A. 1959a. Letter to Mr. Hobbs. 24 February. NAC/RG22/869/40-8-6A/1.

———. 1959b. Letter to the sociology class, Barons Consolidated High School. 13 March. NAC/RG22/335/40-8-23/1.

Hammond, M. 1984. Report of findings on an alleged promise of government to finance the return to their original homes at Port Harrison (Inukjuak) and Pond Inlet. Department of Indian and Northern Affairs, Ottawa.

Harp, E. 1962. The culture history of the central barren grounds. In *Prehistoric cultural relations between the Arctic and temperate zones of northern America,* edited by J. Campbell. Technical Paper No. 11. Montreal: Arctic Institute of Northern America, pp. 69–75.

Harper, F. 1964. *Caribou Eskimos of the Upper Kazan River, Keewatin.* Miscellaneous Publication No. 36. Lawrence: University of Kansas.

Harrington, R. 1952. *The face of the arctic.* New York: Henry Schuman.

Hatt, G. 1916. Moccasins and their relation to Arctic footwear. *American Anthropological Association Memoir* 3:147–250.

HBC [Hudson's Bay Company]. 1935–59. Annual reports of northern stores. HBCA/RG3/80/11-13; RG3/82/1a-22; RG7/NSD accounts.

Head, I. L. 1963. Canadian claims to territorial sovereignty in the Arctic regions. *McGill Law Journal* 9:200–26.

Heath, S. 1981. *Questions of cinema.* Bloomington: Indiana University Press.

Helms, M. 1988. *Ulysses' sail.* Princeton: Princeton University Press.

Henderson, R. 1952. Book reviews. *Library Journal* 77 (15 February):359.

Henry Larsen's sea navigation chart of the Northwest Passage. 1927. NAC/MG30/B75/2/Maps.

Heydte, F. 1935. Discovery, symbolic annexation and virtual effectiveness in international law. *American Journal of International Law* 29:448–71.

Hickling Corporation. 1990. Assessment of the factual basis of certain allegations made before the standing committee on aboriginal affairs concerning the relocation of Inukjuak Inuit families in the 1950s report. Department of Indian Affairs and Northern Development, Northern Program, Ottawa.

Hinds, E. M. 1953a. Welfare teacher's report for May 1953. 31 May. NAC/RG85/1269/1000-304/2.

———. 1953b. Welfare teacher's report for July 1953. 31 July. NAC/RG85/1269/1000-304/2.

———. 1958. *School house in the Arctic.* London: Geoffrey Bles.

Hobbs, M. 1959. Letter to the prime minister. 25 January. NAC/RG22/869/40-8-6A/1.

Houston, J. 1954. Memorandum on Eskimo art and craft work. January. NAC/RG22/324/40-8-5/1.

———. 1955. Ennadai Lake, Northwest Territories—1955. Department of Northern Affairs and National Resources report. Department of Indian Affairs and Northern Development Library, Hull.

———. 1977. Port Harrison, 1948. In *Port Harrison/Inoucdjouac.* Winnipeg: Winnipeg Art Gallery, pp. 7–11.

Howell, M. 1952. Letter to the Northwest Territories Council. 7 October. NAC/RG85/19/20 Farley Mowat.

Ignatieff, M. 1978. *A just measure of pain.* London: The Macmillan Press.

Inch, D.R. 1962. An examination of Canada's claim to sovereignty in the Arctic. *Manitoba Law School Journal* 1, no. 1:31–53.

Inuktitut. 1981. Interview with Anna Nungaq. December, no. 49, pp. 5–14.

Jackson, J. C. 1956. The eastern Arctic patrol 1956, Churchill onward. 4 December. NAC/RG85/1234/201-1-8.

Jackson, P. 1989. *Maps of meaning.* London: Unwin Hyman.

Jacobson, J. V. 1955. Letter to E. Kuhi. 29 November. NAC/RG85/1072/254-3/1.

Jenkin, T. C. 1959. Conditions amongst Eskimos—Resolute Bay detachment area, period ending 31 Dec. 1959. RCMP Resolute Bay detachment report. NAC/RG18/acc. no. 8586-048 box 55/TA-500-8-1-14.

———. 1960. Report to the officer commanding "G" Division, "Relocation of Eskimos—Resolute Bay, NWT." 5 January. NAC/RG18/acc. no. 8586-048 box 55/TA-500-8-1-14.

Jenness, D. 1964. *Eskimo administration: II. Canada.* Technical Paper No. 14. Montreal: Arctic Institute of North America.

———. 1966. The administration of northern peoples: America's Eskimos—pawns of history. In *The Arctic frontier,* edited by R. MacDonald. Toronto: University of Toronto Press, pp. 120–29.

Johnston, H. 1972. *British emigration policy 1815–1830, "Shovelling out paupers."* Oxford: Clarendon Press.

Johnston, R. G. 1952. Report on the eastern Arctic patrol, 1952. NAC/RG85/1207/201-1-8/3.

Kerr, W. 1955. Memorandum to the chief of the Arctic Division. 4 July. NAC/RG22/335/40-8-14/1.

———. 1956. Memorandum to the chief of the Arctic Division. Re: Eskimo—Ennadai Lake, N.W.T. 28 March. NAC/RG85/1267/1000-179/1.

Kitchener Record, The. 1953. Eskimos to be resettled in better hunting areas. 30 July.

Knight, D. 1981. *Ordering the world: A history of classifying man.* London: Burnett Books.

Laliberte, J. 1955. Eskimos in the Ennadai Lake District, NWT. RCMP Churchill detachment report. 8 February. NAC/RG18/acc. no. 8586-048 box 14/G-577-14/3.

———. 1958. Memorandum to the officer commanding, "G" Division, R.C.M. Police. Conditions amongst Eskimos—generally—year ending—December 31, 1957. 7 January 1958. NAC/RG18/acc. no. 8586-048 box 14/G-577-14/3.

Larsen, H. A. 1942. Memorandum to the officer commanding, G Division. Re: General conditions amongst Eskimos, Boothia Peninsula and vicinity as observed whilst on patrol, Feb. 24th to May 6th 1952. NAC/RG18/acc. no. 83-84-048/42/D-1512-2-4-Q-27.

———. 1951. Memorandum to the commissioner, "Responsibility, care, and supervision of Eskimos." 30 October. NWTA/SC/acc. no. N92-023/box 5.

———. 1952a. Memorandum to Commissioner L. H. Nicholson. 8 February. NAC/RG18/acc. no. 8586-048 box 55/TA-500-8-1-13 (1960).

———. 1952b. Memorandum to the commissioner, "Problems affecting Eskimos." 2 May. NAC/RG18/acc. no. 8586-048 box 42/D1512-2-4-Q-27 (1952).

———. 1952c. Memorandum to Commissioner L. H. Nicholson, "Conditions amongst Eskimos—generally." 22 September. NAC/RG18/acc. no. 8485-048 box 42/D1512-2-4-Q-27 (1952).

———. 1952d. Memorandum to Commissioner L. H. Nicholson, "Conditions amongst Eskimos—generally." 29 September. NAC/RG18/acc. no. 8485-048 box 42/D1512-2-4-Q-27 (1952).

———. 1953. Memorandum to F. J. G. Cunningham, director, Northern Administration and Lands Branch. 19 October. NAC/RG22/254/40-8-1/4.

———. 1954a. Memorandum to the director, Northern Administration and Lands Branch. 8 February. NAC/RG85/1474/251-2/4.

————. 1954b. Memorandum to the director, Northern Administration and Lands Branch. 2 June. NAC/RG18/acc. no. 8586-048 box 55/TA-500-8-1-14.

————. 1955a. Memorandum to the commissioner. 13 June. NAC/RG18/acc. no. 8586-048 box 14/G-577-14/3.

————. 1955b. Memorandum to the officer commanding, RCMP "D" Division, Winnipeg, Manitoba. Re: Eskimos in the Ennadai Lake District, NWT— proposed move to Padlei, NWT. 13 June. NAC/RG18/acc. no. 8586-048 box 14/G-577-14/3.

————. 1955c. Memorandum to the director. Eskimos in the Ennadai Lake District, NWT—proposed move to Padlei, NWT. 7 November. NAC/RG18/acc. no. 8586-048 box 14/G-577-14/3.

————. 1956a. Memorandum to the commissioner. Re: Establishment of new Eskimo settlements in the High Arctic. 17 May. NAC/RG85/1070/251-4/2.

————. 1956b. Memorandum to Commissioner L. H. Nicholson. 28 September. RCMP Information Access Directorate, File No. T.1316-16 (1956).

————. 1957. Memorandum to the director, Northern Administration. 16 January. NAC/RG18/acc. no. 8586-048 box 14/G-577-14/3.

————. 1958. Memorandum to the director. Re: Transfer of natives to High Arctic. 16 April. NAC/RG85/1070/251-4/4.

————. 1959. Memorandum to the commissioner. Re: Article by Farley Mowat in *Macleans Magazine*. 26 January. NAC/RG22/335/40-8-23/1.

————. n.d. Memoirs. Unpublished manuscript in the private collection of Doreen Riedel.

LeCapelain, C. K. 1953. Memorandum to Insp. Larsen, "Your file no. 31/181." 8 June. NWTA/SC/acc.no. N92-023/box 10.

Lee, S. 1982. The value of the local area. In *Valued environments*, edited by J. Burgess and J. Gold. London: George Allen and Unwin, pp. 161–69.

Leechman, D. 1952. Review of *People of the deer* by Farley Mowat. *Canadian Geographical Journal* (August).

Lesage, J. 1955. Obligations of White race to the Eskimos. *Ottawa Journal* (23 March).

Ley, D. 1989. Modernism, post-modernism, and the struggle for place. In *The power of place*, edited by J. Agnew and S. Duncan. Boston: Unwin Hyman, pp. 44–65.

Life. 1956. A Mesolithic age today: Caribou Eskimos illustrate its culture. 27 February.

Lloyd, T. 1952. *New York Times*, 30 November, p. 7.

Lucko, G. D. 1964. Conditions amongst Eskimos generally—annual report— year ending 31 Dec. 1964. RCMP Resolute Bay detachment. NAC/RG18/acc. no. 8586-048 box 55/TA-500-8-1-14.

Lysyk, E. R. 1964. Memorandum to the officer commanding, RCMP, Frobisher Bay, NWT. 5 June. NAC/RG18/acc. no. 8586-048 box 55/TA-500-8-1-5.

MacDonald, J. 1993. Tauvijjuaq: The great darkness. *Inuit Art Quarterly* 8, no. 2:19–25.

MacDonald, V. 1950. Report on Canadian sovereignty in the Arctic. Cited in the document "Sovereignty in the Canadian Arctic" from the files of the Advisory Committee on Northern Development for the year 1954. NAC/RG22/544/Rowley-ACND 1954/3.

Macdonell, C. B. 1964. Memorandum to the officer commanding, RCMP, Frobisher Bay, NWT "Conditions amongst Eskimos generally—annual report—year ending 31 December 1963." 21 February 1964. NAC/RG18/acc. no. 8586-048 box 55/TA-500-8-1-5.

Mackinnon, S. 1989. The 1958 government policy reversal in Keewatin. In *For purposes of dominion. Essays in honour of Morris Zaslow*, edited by K. Coates and W. Morrison. North York: Captus Press, pp. 159–70.

Mageean, D. 1991. From Irish countryside to American city: The settlement and mobility of Ulster migrants in Philadelphia. In *Migrants, emigrants and immigrants*, edited by C. Pooley and I. Whyte. London: Routledge, pp. 42–61.

Makivik. 1986. Grise Fiord/Resolute Bay relocation meeting, 13–15 February 1986 in Frobisher Bay. Unpublished transcripts held by Makivik Corporation, Lachine.

Makivik News. 1989a. Interviews with "High Arctic Exiles." Issue 13.

————. 1989b. Interviews with "High Arctic Exiles." Issue 15.

Mannoni, O. 1964. *Prospero and Caliban: The psychology of colonization.* New York: Frederick A. Praeger.

Mansell, G. A. 1950. Condition of Eskimo—District E-9-Port Harrison, Quebec. RCMP Port Harrison detachment report. 24 April. NAC/RG18/acc. no. 8586-048 box 55/TA-500-8-1-13 (1960).

Manvell, R. 1952. *The cinema.* London: Pelican.

Marcus, A. R. 1990. Out in the cold: The legacy of Canada's Inuit relocation experiment in the High Arctic, 1953–1990. Master's thesis, University of Cambridge.

————. 1991. Out in the cold: Canada's experimental Inuit relocation to Grise Fiord and Resolute Bay. *Polar Record* 27, no. 163:285–96.

————. 1992. *Out in the cold: The legacy of Canada's Inuit relocation experiment in the High Arctic.* Monograph, Document 71. Copenhagen: International Work Group for Indigenous Affairs.

————. 1993. Utopia on trial: Perceptions of Canadian government experiments with Inuit relocation. Ph.D. diss., University of Cambridge.

————. 1994. Inuit relocation policies in Canada and other circumpolar countries, 1925–60. A report for the Royal Commission on Aboriginal Peoples. Available from the Royal Commission, Ottawa.

Marshall, C. J. 1953. Report to Graham Rowley, secretary, Advisory Committee on Northern Development, DRD. 9 November. NAC/RG22/254/40-8-1/4.

Mary-Rousselière, G. 1991. *Qitdlarssuaq, the story of a polar migration.* Winnipeg: Wuerz Publishing.

Mascotto, L. 1957. Memorandum to the officer commanding, RCMP "G" Division. Movement of Eskimos from Ennadai Lake, NWT to Henik Lake, NWT.—assistance to Department of Northern Affairs and National Resources. 15 May. NAC/RG18/acc. no. 8586-048 box 14/G-577-14/3.

Mathiassen, T. 1930. The question of the origin of Eskimo culture. *American Anthropologist* 32, no. 4:591–607.

Matthiasson, J. 1992. *Living on the land: Change among the Inuit of Baffin Island.* Peterborough: Broadview Press.

Mauss, M., and M. Beuchat. 1904–1905. Essai sur les variations saisonnières des sociétés Eskimos. *L'Année sociologique* 9:39–130.

Maxwell, M. 1985. *Prehistory of the eastern Arctic.* New York: Academic Press.

McConnell, W. 1973. The dispute on Arctic sovereignty: A Canadian appraisal. *University of Florida Law Review* 25:465–93.

McCook, J. 1959. Eskimos make first appearance on hill. *The Journal,* 26 May 1959.

McKenna, A. 1952. *Wall Street Journal,* 2 December 1952.

Mikkelsen, E. 1927. The colonization of eastern Greenland. *The Geographical Review* 17:207–25.

———. 1933. The Blosseville coast of east Greenland. *The Geographical Journal* 81, no. 5:385–403.

———. 1951. The Eskimos of east Greenland. *Canadian Geographical Journal* 43, no. 2:88–98.

Montreal Gazette. 1954. New homes for Eskimos said success. 26 October.

Moodie, D. 1959. Memorandum to the officer commanding, "G" Division. Re: Relocation of Eskimos Resolute Bay, NWT. 26 September. NAC/RG85/1382/1012-13/5.

Morrison, W. 1985. *Showing the flag: The Mounted Police and Canadian sovereignty in the North, 1894–1925.* Vancouver: University of British Columbia Press.

———. 1986. Canadian sovereignty and the Inuit of the central and eastern Arctic. *Inuit Studies* 10, no. 1–2:245–59.

Mortimer, R. 1952. A new classic of exploration. *Sunday Times,* 24 August.

Mowat, F. 1952. *People of the deer.* Boston: Little, Brown.

———. 1957a. Letter to Mr. B. Sivertz. November. NAC/RG85/5/512/20 Farley Mowat.

———. 1957b. Letter to Mr. Robertson. 17 December. NAC/RG22/485/40-8-6/1.

———. 1958a. Letter to Alvin Hamilton. 19 November. NAC/RG22/869/40-8-6A/1.

———. 1958b. Letter to Ben Sivertz. 8 November. NAC/RG22/869/40-8-6A/1.

———. 1959a. *The desperate people.* Boston: Little, Brown.

———. 1959b. Integration and the Eskimo: A success story. *The Globe Magazine,* 3 January.

———. 1959c. It's time we treated Inuk as a man. *The Telegram,* 20 January.

———. 1959d. Letter to Commissioner Nicholson. 20 January. NWTA/SC/acc. no. N92-023/box 19.

———. 1959e. Letter to Mr. B. Sivertz. 12 January. NAC/RG85/512/20 Farley Mowat.

———. 1959f. The realities: Hunger, disease, death. *The Telegram,* 22 January.

———. 1959g. The two ordeals of Kikkik. *Maclean's Magazine,* 31 January.

———. 1960. Letter to Minister Hamilton. 18 January. NAC/RG22/869/40-8-6A/1.

Müller-Wille, L. 1983. Inuit toponymy and cultural sovereignty. In *Conflict in development in Nouveau-Québec,* edited by L. Müller-Wille. McGill Subarctic Research Paper No. 37. Montreal: Centre for Northern Studies and Research McGill University, pp. 131–50.

Müller-Wille, L., and L. Weber. 1983. Inuit place name inventory of northeastern Québec—Labrador. In: *Conflict in development in Nouveau-Québec,* edited by L. Müller-Wille. Subarctic Research Paper No. 37. Montreal: Centre for Northern Studies and Research McGill University, pp. 151–210.

Nicholas, A. 1956. Eskimos in the Ennadai Lake District, NWT. RCMP

Churchill detachment report. 21 September. NAC/RG18/acc. no. 8586-048 box 14/G-577-14/3/.

———. 1957. Eskimos in the Ennadai Lake District, N.W.T. RCMP Churchill detachment report. 23 February. NAC/RG18/acc. no. 8586-048 box 14/G-577-14/3.

Nichols, P. A. C. 1959. Letter to Mr. Bolger. 13 February. NAC/RG85/1349/1000-179/3.

Nicholson, L. H. 1952. Memorandum to Major-General H. A. Young. 11 February. NAC/acc. 8586-048 box 42/D1512-2-4-Q-27 (1952).

———. 1953. Memorandum to H. A. Young. 24 February. NAC/RG22/254/40-8-1/3.

———. 1957a. Memorandum to the deputy minister, DNANR. Movement of Eskimos from Ennadai Lake, NWT to Henik Lake, NWT. 19 December. NAC/RG22/335/40-8-14/1.

———. 1957b. Memorandum to Robertson. 21 February. NAC/RG22/335/40-8-14/1.

———. 1959a. Memorandum to R. G. Robertson. 13 March. NWTA/SC/acc. no. N92-023/box 19.

———. 1959b. Presentation to the commissioner, Northwest Territories Council Debate. 2 February. NAC/RG85/1514/1012-1/7.

Norton, W. 1989. *Explorations in the understanding of landscape.* New York: Greenwood Press.

Nuttall, M. 1992. *Arctic homeland.* London: Belhaven Press.

Paine, R. 1977. *The white Arctic.* Newfoundland Social and Economic Papers No. 7. St. John's: Memorial University of Newfoundland, Institute of Social and Economic Research.

Petersen, R. 1962. The last Eskimo migration into Greenland. *Folk* 4:95–110.

Phillips, R. A. J. 1955. Eastern Arctic patrol 1955, Montreal to Resolute. NAC/RG22/319/40-2-20/4.

———. 1956. Memorandum for the deputy minister. Eastern Arctic patrol 1956. Montreal to Churchill. NWTA/SC/acc. no. N92-023/box 3.

———. 1958a. Memorandum for the deputy minister. 15 January. NAC/RG85/1511/1000-179/2.

———. 1958b. Memorandum for Stevenson and Rudnicki. Henik Lake Eskimos. 27 February. NAC/RG22/335/40-8-14/1.

———. 1959a. Memorandum for the deputy minister. "The desperate people." 2 October. NAC/RG22/869/40-8-6A/1.

———. 1959b. Slum dwellers of the wide-open spaces. *Weekend Magazine* 9, no. 15:20.

———. 1967. *Canada's North.* Toronto: Macmillan of Canada.

Pilot, B. 1958. Conditions amongst Eskimos generally—annual report—Grise Fiord area, NWT, year ending December 31, 1958. RCMP Grise Fiord detachment report. NAC/RG85/1446/1000-133/1.

———. 1959. Conditions amongst Eskimos generally—annual report—Grise Fiord area, NWT, year ending December 31, 1959. RCMP Grise Fiord detachment report. NAC/RG85/1446/1000-133/1.

Piven, F., and R. Cloward. 1972. *Regulating the poor.* London: Tavistock Publications.

Polar Record. 1957. New Eskimo settlement at Resolute Bay, NWT. Vol. 8, no. 55:370–71.

Porsild, A. 1952a. Letter to Mr. Farquharson. 15 September. NAC/RG22/485/40-8-6/1.

———. 1952b. Review of *People of the deer. The Beaver,* June 1952.

Rae, R. 1951. *Climate of the Canadian Arctic archipelago.* Toronto: Department of Transport, Canada.

Rasmussen, K. 1908. *The people of the polar North: A record.* Edited and compiled by G. Herring. London: K. Paul, Trench, Trübner.

———. 1930. *Observations on the intellectual culture of the Caribou Eskimos.* Report of the Fifth Thule Expedition 1921–24. Vol. 7, no. 2. Copenhagen: Gyldendalske Boghandel Nordisk Forlag.

———. 1931. *The Netsilik Eskimos.* Report of the Fifth Thule Expedition 1921–24. Vol. 8, no. 1. Copenhagen: Gyldendalske Boghandel Nordisk Forlag.

Ray, D. 1984. The Sinuk mission: Experiment in Eskimo relocation and acculturation. *Alaska History* 1, no. 1:27–43.

RCMP [Royal Canadian Mounted Police]. 1957. RCMP arrest and sentencing records of Iootna, Mounik and Oohootok. 30 November. Territorial Justice Department Library in Yellowknife.

Rea, K. 1968. *The political economy of the Canadian North.* Toronto: University of Toronto Press.

Richards, J. 1956a. Memorandum for Mr. B. G. Sivertz. Eskimos Ennadai Lake—proposed transfer to Henik Lake region—southern Keewatin District. 26 April. NAC/RG85/1267/1000-179/1.

———. 1956b. Memorandum for Mr. B. G. Sivertz. Establishment of new Eskimo settlements in the High Arctic. 4 October. NAC/RG85/1070/251-4/3.

Riches, D. 1977. Neighbours in the "Bush": White cliques. In: *The white Arctic,* edited by R. Paine Newfoundland Social and Economic Papers No. 7. Toronto: University of Toronto Press.

———. 1982. *Northern nomadic hunter-gatherers.* London: Academic Press.

Riewe, R. 1977. The utilization of wildlife in the Jones Sound region by the Grise Fiord Inuit. In: *Truelove Lowland, Devon Island, Canada: A High Arctic ecosystem,* edited by L. Bliss. Edmonton: University of Alberta Press, pp. 623–44.

———. 1991. Inuit land use studies and the native claims process. In: *Aboriginal resourse use in Canada: Historical and legal aspects,* edited by K. Abel and J. Friesen. Manitoba Studies in Native History VI. Winnipeg: University of Manitoba Press, pp. 287–99.

Rink, H. J. 1875. *Tales and traditions of the Eskimo.* London: Henry S. King and Company.

Robertson, R. G. 1954a. Memorandum to J. R. Baldwin. 5 November. NAC/RG22/298/40-8-1/5.

———. 1954b. Memorandum for the minister. 5 January. NWTA/SC/acc. no. N92-023/box 16.

———. 1956. Memorandum to Commissioner L. H. Nicholson. 10 May. NAC/RG85/1070/251-4/2.

———. 1957. Memorandum to Commissioner Nicholson. Ennadai Lake Natives. 18 February. NAC/RG22/335/40-8-14/1.

———. 1958a. Letter to Commissioner L. H. Nicholson. 18 February. NAC/RG22/335/40-8-14/1.

————. 1958b. Memorandum for the minister. "Articles and book by Farley Mowat." 18 November. NAC/RG22/869/40-8-6A/1.

————. 1959a. Letter to Farley Mowat. 16 January. NAC/RG22/869/40-8-6A/1.

————. 1959b. Letter to W. Clarke. 2 June. NAC/RG85/653/1012-9/2.

————. 1959c. Memorandum for the minister. "Statements concerning articles by Farley Mowat." 2 February. NAC/RG22/869/40-8-6A/1.

————. 1959d. Memorandum for Mr. Sivertz. 22 January. NAC/RG22/869/40-8-6A/1.

————. 1960. Letter to Mr. Learmonth. 11 January. NAC/RG22/869/40-8-6A/1.

Robinson, D. 1989. The language and significance of place in Latin America. In: *The power of place*, edited by J. Agnew and S. Duncan. Boston: Unwin Hyman, pp. 157–84.

Rombout, L. and others. 1979. *Robert Flaherty: Photographer/filmmaker. The Inuit 1910–1922*. Vancouver: Vancouver Art Gallery.

Rothery, J. 1955a. Eskimos in the Ennadai Lake District, NWT. RCMP Churchill detachment report. 17 January. NAC/RG18/acc. no. 8586-048 box 14/G-577-14/3.

————. 1955b. Eskimos in the Ennadai Lake District, NWT. RCMP Churchill detachment report. 15 February. NAC/RG18/acc. no. 8586-048 box 14/G-577-14/3.

————. 1956. Eskimos in the Ennadai Lake District, NWT. RCMP Churchill detachment report. 13 February. NAC/RG18/acc. no. 8586-048 box 14/G-577-14/3.

Rowley, G. 1953. Memorandum for the members of the ACND: Future of the joint weather stations. Confidential document ND-69-A. 19 November. NAC/MG 30 E 133/294/ACND 1953.

————. 1954. Memorandum for the Advisory Committee on Northern Development: Policy guidance paper for release of information on the North. Document ND-98. 28 May. NAC/RG85/376/1009-3/6.

————. 1956a. Memorandum for the deputy minister. 1 November. NAC/RG22/545/Rowley-1956.

————. 1956b. Memorandum for the deputy minister. Establishment of new Eskimo settlement in the High Arctic. 31 May. NAC/RG85/1070/251-4/2.

————. 1958a. Letter to Geert van den Steenhoven. 7 March. NAC/RG22/545/Rowley–ACND–1958.

————. 1958b. Memorandum for the deputy minister. 29 January. NAC/RG22/335/40-8-14/1.

————. 1958c. Memorandum for the deputy minister. Ennadai Eskimos. 22 January. NAC/RG22/335/40-8-14/1.

Rowley, S. 1985a. Population movements in the Canadian Arctic. *Etudes/Inuit/Studies* 9, no. 1:3–21.

————. 1985b. The significance of migration for the understanding of Inuit cultural development in the Canadian Arctic. Ph.D. diss., University of Cambridge.

Royal Commission on Aboriginal Peoples. 1994. *The High Arctic relocation: A report on the 1953–55 relocation*. Ottawa: Canada Communication Group.

Ruby, J. 1982. *A crack in the mirror: Reflexive perspectives in anthropology*. Philadelphia: University of Pennsylvania Press.

Rudnicki, W. 1960. Memorandum for the director. Creating new communities. 13 December. NAC/RG85/1382/1012-13/5.

Rudnicki, W., and A. Stevenson. 1958. Report—field trip to Eskimo Point, March 1958. Department of Northern Affairs and National Development. Department of Indian Affairs and Northern Development Library, Hull.

Russell, C. 1978. The Devon Island post. *The Beaver*, Spring, Outfit 308.4, pp. 41–47.

Salluviniq, D. 1977. Salluviniq's story. *Nunatsiaq News*, 25 May.

Sanderson, T. 1952. *Saturday Review* no. 35, 17 June, p. 17.

Sargent, G. K. 1953. Eskimo conditions, Craig Harbour area, period ending December 31st, 1953. RCMP detachment, Craig Harbour. NAC/RG85/1446/1000-133/1.

———. 1954. Eskimo conditions, Craig Harbour area. RCMP Craig Harbour detachment report. 31 December. NAC/RG85/1446/1000-133/1.

———. 1955. Eskimo conditions, Craig Harbour area, period ending December 31st, 1955. RCMP detachment, Craig Harbour. NAC/RG85/1446/1000-133/1.

Schuler, M. 1986. The recruitment of African indentured labourers for European colonies in the nineteenth century. In: *Colonialism and migration: Indentured labour before and after slavery*, edited by P. Emmer. Boston: Martinus Nijhoff Publishers, pp. 125–62.

Sharpe, J. 1953. Memorandum to H. A. Young, 30 July. NAC/RG85/10070/251-4/1.

Short, J. 1991. *Imagined country: Environment, culture and society*. London: Routledge.

Simpson, R. N. 1953. Medical report of the eastern Arctic patrol 1953. 4 December. NAC/RG85/376/201-1/29.

Sinclair, G. E. B. [1951]. Memorandum to A. Stevenson. NAC/RG85/80/201-1/26.

Sissons, J. 1968. *Judge of the far North*. Toronto: McClelland and Stewart.

Sivertz, B. G. 1954. Memorandum to Mr. Doyle. 26 August. NAC/RG85/1446/1000-133/1.

———. 1956a. Memorandum to the director, "Eskimo settlements at Resolute and Craig Harbour." 22 October. NAC/RG85/1514/1012-1/5.

———. 1956b. Memorandum for Mr. W. G. Kerr. Eskimo—Ennadai Lake, NWT. 28 September. NAC/RG18/acc. no. 8586-048 box 14/G-577-14/3.

———. 1958a. Letter to Farley Mowat. 4 July. NAC/RG22/869/40-8-6A/1.

———. 1958b. Memorandum for the deputy minister. "Farley Mowat." 14 November. NAC/RG22/869/40-8-6A/1.

———. 1958c. Memorandum to the deputy minister, "Garbage Dumps." 19 May. NAC/RG22/485/40-8-1/9.

———. 1958d. Memorandum for the deputy minister. Relocation of Eskimos. 7 December. NAC/RG85/1382/1012-13/5.

———. 1959a. Draft review of *The desperate people*. NAC/RG22/869/40-8-6A/1.

———. 1959b. Memorandum for the deputy minister. Background of Henik Lake Eskimos. 9 March. NAC/RG85/1349/1000-179/3.

———. 1959c. Memorandum for the deputy minister. Re: "Tragedy on the tundra" by Patrick Karl Lynn—March issue of *The Carleton*. 18 March. NAC/RG85/1349/1000-179/3.

———. 1959d. Memorandum to H. R. Wilson, chief Treasury officer, revision of regulations governing the Eskimo Loan Fund. 12 January. NAC/RG85/1474/251-2/8.

———. 1959e. Memorandum for Mr. Cunningham. Starvation among the Keewatin Eskimos in the winter of 1957–58. 9 March. NAC/RG85/1349/1000-179/3.

———. 1959f. Memorandum for Supt. H. A. Larsen. 4 August. NAC/RG85/1382/1012-13/5.

———. 1959g. Memorandum for Supt. H. A. Larsen. 9 November. NAC/RG85/1382/1012-13/5.

———. 1960a. Memorandum to the deputy minister. 18 November. NAC/RG85/1446/1000-133/1.

———. 1960b. Memorandum to Mr. Bolger, administrator of the Arctic, "Relocation of Eskimo groups in the High Arctic." 25 November. NAC/RG85/1962/A-1012-13/1.

Slowe, P. 1990. Nationhood and statehood in Canada. In: *Shared space: Divided space*, edited by M. Chisholm and D. Smith. London: Unwin Hyman, pp. 67–83.

Smith, D. 1990. Introduction: The sharing and dividing of geographical space. In: *Shared space: Divided space*, edited by M. Chisholm and D. Smith. London: Unwin Hyman, pp. 1–21.

Smith, E. A. 1991. *Inujjuamiut foraging strategies*. New York: Aldine de Gruyter.

Soberman, D. 1991. Report to the Canadian Human Rights Commission on the complaints of the Inuit people relocated from Inukjuak and Pond Inlet to Grise Fiord and Resolute Bay in 1953 and 1955. 11 December. Canadian Human Rights Commission, Ottawa.

Sociology Class. Barons High School. 1959. Letter to the prime minister. 17 February. NAC/RG22/335/40-8-23/1.

Stead, G. W. 1953. Report on tour of the Arctic Islands, September 8–12, 1953. NAC/RG22/176/40-2-20/3.

Steenhoven, G. 1955. Notes of interest, the N.W. Territories and Yukon Radio System. Steenhoven private collection, Hernen.

———. 1962. Leadership and law among the Eskimos of the Keewatin District, NWT. Ph.D. diss., University of Leiden.

Steensby, H. 1917. An anthropogeographical study of the origin of the Eskimo culture. *Meddelelser om Grønland* 53, no. 2:39–228.

Stefansson, E. 1952. Book review. *New York Herald Tribune*, 28 December.

Stevenson, A. 1950. Excerpts from report of the eastern Arctic patrol. NAC/RG85/1127/201-1-8/2A.

———. 1951a. Report of the eastern Arctic patrol, northern section. NAC/RG85/1127/201-1-8/3.

———. 1951b. Wireless message to J. G. Wright. 5 September. NAC/RG85/1127/201-1-8/2A.

———. 1952. Memorandum to J. Cantley. 8 December. NAC/RG85/1234/251-1/2.

———. 1953. Inspection trip eastern and northern Quebec coast and southern Baffin Island—June–July, 1953. NAC/RG85/1207/201-1-8/3.

———. 1954. Note to J. Cantley. 8 February. NAC/RG85/1474/251-2/4.

———. 1959. Memorandum to Mr. Bolger, "Eskimo Loan." 4 February. NAC/RG85/1474-251-2/8.

————. 1968. Letter to F. Bruemmer. 18 April. NWTA/SC/acc. no. N92-023/box 28.

————. 1977. Relocation of Inuit people. November. NWTA/SC/acc. no. N92-023/box 5.

Stevenson, D. 1968. *Problems of Eskimo relocation for industrial employment.* Northern Science Research Group. Ottawa: Department of Indian Affairs and Northern Development.

Stirrat, J. 1958. Autopsy report of the case of Nesha (E1.614). 4 March. Territorial Justice Department Library in Yellowknife.

Sutton, C. 1975. Comments. In: *Migration and development,* edited by H. Sefa and B. Du Toit. The Hague: Mouton Publishers, pp. 175–85.

Svarlien, O. 1960. The sector principle in law and practice. *Polar Record* 10, no. 66:248–63.

Sverdrup, O. 1904. *New land.* London: Longmans Green and Co.

Tassé, R., and M. Simon. 1993. Report to the Royal Commission on Aboriginal Peoples. 1 February. Available from the Royal Commission, Ottawa.

Taylor, W. 1965. Fragments of Eskimo pre-history. *The Beaver,* spring issue, pp. 4–17.

Tester, F., and P. Kulchyski, 1994. *Tammarnitt (mistakes): Inuit relocation in the eastern Arctic 1939–63.* Vancouver: University of British Columbia Press.

Time. 1954. Milestones. 4 October.

Times Literary Supplement. 1952. Book reviews. London, 12 September, p. 599.

Toren, C. 1991. Leonardo's "Last Supper" in Fiji. In: *The myth of primitivism,* edited by S. Hiller. London: Routledge.

Toronto Telegram. 1959. He stayed angry for ten years. 20 January.

Tuan, Y-F. 1977. *Space and place.* London: Edward Arnold.

Tudor, A. 1974. *Image and influence.* London: George Allen & Unwin Ltd.

Tyrrell, J. B. 1897. *Report of the Dubawnt, Kazan and Ferguson Rivers and the north-west coast of Hudson Bay.* Annual report for 1896, vol. 9, report F. Ottawa: Geological Survey of Canada.

Union Oil. 1953. Advertisement in *Newsweek.* 16 February.

Usher, P. 1970. *The Bankslanders: Economy and ecology of a frontier trapping community, volume—history.* Ottawa: Department of Indian Affairs and Northern Development.

————. 1971. *Fur trade posts of the Northwest Territories 1870–1970.* NSRG 71-4. Ottawa: Department of Indian Affairs and Northern Development.

Vancouver Province, The. 1953. Ottawa to move Eskimos. 30 July.

Vitebsky, P. 1986. National discussion and local actuality. *Manchester Papers on Development* 2, no. 2:1–12.

————. 1992. Landscape and self-determination among the Eveny. In: *Bush base: Forest farm,* edited by E. Croll and D. Parkin. London: Routledge, pp. 223–46.

Vitt, V. R. 1965. Conditions amongst Eskimos generally—annual report year ending 31 December 1965. RCMP Grise Fiord detachment report. NAC/RG18/acc. no. 8586-048 box 55/TA-500-8-1-5.

————. 1968. Conditions amongst Eskimos generally—annual report year ending 31 December 1968. RCMP Grise Fiord detachment report. NAC/RG18/acc. no. 8586-048 box 55/TA-500-8-1-5.

Voiles, J. 1952. *San Francisco Chronicle,* 6 April, p. 21.

Wilkinson, D. 1953. Letter to Graham Rowley. 25 August.
  NAC/RG22/544/Rowley-1953.
———. 1956. *Land of the long day.* London: George G. Harrap.
———. 1957. Memorandum for chief, Arctic Division. 25 September.
  NAC/RG85/1511/1000-179/2.
Williamson, R. 1974. *Eskimo underground.* Occasional Papers II. Uppsala:
  Uppsala Universitet.
Williamson, R., and T. Foster. 1974. *Eskimo relocation in Canada.* Saskatoon:
  Institute for Northern Studies.
Willmott, W. E. 1961. *The Eskimo community at Port Harrison P. Q.* Ottawa:
  Department of Northern Affairs and National Resources.
Woodbury, A. 1984. Eskimo and Aleut languages. In: *Handbook of North
  American Indians.* Edited by D. Damas. Vol. 5, *Arctic.* Washington, D.C.:
  Smithsonian Institution, pp. 49–63.
Wright, J. 1950. Letter to Mr. Cheshire. 7 November. NWTA/SC/acc. no.
  N92-023/box 6.
———. 1953. Letter to G. Waring. 30 March. NAC/RG85/1235/251-2/1.
Young, H. A. 1953a. Letter to the editors. 12 January.
  NAC/RG22/485/40-8-6/1.
———. 1953b. Memorandum to J-C. Lessard, deputy minister, D.O.T. 8 June.
  NAC/RG85/80/201-1/28.
———. 1953c. Memorandum to L. H. Nicholson, 20 February.
  NAC/RG22/254/40-8-1/3.
———. 1953d. Memorandum to L. H. Nicholson, 10 March.
  NAC/RG22/254/40-8-1/3.
———. 1953e. Memorandum to L. H. Nicholson, 13 May.
  NAC/RG22/254/40-8-1/3.
Zaslow, M. 1988. *The northward expansion of Canada 1914–1967.* Toronto:
  McClelland and Stewart.

· INDEX ·

UNIVERSITY PRESS OF NEW ENGLAND publishes books under its own imprint and is the publisher for Brandeis University Press, Dartmouth College, Middlebury College Press, University of New Hampshire, University of Rhode Island, Tufts University, University of Vermont, Wesleyan University Press, and Salzburg Seminar.

Library of Congress Cataloging-in-Publication Data

Marcus, Alan R.
  Relocating Eden: the image and politics of Inuit exile in the Canadian Arctic / Alan Rudolph Marcus.
   p.   cm. — (Arctic visions)
  Includes bibliographical references and index.
  ISBN 0–87451–659–5 (pa : alk. paper)
  1. Inuit — Relocation — Canada, Northern. 2. Inuit — Canada — Government relations.   I. Title.   II. Series.
  E99.E7M285 1995
  323.1'1971071—dc20   95–3420

♾